GOLD

first

FIRST CERTIFICATE IN ENGLISH

g coursebook

Jan Bell

Amanda Thomas

CONTENTS

Exam information

The Cambridge First Certificate in English is made up of five papers, each testing a different area of ability in English. Each paper is worth 20 percent of the total mark. There are five grades. A, B and C are pass grades; D and E are fail grades.

Paper 1 Reading (1 hour)

The Reading paper has three parts. Each part tests a different reading skill or skills. There are thirty questions altogether. You write your answers on an answer sheet during the exam.

Part 1 Multiple-choice questions	Focus	Detail, opinion, gist, attitude, deducing meaning, text organisation features (exemplification, comparison, reference), tone, purpose and main idea
	Task	There are eight four-option multiple-choice questions. You have to choose the correct option (A, B, C or D) based on the information in the text.
Part 2 Gapped text	Focus	Understanding text structure, cohesion and coherence
	Task	You read a text from which seven sentences have been removed and placed in jumbled order after the text. There is one extra sentence that you do not need to use.
Part 3 Multiple matching	Focus	Specific information, detail, opinion and attitude
	Task	You read fifteen questions or statements about a text which has been divided into sections, or several short texts. You have to decide which section or text contains the information relating to each question or statement.

Paper 2 Writing (1 hour 20 minutes)

The Writing paper is divided into two parts, and you have to complete one task from each part. Each answer carries equal marks, so you should not spend longer on one than another.

Part 1	Focus	Content, organising information, thinking about a target reader
	Task	Part 1 is compulsory, and there is no choice of questions. You have to write a letter or email based on given information and prompts. It may be informal or semi-formal, and you have to write 120–150 words
Part 2	Focus	Layout, style and register, thinking about a target reader
	Task	Part 2 has four tasks to choose from. The first three options may include any three of the following: • a letter or email • an article • a report • an essay • a story • a review The fourth option has a choice of two tasks based on a background reading text. This can be a letter, article, report, essay or review. You have to write 120–180 words for Part 2.

Paper 3 Use of English (45 minutes)

There are four parts in the Use of English paper, with forty-two questions altogether. You write your answers on an answer sheet during the exam. There is always an example at the beginning of each task to help you.

Part 1 Multiple-choice cloze	Focus	Vocabulary/Lexico-grammatical
	Task	You read a text with twelve gaps. You choose the best word to fit in each gap from a choice of four options (A, B, C or D).
Part 2 Open cloze	Focus	Grammar/Lexico-grammatical
	Task	You read a text with twelve gaps. You have to think of the most appropriate word to fill each gap. You must use one word only. No options are provided.
Part 3 Word formation	Focus	Vocabulary/Lexico-grammatical
	Task	You read a text with ten gaps. You are given the stems of the missing words in capitals at the ends of the lines with gaps. You have to change the form of each word to fit the context.
Part 4 Key word transformations	Focus	Grammar and vocabulary
	Task	There are eight items. You are given a sentence and a 'key word'. You have to complete a second, gapped sentence using the key word. The second sentence has a different grammatical structure but must have a similar meaning to the original.

Paper 4 Listening (approximately 40 minutes)

There are four parts in the Listening paper, with a total of thirty questions. You write your answers on the question paper and then you have five minutes at the end of the exam to transfer them to an answer sheet. In each part you will hear the text(s) twice. The texts may be monologues or exchanges between interacting speakers. There will be a variety of accents.

Part 1 Extracts with multiple-choice questions	Focus	Each extract will have a different focus, which could be: main point, detail, purpose or location of speech, relationship between the speakers, attitude or opinion of the speakers.
	Task	You hear eight short, unrelated extracts of about thirty seconds each. They may be monologues or conversations. You have to answer one three-option multiple-choice question (A, B or C) for each extract.
Part 2 Sentence completion	Focus	Specific information, detail, stated opinion
	Task	You hear a monologue or conversation lasting about three minutes. You complete ten sentences with words from the text.
Part 3 Multiple matching	Focus	As for Part 1
	Task	You hear a series of five monologues or exchanges, lasting about thirty seconds each. The speakers in each extract are different, but the situations or topics are all related to each other. You have to match each speaker to one of six statements or questions (A–F). There is one extra option that you do not need to use.
Part 4 Multiple-choice questions	Focus	Specific information, opinion, attitude, gist, main idea
	Task	You hear a monologue or conversation which lasts about three minutes. There are seven questions. You have to choose the correct option (A, B or C).

Paper 5 Speaking (approximately 14 minutes)

You take the Speaking test with a partner. There are two examiners. One is the 'interlocutor', who speaks to you, and the other is the 'assessor', who just listens. There are four different parts in the test.

Part 1 Interview (3 minutes)	Focus	General interactional and social language
	Task	The interlocutor asks each of you questions about yourself, such as where you come from, what you do in your free time.
Part 2 Individual long turn (4 minutes)	Focus	Organising your ideas, comparing, describing, expressing opinions
	Task	The interlocutor gives you a pair of photographs to compare, and to give a personal reaction to. You speak by yourself for about a minute while your partner listens. Then the interlocutor asks your partner a question related to the topic. Only a short answer is expected. You then change roles.
Part 3 Collaborative task (3 minutes)	Focus	Interacting with your partner, exchanging ideas, expressing and justifying opinions, agreeing and/or disagreeing, suggesting, speculating, evaluating, reaching a decision through negotiation
	Task	You are given a task to discuss together, based on a set of pictures. You should try to reach a conclusion together, but there is no right or wrong answer to the task, and you don't have to agree with each other. It is the interaction between you that is important.
Part 4 Discussion (4 minutes)	Focus	Expressing and justifying opinions, agreeing and disagreeing
	Task	The interlocutor asks you both general questions related to the topic of Part 3, and gives you the chance to give your opinions on other aspects of the same topic.

For more information see the **Writing reference** (page 179), the **General marking guidelines** (page 199) and the **Exam focus** (page 200).

Bands and fans

1

Speaking

1 **Discuss the questions.**

1 Why do people like listening to different kinds of live music?

2 What do you enjoy doing most: playing a musical instrument, listening to music at home or going to a live gig?

3 Are you a fan of a particular band or musical artist? What makes someone a 'fan'?

Vocabulary

free time activities: verb/noun collocations

2 **Match the verbs in A with the activities in B. There may be more than one possibility.**
Example: go to/watch a film

A	do	go (to/out for/on)	have	play	watch

B	the computer	computer games	a DVD	a film	football
	friends round	a gig	the guitar	a pizza	running
	shopping	the theatre	television	yoga	

3 **Add any other free time activities you can think of to list B. Put the verb it goes with in list A.**

Listening and speaking

asking and answering questions

4 ▶ 1.02 **Read and listen to the questions about free time. Underline the words which are stressed.**

1 How do you usually relax when you have some free time?

2 What do you do when you stay in? Where do you go when you go out?

3 Do you like being in a large group or would you rather be with a few close friends?

5 ▶ 1.03 **Listen to the students' answers and complete the gaps.**

I   I usually find .... quite relaxing but it depends on ....

2   I tend to .... on weekdays though I sometimes ....

3   .... is good fun.

4   .... helps me to switch off.

5   I'm really into ....

6   I go out .... now and again.

6   **Work in pairs. Ask and answer the questions in Activity 4.**

Interview (Part I)

listening to and answering questions

▶ **EXAM** FOCUS p.206

7   **In Part 1 of the Speaking paper, you answer some questions in which you give personal information and opinions. Match questions 1–7 to topics A–E.**

1   What kind of music do you enjoy listening to?

2   Do you have any brothers or sisters?

3   What do you like about the place that you were brought up?

4   What subject did you enjoy most at school?

5   What do you think you'll be doing in five years' time?

6   Where do you think you'll go on holiday this year?

7   Tell us about your closest friend.

A   your personal relationships

B   your hometown

C   your job or studies

D   your free time activities

E   your future plans

8   **Add two more questions to each topic A–E. Use question words such as *what (kind), when, how (many), who, why, where*.**

9 ▶ 1.04 **Listen to Julia and Stefan and answer the questions.**

1   Which of the questions in Activity 7 were they each asked?

2   Did they answer them in enough detail?

3   Did they vary their tone of voice?

4   What did Stefan say when he didn't understand the question?

10   **Choose one question from each topic in Activities 7 and 8 and ask your partner.**

▶ **GRAMMAR** REFERENCE p.162

Speaking

1 **Look at the photos and discuss the questions.**

1 When do you think these photos were taken?

2 What kind of music do you think the people were into?

3 Why do groups of young people get together like this?

Gapped text (Part 2)

▶ **EXAM** FOCUS p.201

2 **You are going to read a newspaper article about music sub-cultures. Read the text quickly. How does the writer answer the question in the title?**

ARE MUSIC 'TRIBES' A THING OF THE PAST?

Like-minded music fans have been bonding together for half a century. But is this on its way out?

There was a time when the average person formed their opinions about pop music not just on what they heard, but also on their reaction to the many groups of young people who followed the very different kinds of music. *These impressions* were based on the clothes *they* wore as much as their behaviour in general. The style-conscious mods of the 1960s would <u>roam around</u> on their scooters all day, getting off only for an occasional fight with passing rockers, identified by their powerful motorbikes, greased hair and leather jackets. And in the 70s and 80s, punks would dye their hair pink and terrorise grannies, or at least that is how *they* <u>came across</u> in the media. But when was the last time a new kind of music was associated with a particular group of youths in the same way?

These days you can't always tell what music someone likes just by looking at them. People now seem less likely to hold on tight to their cultural identity, which means that, although tribes still exist, they are looser and broader than before. This change is probably due to the fact that music is now accessed in very different ways, with people able to listen to it at any time. Hardly any young people remember pop culture before the internet, when records were bought rather than streamed or downloaded. **1** *E*

19-year-old Bianca Munyankore agrees that the excitement of listening to a song you waited to buy has probably gone. **2** In any case, saving up to buy a CD means you wouldn't be exploring any other music, and she believes an openness to music is now a natural part of being young.

Music writer and teacher Neil Kulkarni observes that, although sub-cultures still exist, they are no longer participated in with pride or any form of aggression. These days, rather than making any kind of statement, it's just a way for kids to say what kind of music they're into. **3** The internet has made them more prepared to listen to things that they wouldn't necessarily have expected to like and, as a result, there are more connections between sub-cultures.'

4 Author Paul Hodkinson thinks so; he believes the fact that pop tribes have changed over the years means that they've succeeded rather than failed. 'If other people find you odd, and if that makes you unpopular, it's important to connect with other people like you,' he says. 'Being in a tribe's always about being comfortable.'

But surely comfort wasn't important to tribes in the 60s, 70s and 80s? **5** Hodkinson believes that the political aspect was exaggerated. 'The desire to be part of a group is often about far less exciting things such as trying to make friends or having something to do.'

Mass communication has meant that sharing music is now easy. **6** The most underground metal or hip-hop can be found not just on the internet, but even on TV; many musicians make their money from TV or adverts rather than from fans buying music or concert tickets.

Perhaps the biggest change to pop tribes, though, is that they are no longer restricted to young people. Today, audiences for punk gigs or metal nights range in age from 16–60 and mix well together. **7**

3 **Read the first two paragraphs again and answer the questions.**

1 In the first paragraph, what do *these impressions* and *they* in line 5 refer back to? What does *they* refer to in line 12?

2 In the second paragraph, which words in the answer (sentence E) link to the topic and vocabulary? How does *neither* link back? What does *they* refer to?

4 **Seven sentences have been removed from the article. Choose from sentences A–H the one which fits each gap. There is one extra sentence which you do not need to use.**

EXAM TIP

Look for linking words and phrases in the options which link to the ideas and language (e.g. connecting words, synonyms, pronouns which link to nouns) in the sentences before and after each gap.

A So does that mean that tribes are, in fact, expanding, rather than dying?

B Another consequence of this is that all kinds of music are now found much more <u>in the mainstream</u>.

C However, the freedom of simply listening to whatever you want, whenever you want more than <u>makes up for</u> that feeling.

D Which appears to show that, if a pop tribe means anything these days, it seems to be about a set of <u>tastes</u>, rather than a stage of life you go through before reaching adulthood.

E *Neither* have *they* experienced a time when they were limited to <u>tracks</u> they could hear on the radio or get on a cassette from friends.

F Does the lack of very visible teenage tribes matter for the health of pop culture?

G And a lot of youngsters are now finding that their taste overlaps with other groups.

H Wasn't there a spirit of protest that drove angry mods and rockers and rebellious punks?

5 **Compare your answers and give reasons for your choices.**

6 **What sub-cultures exist in your country? In what ways can you identify people in these sub-cultures by the way they dress and the music they like?**

Vocabulary
deducing words in context

7 **Look at these words and phrases and choose the correct meaning. Which clues in the text helped you?**

Example: 'scooters' and 'all day' might help you to understand 'roam around'.

1 *roam around* (para 1)
   A cause trouble
   B travel with no real purpose

2 *come across* (para 1)
   A appear to be
   B find by chance

3 *track* (option E)
   A a narrow path or road
   B a piece of music or a song from a CD

4 *make up for* (option C)
   A improve a bad situation
   B do something to show you are sorry

5 *in the mainstream* (option B)
   A conventional
   B respected

6 *tastes* (option D)
   A experiences of something
   B things you like

Present simple and continuous

1 **Look at the sentences and decide whether they should be in the simple or continuous form. Then discuss why.**

1 My son's *always downloading/always downloads* music instead of getting on with his work.

2 I *work/'m working* overtime this month while the music editor is on sick leave.

3 Someone *plays/'s playing* the piano. Can you hear it?

4 Did you know that band *comes/'s coming* from my home town?

5 I *get/'m getting* better at recognising classical music.

6 I *take/'m taking* my iPod everywhere.

2 **Match the uses of the present simple and present continuous with the examples in Activity 1.**

A repeated actions/habits 6

B permanent situations/facts 4

C an activity happening at the moment of speaking 3

D an activity in progress but not at this exact moment 2

E changing or developing situations 5

F emphasises repetition of typical (often annoying or surprising) behaviour 1

LANGUAGE TIP

Verbs such as *believe, own, belong, like, understand, know, hear* are not usually used in the continuous form because they describe states, not actions.

Some verbs can be used in both the simple and continuous form with different meanings.
I **see** what you mean (see = understand);
I'**m seeing** her next week (see = meet).

3 **Look at the pairs of sentences and say why the speaker has used the present simple or continuous in each case.**

1 A I <u>have</u> a ticket to see Lady Gaga. *states*
 B I'm <u>having</u> a shower. *actions*.

2 A That singer <u>appears</u> to be doing well.
 B Eminem<u>'s appearing</u> at the V Festival.

3 A He<u>'s being</u> really kind.
 B He's really kind.

4 A He<u>'s thinking</u> about joining a band.
 B I <u>think</u> that band is really good.

5 A It <u>depends</u> on how much money I've got.
 B I'm <u>depending</u> on her to organise everything.

6 A This soup <u>tastes</u> good.
 B Joe<u>'s tasting</u> the soup.

4 **Complete the sentences with the present simple or present continuous form of the verb in brackets.**

1 I *don't like* (*not like*) pop music.

2 The band *in appearing* (*appear*) in Manchester all week.

3 I can't hear what you *an doing* (*say*). It's too loud.

4 I *think* (*think*) it's dangerous to listen to your iPod when you're riding a bike.

5 You can never have a conversation with her – she *always* *in checking* (*always check*) her phone for messages.

6 That band *in setting* (*get*) more and more popular.

7 We *often go* (*often go*) to a jazz club on Friday nights.

8 You .... (*be*) very difficult today!

5 **Write sentences about three things that**

1 you do on a regular basis.

2 you are doing now (but not at this exact moment).

6 **Compare your sentences in pairs. Do you have anything in common?**

▶ **GRAMMAR** REFERENCE p.176

Vocabulary

phrasal verbs with *take*

1 Match the phrasal verbs in 1–5 with meanings A–E.

1 His career *took off* as soon as he won the prize: he's so talented.

2 He *takes after* his father, who's also really musical.

3 I *took up* playing the saxophone last year.

4 Tom *took over* as the band's manager when Sam left.

5 I made him *take back* what he said about my taste in music.

A have similar characteristics 2

B become responsible for something 4

C start an activity 3

D admit you are wrong 5

E become successful 1

Multiple-choice cloze (Part I)

▶ **EXAM** FOCUS p.202

2 Read the text about a musician quickly and say what is different about Josh Freese's relationship with his fans. Don't worry about the gaps yet.

3 Look at the example. Why are options A, B and D wrong?

4 Now look at the options for gap 1 and answer the questions.

1 Which of verbs A–D can be followed by *of*?

2 Choose the phrase which means *familiar with*.

5 For questions 2–12, decide which answer (A, B, C or D) best fits each gap.

EXAM TIP

Think about which word might fit the gap before looking at the options. Check each side of the gap to make sure that the option you choose goes with the other words.

6 Look at questions 5 and 12 again and check you have chosen the correct phrasal verb.

7 Discuss the questions.

1 Do you think this is a good way for artists to promote their music?

2 Would any of these offers attract you?

Drumming up business

Josh Freese is a very successful session drummer (**0**) ..*C...based*... in Los Angeles. You probably won't have (**1**) .... of him but he's played with some very successful bands. When Freese (**2**) .... his first solo album, called *Since 1972*, he decided to (**3**) .... up a system where fans could buy something unique. By (**4**) .... with fans directly, he hoped to sell more of his music.

The CD didn't cost much but if you paid $50 for it, you would also get a personal five-minute 'thank you' phone call. Sales of the album quickly took (**5**) .... But there were other limited options which gave fans the opportunity to meet Freese in (6) .... The option to have lunch with Freese for $250 (**7**) .... out in about a week.

For $2500 a fan could (**8**) .... an individual drum lesson from Freese, which (**9**) .... one of his snare drums to take home. At $10,000, you'd have the (**10**) .... to spend the day with Freese and one of his rock-star friends. There were also various $20,000 and $75,000 options (**11**) .... Not all of these were taken (**12**) .... by fans, but a teenager from Florida actually purchased the $20,000 option, and spent a week on tour with Freese.

0	A situated	B located	C based	D lived
1	A recognised	B noticed	C heard	D known
2	A released	B sent	C presented	D brought
3	A put	B get	C set	D go
4	A joining	B discussing	C contacting	D communicating
5	A after	B back	C off	D up
6	A person	B front	C life	D face
7	A stayed	B gave	C sold	D let
8	A achieve	B receive	C collect	D gain
9	A proposed	B involved	C contained	D included
10	A chance	B choice	C time	D luck
11	A available	B offer	C ready	D open
12	A over	B back	C off	D up

Multiple matching (Part 3)

▶ **EXAM** FOCUS p.205

1 **Tick the statements which are true for you. Then compare with a partner.**

A I like following band members on Facebook and Twitter.

B These days I only download music that's free.

C I think the videos a band makes are just as important as their music.

D Most people haven't heard of the music I like.

E My music tastes are quite varied.

F I often discover new bands through personal recommendations.

2 ▶ 1.05 **You will hear five people talking about listening to music. Listen to Speaker 1. Which things does he mention?**

Twitter	video	new bands	his taste in music

3 **Look at extracts from Speaker 1 (1–4). Which one matches one of the statements A–F in Activity 1?**

1 Now I'm just into the same stuff as my friends – hip hop mainly.

2 I don't usually bother with Twitter or Facebook.

3 My friends are always sharing music files and telling each other about new discoveries. I've found a lot of new bands that way.

4 They'll only listen to new bands that no one's heard of. It's just a way of showing off, I think.

4 ▶ 1.06 **Now listen to Speakers 2–5. Choose from the list A–F (in Activity 1) what each speaker says. Use the letters only once. There is one extra letter which you do not need to use.**

EXAM TIP

Listen for words and phrases that are synonyms or paraphrases of the key words in the statements.

5 **Compare your answers in pairs. Then listen again to check.**

Speaking

6 **Work in pairs and discuss the questions.**

1 Which speaker's opinions are the most similar to yours?

2 How are your listening habits and attitudes to music similar to or different from your partner's?

Habit in the past

21:55

used to/would

▶ **GRAMMAR** REFERENCE p.168

1 **Look at the sentences and answer the questions.**

I <u>used to be obsessed</u> with music videos.

When I was growing up, my mum <u>would play</u> 1970s music and dance around the kitchen.

1 Is she still obsessed with music videos?

2 Did her mother often listen to 1970s music?

3 Which underlined verb describes a past state?

4 Which underlined verb describes a past habit?

5 Which of the underlined verbs can you use to describe <u>both</u> past states and habits?

LANGUAGE TIP

Be careful not to confuse *used to do* (describing past habit) with *be/get used to doing* (be accustomed to something in the present).

I **used to** hate classical music (= but now I like it).

I **am used to** being alone (= It's something that happens a lot and I don't mind it).

---

2 **Look at sentences 1–4. Is it possible to use both *would* and *used to*?**

1 My parents would always listen to classical music while we were having dinner.

2 My parents used to go to a jazz festival every year.

3 My dad used to have a really old radio.

4 My mum used to know all the words to every song by Madonna.

3 **Complete the text with the present simple, present continuous, *used to* or *would* forms of the verbs in brackets. Sometimes more than one is possible.**

Speaking

4 **Discuss the questions with a partner.**

1 How do you think the writer's children feel about her taste in music?

2 What kind of music did you use to listen to when you were younger? What did your parents think of it?

3 How do you think your taste in music will change as you get older?

My life as a punk

Insurance broker Sarah Collins might have a boring day job, but she's a punk at heart.

I always say that the best time of my life was when I **(1)** ~~had been~~ *was* (be) a punk. It's a time that I look back on fondly and I still **(2)** *smile* (smile) when I think of those wonderful people, their fantastic haircuts and clothes and their great personalities.

On Saturdays I **(3)** *went* (go) down the Kings Road in London. I **(4)** *met* (meet) punks from all over and we **(5)** *would* (just walk around), sit in the pubs, look in the shops and get searched by the police. That was a very good way to spend a Saturday.

Now I'm in my fifties. I **(6)** *am working* (work) in insurance and I've got three children. But just recently I've started to return to my punk roots. Although I **(7)** *got* (get) older, I've realised I still **(8)** *love* (love) going to gigs and hanging around with punks. I **(9)** *discover* (discover) fantastic new bands and I **(10)** *am enjoying* (enjoy) myself so much!

Informal email (Part 1)

▶ **WRITING** REFERENCE p.185

1 **How do you decide which bands you want to go and see?**

2 **Read the exam task. Who do you have to write to? Why are you writing?**

> You want to see this band which is performing soon but you don't want to go alone. You decide to invite your friend Josh to come with you. Read the information about the concert and the notes you have made. Then write an email to Josh inviting him to the concert.

say why you want to see them

prefer 26th because ...

MYSTERY JETS

By popular demand the Mystery Jets have extended their tour dates at Junction1 to include the 26th October as well as the 25th. Tickets are currently still available for both dates but are expected to sell out well in advance. Tickets can be booked online at Junction1gigs.com or from the Junction1 box office. All tickets are priced at £12.50. Doors open at 9p.m. This is a standing only event so get there early if you want to be near the stage!

offer to get tickets

ends late – suggest a place to stay

3 **Complete the sentences with a word or a phrase.**

Inviting	1 .... *would* you like to come to a gig with me?
Stating preferences	2 I'd prefer *watching* the concert on TV.
	3 I'd rather *play* at home.
Making offers	4 I *don't* mind paying for you.
	5 I *could* drive you home after the gig, if you like.
Making suggestions	6 Why *don't* see if there's any live music on tonight?
	7 *what* about staying in and watching a movie this evening?

4 **Complete the email to Josh with your own ideas.**

> Hi Josh
>
> Hope you're well. I've just found out that The Mystery Jets are playing next month. I really want to see them because *I love them!!!* (give a reason). *Do would you like to came* (invite Josh).
> They're playing on the 25th and 26th. *I'd rather prefer on 26th because I like* (say which prefer and why). Are you free then? We need to get tickets soon as they'll sell out really quickly. So let me know as soon as possible and *I'll buy* (offer to get tickets).
> It ends quite late so we may miss the train home. *I came No.1 on of my friend* (suggest a place to stay). Do you think that's a good idea?
> Please get back to me as soon as you can.
> All the best
> .... (name)

5 **Check that your email is between 120 and 150 words. You may need to cut or add some words.**

1 Complete the second sentence so that it has a similar meaning to the first sentence. Use between two and five words, including the word given.

Example:
I was given responsibility for booking gigs for our band.
OVER
Last month I took over booking gigs for our band.

1 I enjoyed learning to play the guitar and I'd like to take it up again one day.
USED
I .... learning to play the guitar and I'd like to take it up again one day.

2 We always went to the jazz festival every July.
WOULD
We .... to the jazz festival every July.

3 I perform in front of people all the time so I don't mind doing it.
USED
I .... in front of people, so I don't mind doing it.

4 Her career was an instant success as soon as she appeared on a TV advert.
TOOK
Her career .... as soon as she appeared on a TV advert.

5 Unfortunately I'm not like my grandfather, who could play the piano really well.
AFTER
Unfortunately, I .... my grandfather, who could play the piano really well.

6 When we started going out, I hated my boyfriend's taste in music but it's becoming less of a problem.
USED
I .... my boyfriend's taste in music.

2 Put the verbs in brackets into the present simple or present continuous form.

1 I .... (not like) classical music.
2 I don't understand what you .... (say). Can you say it again, please?
3 I .... (think) it's a good idea to learn an instrument when you're too young.
4 She's never at home. She .... (always do) something in the evening.
5 Traditional music .... (get) more and more popular.
6 You .... (play) really well today.

3 Choose the correct word to complete the sentences.

1 I try and .... running as often as I can.
   A go   B do   C doing   D going
2 I often have friends .... in the evening.
   A in   B round   C along   D down
3 Let's go .... the theatre soon.
   A out   B for   C to   D at
4 He's always .... on the computer to check his messages.
   A doing   B having   C going   D watching

4 Complete the text with the words in the box.

| available | collection | concerts | downloaded |
| fans | once | released | tastes |

MP3s have ruined our listening habits

Sometimes I feel the rise of MP3s has made music too easy to obtain. Instead of taking time to appreciate good music, most **(1)** .... now consume as much music as they possibly can. My music **(2)** .... feels increasingly impersonal, to the point where I don't even know if I've **(3)** .... an album or not. Sometimes I'll listen to an album I like only **(4)** .... The problem is there's just not enough time to give every album the same attention because there's always a new band that's just **(5)** .... their first album that I want to listen to.

And another problem is that, despite the huge variety of music **(6)** .... , I feel like people's **(7)** .... are actually narrowing because they generally only go to **(8)** .... where bands sound exactly like all the others they enjoy listening to.

Relative values

2

Speaking

1 **Discuss the questions.**

1 How do you think your friends would describe your personality?

2 What personality characteristics do you share with other members of your family?

2 **Do the personality quiz.**

PERSONALITY QUIZ	How likely are you to...	Very likely	Quite likely	Neither likely nor unlikely	Quite unlikely	Very unlikely
	1 start a conversation with a stranger?					X
	2 give advice to other people?			X		
	3 use difficult words?				X	
	4 change your mind about things?				X	
	5 organise social events?					X
	6 worry about being late?	X				

3 **Turn to page 157 to get your results. Then complete sentences 1–4 so they're true for you.**

1 I'm (very/quite) (un)likely to …

2 I tend to …

3 I'm good at … -*ing*.

4 I find it difficult to …

4 **Compare your sentences with a partner's and discuss the questions.**

1 How much do you have in common?

2 What did you learn from your results?

3 Do you think this is an accurate test of personality?

Vocabulary
formation of adjectives

5 Copy and complete the table with the adjective forms of the nouns in the box.

caution	comfort	drama	emotion	generosity	harm	hope
love	meaning	person	pessimist	prediction	reliability	sympathy

-able	-ous	-ic	-al	-ful
sociable	adventurous	realistic	practical	thoughtful

6 ▶ 1.07 Mark the stress on each adjective, then listen and check. Practise saying the words. Which ones stress different syllables to the noun form?

7 Which adjectives use the suffix *-less* or the prefix *un-* to form the negative?

Examples: hopeless, uncomfortable

Word formation (Part 3)

▶ **EXAM** FOCUS p.203

▶ EXAM FOCUS p.203

EXAM TIP

It's important to think about the meaning, not just the grammar. Sometimes you have to decide if an adjective is positive or negative.

8 Read the text quickly without worrying about the gaps. What problem with describing people's personalities is mentioned?

How well do you know yourself?

When trying to understand our own or other people's

(0) *behaviour* , we tend to over-simplify things. We use   **BEHAVE**

one or two adjectives to sum each other up. We think of one

friend as having a generally **(1)** .... and positive outlook,   **HOPE**

while another friend is considered **(2)** .... and negative.   **PESSIMIST**

Of course, in **(3)** .... none of us is so easily defined.   **REAL**

The truth is that we are all made up of inconsistent and

contradictory **(4)** ....; we can be quiet and serious with   **CHARACTER**

our colleagues at work but in our personal relationships

at home we are quite **(5)** .... and emotional. With some   **PREDICT**

friends we can be **(6)** .... and controlling, while we are   **CAUTION**

(7) .... thrill-seekers with other friends.   **ADVENTURE**

So can people be neatly **(8)** .... into personality types?   **DIVISION**

Or, do we alter our personality according to the **(9)** .... in   **DIFFERENT**

our changing moods and situations? Perhaps the idea of a

fixed personality is just a **(10)** .... misconception. Maybe   **MEANING**

we can never truly understand ourselves or other people.

9 What part of speech goes in each gap? If it's a noun, is it singular or plural?

10 Use the word given in capitals at the end of some of the lines to form a word that fits in the gap in the same line.

Multiple choice (Part 4)

▶ **EXAM** FOCUS p.205

1 **Discuss the questions.**

1 What do you think is the ideal number of children in a family? Why?

2 Are older children more or less independent than their younger siblings? Why?

2 **You're going to listen to a radio discussion about birth order. Read the first question in Activity 4 and underline the key words in the statement and the options.**

3 ▶ 1.08 **Listen to the first part of the discussion.**

1 Which key words, or words with a similar meaning to the statement and options, did you hear?

2 Which option correctly completes the statement?

4 ▶ 1.09 **Read through questions 2–7 and underline the key words. Then listen and choose the best answer, A, B or C.**

EXAM TIP

The radio presenter's questions will help you to follow the discussion, so you know which question you should be listening for.

1 Max says that people mistakenly believe that oldest children

A are likely to do well in the future.

B will be happier than their siblings.

C are often very independent at a young age.

2 What explanation is given for oldest children's results in intelligence tests?

A Parents expect more from the oldest child.

B Oldest children spend more time alone.

C The oldest child benefits from teaching younger siblings.

3 What typical characteristic of oldest children does Max share?

A He is very competitive.

B He experienced jealousy of a sibling.

C He always wanted to please his parents.

4 Max says that youngest children can often be

A confident.

B creative.

C cautious.

5 What do some psychologists believe is likely to increase the 'birth order effect'?

A a large age-gap between siblings

B families with three or more siblings

C having siblings of the same sex

6 What is recommended as the best combination for a successful marriage?

A two oldest children

B two middle children

C two third-born children

7 According to Max, why should we be cautious about the 'birth order effect'?

A Personality can also be affected by other things.

B Personality can change when people are away from their families.

C Personality is too complicated to define simply.

5 **Compare your answers with a partner. Then listen again to check.**

Speaking

6 **Work in pairs. How well do you get on with your siblings? What impact has the 'birth order effect' had on your family?**

Adverbs

▶ **GRAMMAR** REFERENCE p.161

1 **Underline the adverbs in sentences A–D. Then answer the questions.**

A They will have to work very hard to make their marriage work.

B It could be difficult for them to get on well.

C They are allowed to grow up more slowly.

D It can have hardly any impact on large families.

1 Which adverbs are irregular?

2 Which words can be both an adverb and an adjective?

2 **Choose the correct adverb.**

1 I *hardly/hard* know my brother because he's so much older than me.

2 I try *hard/hardly* to get on with my brothers and sisters.

3 He's been feeling depressed *late/lately*.

4 My mother had children *lately/late* in life.

5 My parents live *closely/close* to me.

6 We studied the results of the test *close/closely*.

Vocabulary

extreme adjectives

3 **Match adjectives 1–6 with extreme versions A–F.**

1 difficult
2 intelligent
3 angry
4 frightened
5 tired
6 big

A enormous
B terrified
C exhausted
D impossible
E brilliant
F furious

4 **Which adverbs in the box give the sentence a similar meaning?**

| fairly | completely | a bit | absolutely |
| very | | | |

1 He's *quite* intelligent.

2 He's *really* cautious.

3 She's *really* impossible to get on with.

4 She's a *really* good person.

5 He's a *really* amazing person.

6 He can be *quite* difficult.

5 **Choose the correct adverb(s) to form the rules.**

1 *Really/Very* can be used with any adjective in order to intensify meaning.

2 *Completely* and *absolutely/Really* and *very* are only used with extreme adjectives.

3 *Quite/A bit* is only used when making a criticism with adjectives with a negative meaning.

Speaking

6 **Complete sentences 1–3 with phrases A–C to make statements you agree with. Discuss your sentences with a partner. Do you agree?**

1 It's fairly easy …

2 It's quite hard …

3 It's absolutely impossible …

A … to judge a person's character from their appearance.

B … to get on with everyone in your family.

C … for parents to treat all their children equally.

Colin Firth in *The King's Speech*

Speaking

1 How would you feel if you had a brother or sister who was gifted or famous?

Multiple matching (Part 3)

▶ **EXAM** FOCUS p.201

2 You are going to read an article in which four people talk about their relationship with their brother or sister. Read the text quickly and find out which person is

1   a twin?
2   the oldest?
3   a middle child?
4   the youngest of four?

3 Look at the underlined words in Activity 4, question 1. What information would you expect to find in the text? Check your answer in extract A.

> **EXAM TIP**
>
> Underline the key words in the options and then read through the texts quickly to find a similar word or expression which says the same thing in a different way.

4 For questions 2–14, choose from the people (A–D). The people may be chosen more than once.

Which person

remembers having <u>mixed feelings</u> about the <u>success of a sibling</u>?	1 A
used to try not to get involved when their sibling behaved badly?	2 A
once stopped doing something because of sibling rivalry?	3 B
values the relationship with their sibling more than they used to?	4 C
used to feel their sibling was more special to their parents?	5 B
says their sibling still treats them as if they hadn't grown up?	6 C
feels differently about being famous from their sibling?	7 B
was too cautious to take up a career that they really wanted?	8 A
could depend on their sibling for practical advice as a child?	9 C
thinks people can get labelled too easily?	10 D
was looked after by their sibling at school?	11 A
was a bit annoyed when their sibling was born?	12 D
says their sibling used to be more friendly than them?	13 A
thinks their sibling is the most efficient person in the family?	14 C
admired their sibling for their determination?	15 A

5 Which sibling relationship in the article did you find most interesting? Why?

Vocabulary

phrasal verbs

6 Match the phrasal verbs underlined in the article to meanings 1–8.

1 organise something
2 escape
3 succeed
4 make (someone) leave
5 be determined
6 suddenly become successful
7 admire
8 arrive unexpectedly

7 Work in pairs and discuss the questions.

1   Who do you look up to?
2   Have you ever set your heart on something?
3   Do you sort out your possessions regularly and get rid of things you don't need?
4   Where would you like to get away to?

RELATIONSHIPS

Friend or enemy?

Can siblings ever really be friends?

A Kate Firth, voice coach; sister to film star Colin

As the older brother, Colin was protective of me; when I was very young he'd collect me from the classroom and make sure I had enough money to buy a chocolate bar at break. As a teenager, I looked up to him because he was much more capable and confident than me. I was jealous of his arty friends because I felt I had to be safe and conventional and go to university as our parents expected us to. Colin could have gone but he had set his heart on drama school. I desperately wanted to act too but never had his courage, although I did act for a while, as did my younger brother, Jonathan. Our parents didn't think that success as an actor was a real possibility but Colin and I shared a strong belief that one day we would make it. I knew Colin was talented because I saw him in school plays and at the Drama centre. In my first year at university he did Hamlet and I sat there feeling terribly proud and jealous at the same time because he was doing exactly what I wanted to do. After that his career took off.

B Jonathan Self, journalist and author; brother to novelist and broadcaster Will

When Will was three, he packed a suitcase with toys and ran away from home. I think he only got about four kilometres down the road before he was found but I remember feeling delighted that we had finally got rid of him. I hadn't been at all pleased, at the age of two, when a new child turned up. Even so, we played a lot together as kids and I remember finding him very lovable. But I saw how he became the favourite as soon as my parents, who valued intellect enormously, discovered what an incredible brain he had. When I started working on my first book, I found out that he was doing the same. I felt very competitive and when I read his I thought 'I'll never be as good as that' and gave up. Now I've established myself as a writer, I don't feel like that any more and I'm pleased with Will's success. Unlike me, I think he quite likes being in the public eye.

C Zoë Heller, author and journalist; sister to headhunter, Emily

Unlike me, Emily has always been grown up for her age. She's only three years older than me but she looked after me a lot when we were growing up. She taught me how to write a cheque and would rescue me when I got lost on the underground. And even today she always knows where everything is so if I or my two other older siblings need a document or a family photograph, she's the one you'll call. Although the gap does get smaller as you get older, Emily still can't accept I'm now a mature woman with children; when she visits me she still tidies my flat and sorts out my filing system. I've come to understand the importance of family rather late in life. During my twenties I just wanted to get away. I've lived in New York for years, yet now the first thing I do when I get back to London is have dinner with Emily.

D Will Young, singer-songwriter and actor; brother to Rupert, founder of a charity which helps people with depression

The problem with being twins is that you constantly get compared, and one twin can suffer. I remember when we went to school it was decided that I was the clever one and Rupert was the sporty one. I think he gave up a bit because of the comparison. But we ended up getting more or less the same exam results – it's just that people put you in a certain box and it's difficult to get away from that. Rupert was more of a tearaway than me and I'd get annoyed by teachers who tried to make me responsible for him. As we got older, Rupert was more sociable, and at eighteen I wished I was as good at parties as he was. He'd get on the dance floor, whereas I was very self-conscious. He was going out with lots of girls and was very handsome, which I wasn't. It's funny that I'm now the performer. ■

Listening

1 **Work in pairs and discuss the questions.**

1 Do you have a lot of relations?

2 Which ones do you get on well/badly with?

2 ▶ **1.10** **Listen to five people talking about one of their relations. Match Speakers 1–5 to comments A–E.**

A We'd like him to move house.

B It's a waste of time saying anything to him.

C I once felt worried about being alone with him.

D We enjoy doing the same things.

E I've offered to teach him a sport.

Verb patterns: -ing/infinitive

▶ **GRAMMAR** REFERENCE p.178

3 **Match examples A–E in Activity 2 with rules 1–5.**

Use -ing

1 after some verbs (___D___)

2 after prepositions (...............)

3 after some expressions (...............)

Use infinitive

4 After some verbs (...............)

5 After some verbs + object (...............)

LANGUAGE TIP

Some verbs (e.g. *make, let*) are followed by object plus infinitive without *to*: I **made her tidy up**.

Some verbs (e.g. *love*) can be followed by *-ing* or infinitive with little or no change in meaning: I love **riding/to ride**.

To form a negative, use *not* before the verb: I hate **not** going./He told me **not** to go.

---

verbs with -ing or infinitive with a change of meaning

4 **For sentence pairs 1–5, choose the correct options and explain the difference in meaning between each pair.**

1 A My mother stopped *making/to make* lunch because the phone rang.

B My mother stopped *making/to make* lunch because we were hungry.

2 A Dad tried *phoning/to phone* but nobody answered.

B Dad tried *phoning/to phone* but he couldn't remember the number so he gave up.

3 A The kids remembered *buying/to buy* Grandma a present and write a card for her.

B The kids remembered *buying/to buy* Grandma a present but couldn't find it again later.

4 A My father went on *having/to have* children until he was in his sixties.

B My father went on *having/to have* children with my stepmother.

5 A I regret *telling/to tell* you that all train services have been cancelled.

B I regret *telling/to tell* you because now you're upset.

5 **Read the article quickly. What did Ben like and dislike about having famous parents?**

6 **Complete the text with the -ing form or the infinitive of the verb in brackets.**

7 **Work in pairs. Imagine you have become a celebrity. Talk about what you love, can afford, regret, don't mind, can't stand, etc.**

Ben Taylor: My famous parents

The son of singers James Taylor and Carly Simon talks about his childhood.

As a child, I remember (**1**) .... (*go*) on tour with my dad. It was awesome and I particularly loved (**2**) .... (*sleep*) on the tour bus. He encouraged me (**3**) .... (*travel*) with him on holiday, too – we've been everywhere together.

I didn't mind my parents (**4**) .... (*split up*) because, although I lived with my mother, I still saw my dad a lot. I never regretted (**5**) .... (*have*) celebrity parents because there are lots of advantages, too, although I didn't like people (**6**) .... (*introduce*) me as their son.

I started (**7**) .... (*play*) the guitar myself when I was about ten, just because I wanted (**8**) .... (*know*) if I could do it. I asked my father (**9**) .... (*teach*) me. If he thinks I'm keen on (**10**) .... (*do*) something, he's always very supportive.

Now I'm an adult, I still try (**11**) .... (*go*) on holiday with my dad whenever I can. Sometimes my sister comes with us but I prefer (**12**) .... (*be*) on my own with him. There's always been a lot of rivalry between us for my father's attention.

Listening

1 Look at the photos and read the task below. What relationship does each photo show?

> Talk to each other about the effect these relationships can have on people's lives. Then decide which relationship has the most influence.

2 ▶ **1.11** Listen to Alana and Federico. Which relationships are they discussing? Why do they think they are important?

Collaborative task and discussion (Parts 3 and 4)

agreeing and disagreeing

▶ **EXAM** FOCUS P.207

3 Copy and complete the table with the phrases in the box. Which of the expressions of agreement are uncertain?

So do I/Neither do I   I'm not convinced
That's very true   Good point   I'm not sure about that.
I see what you mean, but…   I suppose so   OK, but…
What about you?   What's your view on that?
I hadn't thought of that.   Exactly!   Well, actually…

Agreeing	Disagreeing politely	Asking opinions

4 Work in pairs and do the task in Activity 1. Talk for three minutes.

EXAM TIP

Give your opinions but make sure you also listen to your partner. Ask about their opinions and respond to what they say.

5 Discuss the following questions.

1 Which people do you think have had the most influence on different stages of your life?

2 Do families sometimes get closer as they get older? Why/Why not?

3 Is it better to have older or younger parents?

4 What are the advantages and disadvantages of belonging to a big family?

Semi-formal letter (Part 1)

▶ **WRITING** REFERENCE p.182

1 Read the exam task and answer the questions.

1 Who must you write to?
2 Why are you writing?
3 Which style do you need to write in?

> You are planning to study at a college in England this summer. Read the letter from the accommodation officer at the college and the notes you have made on it.

say which prefer and why

request a visit to ...

Dear Student

I'm writing to you regarding your placement with a family this summer. We try very hard to match our students with the most appropriate family, so I'd be grateful if you could provide the following information:

• whether you would prefer to stay with a family in an apartment in the city centre or in a house in the suburbs
• a short description of your interests
• suggestions of somewhere you would like to visit with the family during your first weekend.
• whether you would like the family to meet you at the airport

I look forward to hearing from you soon.

Yours faithfully

Emma Brookes

Accommodation Officer
Wentworth College

sports? shopping?

not necessary because ...

2 Underline phrases in the letter which

1 request something politely.
2 state the purpose of the letter.
3 ask for a prompt reply.
4 end the letter appropriately.

3 Say whether the following phrases would be appropriate for a) an informal letter/email, b) a semi-formal letter/email or c) both.

1 I'd prefer to stay …
2 I'd rather stay …
3 My preference would be to stay …
4 My interests include …
5 I enjoy playing …
6 Would it be possible to visit …?
7 I'd be really interested in visiting … if at all possible.
8 It would be absolutely amazing to see …
9 It isn't necessary for the family to collect me because …
10 Don't worry about collecting me because …

4 Write your letter to the Accommodation Officer, using all your notes.
Write 120–150 words.

> **EXAM TIP**
>
> You DON'T need to put your address at the top of your letter.

> **LANGUAGE TIP**
>
> In a semi-formal/formal letter to someone you don't know use their title (*Mr, Mrs, Miss, Ms*) and their surname only. If you're not sure if a woman is married you should use Ms (e.g. *Dear **Ms** Brookes*).

5 Check your work using the writing checklist on page 179.

1 Complete the second sentence with between two and five words, including the word given, so that it has a similar meaning to the first sentence.

1 I'm going to throw away all those old newspapers tomorrow.
   RID
   I'm going to *get rid off* all those old newspapers tomorrow.

2 Peter has always admired his uncle for everything he has achieved.
   LOOK
   Peter has always *look after up to* his uncle for everything he has achieved.

3 She didn't know I was coming – I just arrived unexpectedly on her doorstep.
   TURN
   She didn't know I was coming – I just *turn up* on her doorstep.

4 After fifteen years, the company suddenly became successful.
   TAKE
   The company suddenly *took off* after it had been running for fifteen years.

5 Not many people become successful in the world of acting.
   MAKE
   Not many people *make up* in the world of acting.

6 Olivia has told me she wants to escape to a hot country this summer.
   GET
   Olivia has told me she wants to *get away* to a hot country this summer.

2 Correct the mistake in each of the sentences.

1 He's tried really hardly to get tickets for you.
2 The cinema is fairly closely to the station.
3 The football results were absolutely close.
4 She finished late and I was very furious with her.
5 They spoke free about their difficult childhood.
6 It was hardly dark but he was completely frightened.
7 It would be a bit brilliant if we won the Cup Final.
8 She's been working very hardly lately.

3 Complete the sentences with the adjectives in the box.

cautious   confident   creative
independent   practical   sociable

1 Whereas I'm quite shy about speaking in public, my brother's always been *confident*
2 Even at the age of eighty-five, my gran never likes relying on other people. She's very *independent*
3 My husband's not very good at doing things with his hands. He's not at all *practical*
4 I prefer my own company but my sisters are the opposite; they're all really *sociable*
5 My father paints and writes really well. He's always been really *creative*
6 I am not prepared to take risks any more. I'm getting more and more *cautious*

4 Complete the sentences, using the correct form of the word in capitals.

1 My new car isn't as *reliable* as I hoped it would be. **RELY**
2 Molly's story is very *imaginative* I don't know where she gets her ideas from. **IMAGINE**
3 My children will never try any new food. They are very .... **ADVENTURE**
4 I don't think you're being very *realistic* about how much we can finish. **REAL**
5 I'm absolutely *hopeless* at languages. I just can't do them. **HOPE**
6 I explained I'd been ill but the boss wasn't at all *sympathetic* **SYMPATHY**

5 Complete the sentences with the correct alternative.

1 I regretted not *having/to have* a car to drive.
2 He'd like us *working/to work* late this evening.
3 I'm not very good at *running/to run*.
4 Have you remembered *locking/to lock* the door?
5 Melanie has promised *inviting/to invite us* to stay.
6 She stopped *working/to work* and had a rest.
7 The teacher made me *to finish/finish* my work before I left.
8 Jim asked me *not to/to not* speak.

Things that matter

Multiple choice (Part 1)

▶ **EXAM** FOCUS p.200

1 What matters to you? Put the things in order of importance.

family   friends   interests   education/career   possessions

EXAM TIP

Read the question stems and highlight the part of the text which answers each question. Then read the four options very carefully and decide on the answer.

2 Read the title and first paragraph of the newspaper article and guess what it will be about. Then read the rest of the article and check.

3 Read the article again. For questions 1–8, choose the answer (A, B, C or D) which you think fits best according to the text.

1 What is the writer's attitude towards football fans at matches?

  A She's impressed by their behaviour.

  B She's astonished by how they can afford tickets.

  C She's embarrassed by how irresponsible they are.

  D She's sympathetic towards the strength of their emotions.

2 What does *it* refer to in line 13?

  A an ugly side   **B** passion   **C** football   **D** a penalty shoot-out

3 What does the writer suggest is the main characteristic of obsessive people?

  A They're fascinated by famous people.

  B They find it easier to use technology to communicate.

  C They are out of touch with reality.

  D They are completely normal for most of the time.

4 The writer thinks everyone should have a passion because

  A it puts them in touch with their basic emotions.

  B it encourages affectionate behaviour.

  C it gives them an excuse to take time off work.

  D it makes everything else in life seem unimportant.

5 What does *'thin on the ground'* mean in line 77?

  A unimpressive   **B** infrequent   **C** inflexible   **D** unexpected

LIFESTYLE | 27

All you need is love (and a scarf)

Grown men with their heads buried in each other's shoulders or hidden behind shaking hands. Young mothers shouting with joy. This is what last Saturday's penalty shoot-out for the European Cup produced. If you missed the semi-final, then try and catch the European Cup Final on television tomorrow. Then you'll see what passion does to people. And, while having an ugly side, it is in fact more likely to enrich our lives and make us better people.

Today, supporters are gathering for the big match. Fans who could not afford the fare to travel abroad have sold their car. Others have borrowed from relatives they once promised themselves they would never borrow from again. And many will turn up without any accommodation or even a match ticket. Despite this, they will be relieved just to be there, to be part of it all. It might sound like madness but, as one who is going and is incredibly excited about it, I can tell you I feel extremely fortunate.

Passion should not be confused with obsession. There are those who live in a dream state, madly in love with someone they will never meet – because he is a dead singer or a famous actor who is unlikely ever to visit their hometown – and therefore unable to form real relationships. There are those who spend every waking hour logged on to chat rooms where the only topic of conversation is Star Wars. However, there are also ordinary people – sensible parents, husbands, employees and employers – whose interests are much more healthy and straightforward. Their emotions are also linked to forces they cannot control, but they are to be admired for it.

Maybe some people are incapable of finding a passion, but if so they are missing out. Passions are deep, full of joy and pain, teaching you how to sob when you feel hurt, how to deal with disappointment, how to sing with enthusiasm in public

(not easy). Because of them you might end up hugging a complete stranger or making new friends. They help you to feel part of a community and have something to tease your neighbour about. They are a great way for families to bond together; many dads insist that they are spending their time fishing or playing chess because their child is keen, when actually they are delighted to become absorbed by something outside home, job or money worries.

Explosions of joy are normally thin on the ground. The birth *line 77* of your child, your wedding day, a pay rise are all lovely and a reason to do something special, but they do not happen every week. If you happen to follow a football or rugby team, there are celebrations all the time.

For some, a passion can be switched on and off – which is better than not having a passion at all, I suppose. Witness the behaviour that tennis brings about at the annual two-week UK tennis tournament at Wimbledon. Calm, controlled middle-aged women are suddenly prepared to camp overnight on damp pavements in London and squeal encouragement. Otherwise cool, fashionable students are happy to wave at the TV cameras while wearing silly hats and sunglasses that spurt water.

I had a nightmare two nights ago. In the nightmare, Liverpool's match against AC Milan went to a penalty shoot-out and Liverpool lost. 'That's not a nightmare,' said my husband. But isn't that the point? If I can wake up in a sweat about football, it means I'm not waking up trembling from a dream in which I crashed my car or lost my job.

In the end, what defines us as human is not only language. It is the ability to care about something that does not directly affect our health or wealth or importance. Passions are a rehearsal for life, a distraction from boredom and most of all they are fun – even when they let you down.

6 The writer mentions Wimbledon to show that
  A it's not only football which inspires strong feelings.
  B a wide range of people enjoy this kind of event.
  C sports spectators can behave uncharacteristically.
  D people often behave badly to get on TV.

7 The writer describes her nightmare to emphasise that
  A she takes football extremely seriously.
  B supporting football can be stressful.
  C being a football fan can cause domestic arguments.
  D worrying about football can be a useful distraction.

8 The writer's main purpose is to encourage her readers to
  A become sports fans.
  B have an enthusiasm for something.
  C show their emotions openly.
  D enjoy themselves more.

4 Work in pairs. Do you know anybody who has a passion for something? Have you ever had a passion in common with a member of your family?

Vocabulary

-ed adjectives and prepositions

5 Choose the correct preposition. Then ask your partner these questions.

1 What are you interested *in/at*? What do you find boring?
2 Who are you frightened *with/of*? What do you find frightening?
3 What do you sometimes feel worried *about/in*?
4 Who or what do you get annoyed *of/by*?
5 What do you sometimes feel embarrassed *in/by*? Who do you find embarrassing?
6 What do you get excited *with/about*?

LANGUAGE TIP

-ed adjectives describe how you feel about something.
I'm **bored** with this TV programme.

-ing adjectives describe the noun.
This programme's so **boring**.

Present perfect and past simple

▶ **GRAMMAR** REFERENCE p.176–7

| Home | Archive | News | Members | Search |

I've been mad about horses for most of my life. I've never owned one, but my friend and I used to help out every weekend at the local riding stables and then the owner would let us ride the ponies. But I haven't been back there since I left home to go to college five years ago. Last month a colleague at work persuaded me to take up riding again so I've been having lessons with her. I've only had four so far but I've just got my confidence back so I'll definitely keep it up.

1 **Read Anna's blog, in which she talks about her passion. Answer questions 1–5.**

1 How long has Anna loved horses?
2 Does she still help out at the stables?
3 When did she start riding again? Why?
4 How long has she been riding again?
5 How many lessons has she had?

2 **Look at the verb forms underlined in the text. Which ones describe**

1 completed actions in the past?
2 past habits which are now finished?

3 **Look at the highlighted example of the present perfect simple in the blog. Circle four more examples.**

4 **Match examples 1–3 with uses of the present perfect described in A–C.**

1 *I've just got my confidence back.*
2 *I've never owned one.*
3 *I've been mad about horses for most of my life.*

A began in the past and is still continuing
B has recently happened and is relevant to the present
C refers to indefinite time in the past

5 **Look at the sentences. Which of the time expressions underlined refers to a period of time and which to a point in time?**

1 *I've been mad about horses <u>for</u> most of my life.*
2 *I haven't been back there <u>since</u> I left home to go to college five years ago.*

6 **Divide these time expressions into those which are usually used with**

1 the past simple
2 the present perfect

yet	so far	already	in 2010
never	once	just	last month
ago	this month	at lunchtime	

present perfect simple or continuous?

7 **Look at the sentences from the blog. Which one describes**

1 a completed activity?
2 an activity over a period of time (which may or may not be finished)?

A *I've been having lessons.*
B *I've had four lessons.*

8 **Complete the sentences below with simple past, present perfect simple or present perfect continuous. There may be more than one possibility.**

1 I .... (*ride*) a motorbike since I was seventeen.
2 I .... (*once witness*) a crime.
3 I .... (*live*) abroad when I was a child.
4 I .... (*have*) an operation a few years ago.
5 I .... (*never go*) camping.
6 I .... (*just win*) a competition.

9 **Work in pairs. Ask and answer questions with *Have you ever …?* and *How long …?***

Use the ideas in Activity 8 to help you. If appropriate, ask for more details, using *When? Why?* etc.

Grammar *as/like*

▶ **GRAMMAR** REFERENCE p.164

1 **Complete sentences 1–6 with *as* or *like*.**

1 Was that film .... all his other ones?

2 Shall we still have lunch together, ... we said yesterday?

3 I've always regarded you .... a friend.

4 A job .... that one takes a long time to finish.

5 He's working .... a waiter in the holidays.

6 Please do it carefully .... I asked you.

LANGUAGE TIP

as + noun, for a role or purpose:
*She works **as a musician**. I use that room **as a study**.*

as + noun clause, for manner: *I treated him **as my son**.*

like + noun, for comparison:
*You're just **like Tony**; **Like you**, I love jazz.*

like + noun for informal examples:
*Food **like that risotto** is worth waiting for.*

Open cloze (Part 2)

▶ **EXAM** FOCUS p.202

2 **Work in pairs and discuss the questions.**

1 What do you do to cheer yourself up when you're depressed?

2 What makes you really happy?

3 **Read the text quickly. Underline three things that make Pixie happy. Are you like her?**

4 **Look at the example (0). What part of speech is it? Now look at gaps 1–12. What kind of word is missing?**

5 **Read the text again and think of the word which best fits each gap. Use only one word in each gap.**

EXAM TIP

Read the whole sentence, especially the words before and after each gap. Think about what kind of word is missing (e.g. a preposition, a pronoun).

6 **Compare your answers with a partner.**

Pixie Lott: What makes me happy

The London-based singer tells us about the things that make her smile.

I'm at my happiest when I'm (0) ......*on*...... stage or writing music. Music, for me, is medicine and writing songs is a kind of therapy. And, (1) .... lots of people, even just listening (2) .... music makes me happy. If I'm fed up or worried (3) .... something, I put my iPod on loud and it changes my mood at once. I use it (4) .... a way of relaxing and there's always a song that matches my mood. But the song I like best is a 1980s tune, (5) .... my friends and I play at full volume (6) .... we're getting ready to go out. We all love it. I've got some very happy memories associated with that song When I (7) .... had a bad day or feel unhappy, I usually go to the piano and write (8) .... song. Sometimes I'm almost crying at the time but I always feel much (9) .... cheerful afterwards. The emotion is real and it really helps me. I am not really sure why music connects so strongly with me, but it always (10) .... these days.

I guess I'm a naturally happy person. Apart from my music, I also love being (11) .... home with my friends and my family. I know I am so lucky to have (12) .... all living so near.

LIFE-OF-LUXURY.CO.UK

Sign in | Email updates | Shopping bag

WHAT'S NEW   BOUTIQUE   GIFTS   ACCESSORIES   MAGAZINE   DESIGNERS   **CONTACT**

VIEW DETAILS ▶   ADD TO BASKET ▶

Speaking and vocabulary
money

1 Match the price tags to the things in the pictures. Then see if your partner agrees. Decide whether each thing is

1 worth the money.
2 good value for money.
3 a waste of money.

| £675 | $102.3 million | $158,500 |
| £35,000 | €4,200 | |

2 Match the two halves of the expressions. Then discuss what they mean with a partner. Do you have similar expressions in your language?

1 He's got more money   A   to burn.
2 Put your money where   B   not made of money.
3 I'm a bit short   C   a fortune.
4 Money's a bit   D   your mouth is.
5 She's got money   E   tight at the moment.
6 He's worth   F   to make ends meet.
7 My mum always says she's   G   of money this month.
8 It's sometimes hard   H   than sense.

3 Complete the sentences with a preposition from the box. Which of the statements do you agree with and why?

| on | within | of | away | to | in |

1 It's difficult to live .... your means when you're a student.
2 You should always avoid being .... debt.
3 Having to live .... a tight budget is boring.
4 Very rich people should give most of their money ....
5 It's not a good idea to lend your credit card .... a friend.
6 Young people today have a higher standard .... living than their grandparents' generation.

Sentence completion (Part 2)

▶ **EXAM** FOCUS p.204

4 You're going to hear a multi-millionaire called Gavin Norris talking about his life. Read the gapped sentences in Activity 7. Which of A–E do you expect to hear?

A   how he made his fortune
B   his attitude to money
C   his typical working day
D   what he spends his money on
E   where he lives

5 ▶ 1.12 **Listen and check.**

6 Look at the gap in each sentence. Where do you think you can put

1   a number?
2   a noun?
3   a plural form?
4   only one word?

EXAM TIP

Usually you only have to write one or two words or a number in the gap. Occasionally you may need to write three words.

7 ▶ 1.12 **Listen again and complete the gapped sentences.**

8 Compare your answers in pairs. Then listen again to check. Make sure you have spelt the words correctly.

9 Work in pairs and discuss the questions.

1   How do you think Gavin's children feel about his decision to give all his money away?
2   What problems can people have if they inherit a lot of money?

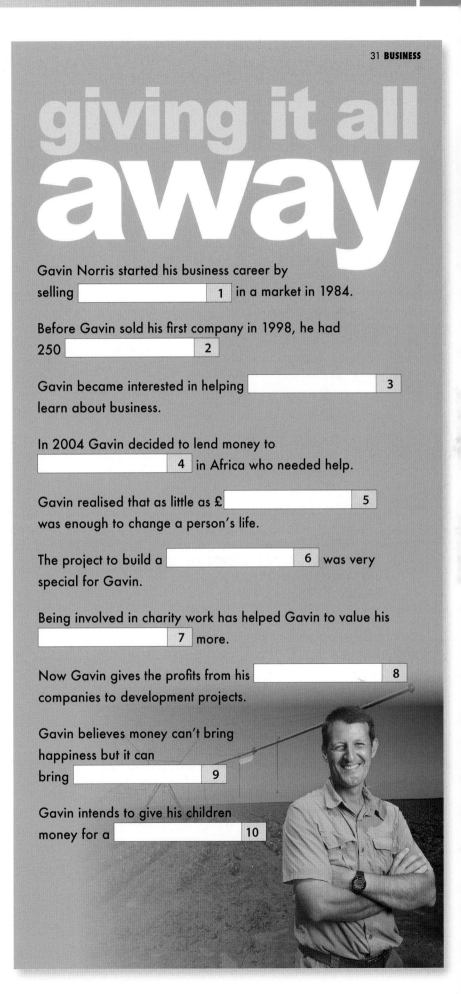

31 **BUSINESS**

giving it all away

Gavin Norris started his business career by selling [_____ 1] in a market in 1984.

Before Gavin sold his first company in 1998, he had 250 [_____ 2]

Gavin became interested in helping [_____ 3] learn about business.

In 2004 Gavin decided to lend money to [_____ 4] in Africa who needed help.

Gavin realised that as little as £[_____ 5] was enough to change a person's life.

The project to build a [_____ 6] was very special for Gavin.

Being involved in charity work has helped Gavin to value his [_____ 7] more.

Now Gavin gives the profits from his [_____ 8] companies to development projects.

Gavin believes money can't bring happiness but it can bring [_____ 9]

Gavin intends to give his children money for a [_____ 10]

Comparing

▶ **GRAMMAR** REFERENCE p.165

1 ▶ 1.13 **Look at sentences 1–3 taken from the listening on page 31 and complete them with the correct comparative or superlative form. Then listen and check.**

1 I'm .... I used to be in holidays. (*interested*)

2 Building the hospital was .... experience of my life. (*satisfying*)

3 I'm .... I was twenty years ago. (*happy*)

2 **Decide which pairs of sentences have a similar meaning, and which have a different meaning.**

1 **A** I've never been as happy as I am now.
  B I'm just as happy now as I ever was.

2 **A** My car was by far the most expensive thing I've ever bought.
  B My car was a lot more expensive than anything else I've ever bought.

3 **A** My grandfather is one of the most generous people I know.
  B There aren't many people who are as generous as my grandfather.

3 **Complete the second sentence so that it has a similar meaning to the first, using the word given in bold.**

Example: A scooter isn't nearly as expensive as a sports car. **LOT**
A sports car is **a lot more expensive than** *a scooter.*

1 Our standard of living is a bit lower than it was. **QUITE**
  Our standard of living is not .... it was.

2 There aren't many cities which are as exciting as Rio de Janeiro. **ONE**
  Rio de Janeiro is .... exciting cities.

3 She doesn't have nearly as much free time now. **LESS**
  She has .... free time than before.

4 Not many people earn such a high salary as he does. **THAN**
  His salary is .... most people's.

5 He's almost as wealthy as she is. **BIT**
  She's .... him.

6 It's getting much more difficult to get a bank loan. **AS**
  It is .... to get a bank loan now.

Speaking comparing quantities

4 **Use the table to make six sentences that are true about you.**

I spend	most	
	a large amount	
	quite a lot	of my money on…
	hardly any	of my time -ing
I don't spend	much	
	any	

5 **Compare your answers in groups and write a paragraph about how your group spends time and money.**

Example: The thing we spend most/least time/money on is … More/Less than half of us spend a large amount on …

Long turn (Part 2)

comparing

▶ **EXAM** FOCUS p.206

1 **What do these photos have in common? Choose A or B.**

A They show things which are important to people.

B They show people in unusual situations.

2 **Make a list of the similarities and differences between the two pictures.**

3 ▶ **1.14** **Listen to a student comparing the two photographs. Does she mention any of the points on your list?**

4 **Complete the sentences with *like* or *as if/as though*. In which sentences is it only possible to use *like*? Why?**

1 It looks .... a graduation ceremony.

2 The man looks .... he's very proud of his car.

3 It looks .... hard work.

4 He looks .... he's a bit obsessive.

5 She looks .... she's having more fun than the man.

▶ **GRAMMAR** REFERENCE p.164

5 **Look at sentences A and B and answer questions 1–3 about *whereas* and *while*.**

A *While* the man may have a passion for his car, it's probably not something that will last for his whole life.

B The first picture is celebrating an achievement *whereas* the second picture shows someone who values an important possession.

1 Which sentence is making a comparison and showing how the two things are different?

2 In which sentence is it possible to use both *whereas* and *while*?

3 In which sentence could you use *although* instead of *while/whereas*?

6 **Make sentences with *both, too* or *also*. Where can you put these words in the sentence? There may be more than one possibility.**

1 the pictures show an achievement (*both*)

2 the man looks happy (*also*)

3 the man seems to be enjoying himself (*too*)

7 **Work with a partner.**

Student A: look at the photos on page 152.

Student B: look at the photos on page 154.

Take turns to compare your photos. Try to use expressions such as *whereas, while, both, also, too, like, as if/as though*.

EXAM TIP

Don't describe what's in the pictures. Focus on the main topic and compare the main similarity and any differences between the pictures.

8 **Work in pairs. Do you agree with this statement?**

Happiness is not having what you want but wanting what you have.

Article (Part 2)

▶ **WRITING** REFERENCE p.187

1 **Look at the exam task and answer the questions.**

1 What kind of style will you write it in? How do you know?

2 What information do you need to include?

> You have seen the following advertisement in a magazine for young people.
>
> > **An object that matters to me**
> >
> > Write us an article, describing something you own and explaining why it's important to you.
> >
> > The best article will be published in the magazine next month.
>
> Write your **article** in **120–180 words**.

2 **Look at opening paragraphs A and B. Which one is most effective? Think about**

1 how eye-catching the title is.

2 how appropriate the style is.

3 how varied the language is.

EXAM TIP

Try to 'speak' directly to the reader for maximum impact.

Paragraph A

> What I'd save in a fire
> Have you ever thought about which one thing you'd save if you were in a fire? Well, for me it would definitely be my laptop. Obviously, I'd rescue my family and pets first but after that it would be my precious computer.

Paragraph B

> My most important possession
> My laptop is very important to me and I would be very upset if it got lost or damaged. I spend hours every day using my laptop and I would be lost without it. I think most people feel the same way about their laptops.

3 **Look at notes A–H and choose whether to include them in Paragraph two: a simple description of the object or Paragraph three: the reasons why it's special to you.**

A eighteenth birthday present from parents

B not expensive and very ordinary to look at

C two years old

D used to have to share my brother's computer

E all my photographs are on it

F made by Toshiba

G user-friendly

H contains friends' details

4 **Work in pairs. Write paragraphs two and three, using the ideas in Activity 3.**

5 **Write one or two concluding sentences to finish the article. You could explain, for example, that it has sentimental value and contains memories that couldn't be replaced.**

6 **Make notes on your own response to the advert. Choose a favourite possession and divide your notes into four paragraphs:**

1 Introduction (a title and introduction to get the readers' attention)

2 Background (a description of the object)

3 Opinion (the reasons why it is important to you)

4 Conclusion (a brief conclusion)

LANGUAGE TIP

Use extreme adjectives such as *amazing*, and extreme adverbs such as *absolutely* and *incredibly* for emphasis.

7 **Write your article in 120–180 words. Then check it for spelling and punctuation. Write another draft if necessary.**

8 **Read other students' articles and choose which ones to include in the magazine.**

1 Choose the best alternative to complete the following sentences.

1 A .... standard of living is important to me.
   A tall   **B** big   **C** great   **D** high

2 The house they live in must be worth a ....
   A treasure   **B** fortune   **C** resource   **D** wealth

3 When I was at college I had to learn to live .... a budget.
   A on   **B** in   **C** from   **D** at

4 I'm afraid I can't come because I'm .... of money.
   A low   **B** lacking   **C** short   **D** tight

5 She is always .... debt at the end of the term.
   A on   **B** at   **C** with   **D** in

6 I'm still learning to live .... my means.
   A between   **B** within   **C** under   **D** at

2 Complete the gap in the second sentence so that it means the same as the first sentence. Use between two and five words, including the word given.

1 Rebecca started living here five years ago. **FOR**
   Rebecca .... five years.

2 I last saw Mike in 2006. **SINCE**
   I .... 2006.

3 This is my first visit to India. **TIME**
   This is the first .... to India.

4 It's kind of you but I had a coffee earlier. **ALREADY**
   It's kind of you but I .... a coffee.

5 I don't spend much money on clothes these days. **ANY**
   I .... money on clothes these days.

6 This hotel isn't nearly as expensive as the other one. **FAR**
   The other hotel is .... this one.

7 Both Tom and Zak are equally friendly. **JUST**
   Tom is .... Zak.

8 There aren't many fashion designers that are as expensive as Prada. **ONE**
   Prada is .... fashion designers.

3 Complete the sentences with a word formed from the word in capitals.

1 I haven't got much money but I'm not .... about it. **WORRY**

2 Golf is not a very .... sport to watch on TV. **INTEREST**

3 Having a passion can make life more .... **EXCITE**

4 I'm really .... by my obsession with that actor. **EMBARRASS**

5 What is the most .... film you have ever seen? **FRIGHTEN**

6 I'm .... that the Cup Final is over at last. **RELIEF**

4 Complete the gaps with one word.

Letting go

When I was younger I used to worry **(1)** .... all kinds of things. I knew I would never look **(2)** .... my sister, who was **(3)** .... more attractive than me and just **(4)** .... intelligent as me, but I still felt jealous. I was also embarrassed **(5)** .... my father, who worked **(6)** .... an actor, instead of having a 'normal' job. However, I have always **(7)** .... very close to **(8)** .... of my parents and know I am very lucky to have them.

Battling nature

4

Speaking

1 **How much do you know about Antarctica? Do the quiz. Then turn to page 160 and check your answers.**

1 Antarctica has the world's largest

   A volcano   **B** desert   **C** mountain range

2 Has Antarctica always been cold?

   A No, it used to be tropical.

   B Yes, it's always been covered in thick ice.

   C Yes, but the ice used to be a lot thinner.

3 Which of these animals do you NOT get in Antarctica?

   A penguins   **B** seals   **C** polar bears

4 Who led the first team to reach the South Pole in 1911?

   A Roald Amundsen

   B Robert Falcon Scott

   C Ernest Shackleton

5 Why is Ernest Shackleton's 1908 expedition famous?

   A Everyone except Shackleton survived the trip.

   B The men survived but they didn't get to the South Pole.

   C All the men died on the way back from the South Pole.

Multiple choice (Part 4)

▶ **EXAM** FOCUS p.205

2 You are going to hear a review of a book about two journeys to the South Pole. Before you listen, read the questions and underline the key words.

1 What does Leo say about Henry Worsley's team?
  A They had never considered doing a trip to the South Pole before.
  B They had personal reasons for wanting to complete the journey.
  C They were trying to break a world record.

2 What does Leo say was the hardest thing for Worsley's team before the expedition?
  A organising the finance
  B preparing mentally
  C getting physically fit

3 What was easier for the twenty-first century expedition than for Shackleton's expedition?
  A planning their daily route
  B doing the cooking
  C carrying their equipment

4 What problem did both expeditions experience?
  A running out of food
  B a serious illness
  C bad weather

5 How did Worsley feel when he was crossing the Antarctic plateau?
  A He hadn't expected it to be so difficult.
  B He was worried they wouldn't reach the South Pole.
  C He doubted his skills as a leader.

6 The part of the book Leo enjoyed most was when Worsley
  A reached the South Pole.
  B arrived at the point Shackleton had got to.
  C completed the trip.

7 What does Leo admire about Shackleton?
  A his determination
  B his ambition
  C his bravery

EXAM TIP

The information on the recording will be in the same order as questions 1–7.

3 ▶ **1.15 Listen to the review and answer questions 1–7.**

4 Check your answers in pairs. Then listen again. What words or phrases did you hear to justify choosing A, B or C for each question?

5 Discuss the questions.

1 What would you find hard about a trip like this?
2 Shackleton is considered a hero and a role model by many people. Who are your heroes and role models?
3 Where would you most like to travel to? Why?

Vocabulary

idioms: the body

6 Match the underlined idioms 1–10 with meanings A–J.

1 The hardest part was getting their heads around doing a 900 mile journey.
2 When he came face to face with conditions there, Shackleton began to doubt he'd ever reach the Pole.
3 He's always putting his foot in it. He just doesn't know when to keep his mouth shut.
4 My father and I don't see eye to eye. Perhaps our relationship will improve when I leave home.
5 Something in the distance caught my eye.
6 I must keep an eye on the time. I don't want to be late.
7 It was really difficult to keep a straight face; he looked so silly.
8 I'm beginning to get cold feet about the whole idea.
9 I can't face going to work. I feel terrible.
10 You need to put your foot down. Don't agree to working late every evening.

A pay attention to
B look serious
C attract your attention
D change your mind
E get on with each other
F feel unable to
G very close to
H say the wrong thing
I say no to something
J understand/accept an idea

7 When was the last time you

1 put your foot in it?
2 couldn't face doing something?
3 put your foot down?
4 couldn't keep a straight face?

Narrative forms

past simple, past continuous and
past perfect

▶ **GRAMMAR** REFERENCE p.177

1 You are going to read a story about a man who was
shipwrecked on a desert island. Read Paragraph 1
and predict what happens next.

(1) Last October, 79-year-old
Mark Richards <u>set off</u> from
Florida in his cabin cruiser. He
<u>had planned</u> to sail to Nassau
in the Bahamas in twelve
hours. However, while he <u>was
sailing</u> there, a storm blew up
and he was shipwrecked on a
small island.

2 Read Paragraph 1 again. Which of the underlined
forms is

1 past simple?

2 past continuous?

3 past perfect?

3 Which one

1 refers to a finished event?

2 describes a situation which happened before another past
action?

3 describes an action already in progress when something else
happened?

4 Read the rest of the story quickly. Don't worry about
the gaps yet. How well did you predict the ending?

His family realised he (1) .... (*miss*) and a massive
search was launched. But they (2) .... (*have to*) wait
there for three long days before they finally (3) ....
(*hear*) that some fishermen (4) .... (*rescue*) him.
Mr Richards survived for three days on a mixture of
dried noodles and snack bars which (5) .... (*float*)
ashore from his boat. Mr Richards knew he would be
rescued eventually because there were a lot of boats in
the area. 'I wasn't frightened but I was pleased to be
rescued on the third day because I (6) .... (*start*) to
feel quite hungry,' he said.

5 Now fill each gap with the correct form
of the verb in brackets.

past perfect simple and past perfect
continuous

6 Complete the sentences with past
perfect or past perfect continuous.
Match the examples to one of the
statements, A or B.

1 He .... (*work*) as a life guard for ten years but
.... (*never need*) to rescue anyone until last
week.

2 Andy's leg .... (*hurt*) for ages before he went
to the doctor.

3 We .... (*never see*) a glacier before.

4 I .... (*not hear*) the news until Sophie rang me.

A Only the simple form is possible here.

B It is more natural to use the continuous form
here because the action continues over a period
of time (although it isn't wrong to use the simple
form).

7 Complete the gaps so that B has the
same meaning as A. Sometimes more
than one form is possible.

1 A Jack was hoping to compete in the Olympics.
Then he hurt his back.

   B Before he .... (*hurt*) his back,
Jack .... (*hope*) to compete in the
Olympics.

2 A Luke spent six months in hospital. He studied
to be a lawyer during this time.

   B While Luke .... (*recover*) in hospital,
he .... (*study*) to be a lawyer.

3 A During his swim to the island Lewis cut his
knee badly on a rock.

   B Lewis .... (*swim*) to the island when
he .... (*cut*) his knee on a rock.

4 A Fauzia didn't feel well all day. So she decided
not to go to Zhara's party last night.

   B Because she .... (*feel*) well all day,
Fauzia .... (*decide*) not to go to
Zhara's party last night.

Collaborative task (Part 3)

ranking

▶ **EXAM** FOCUS p.207

1 **You're going to hear two students talking about survival skills. First match the activities to the pictures.**

A giving first aid

B building a shelter

C fishing with your bare hands

D lighting a fire

E building a raft

2 ▶ 1.16 **Listen and answer the question.**

1 What two things do the students have to do?

3 ▶ 1.17 **Listen and complete the expressions the students used for ranking in their discussion.**

Marc: For me **(1)** .... is fishing with your bare hands.

Alice: I think **(2)** .... I'd want to learn.

Marc: Another reason for putting this **(3)** .... is that it's not a useful skill when you leave the island because everyone uses a fishing rod to catch fish.

Alice: So basically we're saying **(4)** ....

4 **Work in pairs. Look at the task and follow the instructions.**

> Talk together for about three minutes. I'd like you to imagine that you are going on an expedition to a desert island. Here are some survival skills you might need on the island. First, discuss how difficult it would be to learn these survival skills. Then decide which one would be the most useful on the island.

EXAM TIP

You shouldn't try to reach a decision too quickly.

1 In this task, you should spend at least two of the three minutes talking about:
  • how difficult you think each skill would be to learn
  • the advantage of learning each skill
  • which skills would/wouldn't be useful on the island and why

2 Discuss which skill you think would be the most useful. You don't have to agree.

Discussion (Part 4)

5 **Work in pairs and discuss the Part 4 questions.**

1 What kind of person do you need to be to survive on a desert island?

2 How essential is it for people to know how to survive in the wild?

3 Do you think most people today have lost touch with nature?

4 In what ways can the natural world be a threat to humans?

Speaking

1 **Look at the paragraph headings in the article. Discuss questions 1–4 with a partner.**

1 Which of these experiences do you think would be the most frightening?

2 Which of these experiences might give you shock, frostbite or hypothermia?

3 Which could give you injuries such as broken bones?

4 What other kinds of extreme weather conditions can you think of?

Multiple matching (Part 3)

▶ **EXAM** FOCUS p.201

2 **Read the article. Did anyone have serious injuries as a result of their experiences?**

3 **Read the questions and underline the key words or phrases. Then scan the texts for words and expressions which have the same meaning. The first one is done for you.**

EXAM TIP

Be careful! There might seem to be similar information in more than one text. Make sure the word or expression you choose has the same meaning as in the question.

4 **For questions 2–15, choose from the people A–D. Some of the people may be chosen more than once.**

Which person

completely <u>panicked</u> when the incident happened?	1	A
tried to focus on staying awake during the incident?	2	
fainted during the incident?	3	
describes being in pain all over afterwards?	4	
is aware of the potential psychological consequences of the incident?	5	
was thrown up into the air during the incident?	6	
feels he has changed for the better after what he went through?	7	
helped to save his own life by crying?	8	
had multiple injuries as a result of the incident?	9	
had a long wait before he was rescued?	10	

experienced deafness during the incident?	11
felt cold for a long time after the incident?	12
found it difficult to relate to his rescuers?	13
experienced big variations in body temperature during the incident?	14
realises that a part of his brain has been affected as a result of what happened?	15

5 **Work in pairs and discuss the questions.**

1 Which person do you think had the luckiest escape?

2 How do you think you would react in these situations?

3 Do you know of any disaster films connected to the weather? What happens?

Vocabulary

collocations and idioms: weather

6 **Match the words in column A with their collocations in column B.**

Column A	Column B
1 freezing	A wet
2 boiling	B black
3 soaking	C frozen
4 pitch	D cold
5 absolutely	E hot
6 thick/dense	F wind/sun
7 torrential/heavy	G sea
8 strong	H frost
9 a rough	I rain
10 a hard	J fog

7 **How would someone be feeling if**

1 they froze when they saw something?

2 they stormed out of somewhere?

3 they moved like lightning?

4 they were icy with someone?

5 their face clouded over?

6 their face was like thunder?

Battling with nature

FOUR PEOPLE TALK ABOUT THEIR STORIES OF SURVIVAL

A **Lester Morlang was buried in an avalanche in Colorado.**

There was no warning. It was instant. All of a sudden I was curled up in a ball. Then it was over and I was buried under about fifty feet of snow. It was totally dark. My mouth was packed with snow and the pressure was enormous. It was hard to breathe and I didn't know which direction was up. I thought I was already dead. Luckily I had my hands over my face so I cleared the snow out of my mouth and then I started screaming. I absolutely lost it – I was out of my mind, and then I noticed my tears were running across my face so I realised I must be lying kind of upside down. Now I felt determined to get out. I dug for twenty-two hours, and when I finally saw the first little bit of light I was over the moon, although it was fourteen hours before anyone found me. My misfortune has made me a better person; trivial things don't worry me any more. ■

B **Rod Herd was on a boat with the New Zealand Police Search and Rescue team when he nearly drowned.**

When we hit the wave, I was thrown against the window, which smashed and let in a tremendous volume of water. There was no air, just pitch darkness, noise, and violent movement. I had no idea the boat had overturned. I felt sad, anxious and despairing, and the fear of drowning was unbearable. I couldn't hold my breath any longer and at this point I had a vision of my wife and sons waving me goodbye, and I felt at peace. But then I grabbed a stair rail and found myself back in the real world. I managed to pull myself up to the surface and then had to deal with the shock and hypothermia. Periods of shivering became painful. Trying to stay afloat kept my mind off it, although I had to fight the desire to go to sleep. When the helicopter arrived soon afterwards, I vividly remember feeling disconnected from the people who were there to save me. And in the months afterwards I never felt completely warm. Being afraid of dying was the most terrifying thing. It's impossible for someone to understand what it feels like and I'm still not sure how long the emotional after-effects will last. ■

C **John Neidigh survived a tornado in Mississippi.**

I heard the warning on the television and had just enough time to lie down and cover my head with my arms. The feel of a twister approaching is like a goods train – that low, ever-louder howl and the shuddering ground. First, a sheet of rain sprayed against the side of my trailer like machine-gun fire. I could hear trees snapping, and the roof began to come off as the trailer started moving up and down. Just as I felt the entire trailer lift off the ground, I lost consciousness and woke up twenty minutes later face-down outside. The evening was completely quiet, no wind, no cars, no insect noises. I had gone through the trailer wall, ended up thirty feet up in a tree, and then dropped to the ground. I had concussion, a collapsed lung, cracked ribs and a shattered leg. My injuries should have killed me but the surgeons sewed me back together again. ■

D **Max Dearing was on the golf course in North Carolina when lightning struck.**

It happened on a lovely July afternoon while I was playing golf with friends from work. When it started to drizzle, we decided to get under a shelter. We were standing there teasing each other and I remember the air had an unusual sweet smell. When the lightning struck, I felt absolutely frozen, but then part of me was boiling hot too. I saw these flashing lights and there was such an incredibly loud noise that I couldn't hear anything for a while. My arms and legs felt heavy. Every bit of my body – including my hair, my eyelashes – hurt. It was a dull ache and yet so sharp at the same time, like a bad headache and needles being stuck in every part of your body. The lightning bolt went up through me and left an exit wound in my head. Now I have a hard time adding simple numbers, although I have no problem with more complex calculations. ■

Articles

definite, indefinite and zero articles

▶ **GRAMMAR** REFERENCE p.163

1 **Choose the correct option *a/an, the* or (-) for no article to complete rules 1–8. Use the text on page 40–41 to help you.**

1 We use *a/an/the/*(-) when there is only one of something in existence.

2 We use *a/an/the/*(-) when there is only one of something in this context.

3 We use *a/an/the/*(-) to talk about plural countable nouns in general.

4 We use *a/an/the/*(-) to refer back to nouns mentioned before (or where the meaning is clear from the context).

5 We use *a/an/the/*(-) with superlative forms.

6 We use *a/an/the/*(-) with many common expressions such as *home, school* etc.

7 We use *a/an/the/*(-) with singular countable nouns when mentioned for the first time, or when it is not important which one.

8 We use *a/an/the/*(-) with uncountable and abstract nouns.

2 **Match rules 1–8 from Activity 1 to extracts A–H from the text on page 40–41.**

A I grabbed *a stair rail* and found myself…

B … back in *the real world*.

C Being afraid of dying was *the most terrifying thing*.

D I could hear *trees* snapping.

E … and *the roof* began to come off.

F My mouth was packed with *snow* and the pressure was enormous.

G I cleared *the snow* out of my mouth.

H I was *playing golf* with friends *from work*.

LANGUAGE TIP

We normally use possessives, not articles for parts of the body, e.g. **my** *face* NOT **the** *face*.

---

3 **Complete the gaps in the story with *a/an, the* or (-).**

Speaking

4 **Work in groups. Find somebody who has had one of the following experiences. Tell the class about it.**

Have you ever

1 been afraid of a storm?

2 been snowed in?

3 had heatstroke?

4 been in a flood?

5 skidded on a patch of ice?

6 seen lightening strike?

7 lost your way in fog?

8 been in or on a rough sea?

A pilot's story

As pilots, we have to get used to (1) .... storms and (2) .... severe weather and we are obviously prepared for (3) .... emergencies. However, sometimes they can take you by (4) .... surprise. A year ago, I was flying to (5) .... United States and we were over (6) .... Atlantic Ocean when a ball of lightning struck (7) .... aircraft I was flying. Within seconds, (8) .... bright blue ball of light with (9) .... yellow tail filled (10) .... windscreen and there was (11) .... loud bang. My colleague said it felt as if (12) .... cat had brushed against his leg as (13) .... lightning struck. Fortunately, after a lot of violent shaking, (14) .... things soon returned to (15) .... normal.

Vocabulary
negative prefixes

1 **In each sentence, underline the prefix which makes a word negative.**

1 The first expedition was unsuccessful.

2 The Antarctic is the most incredible place I have been to.

3 The group on the expedition felt discouraged at times.

4 It's impossible to think of living in such freezing conditions.

5 They misunderstood our instructions and went the wrong way.

6 Some people thought it was irresponsible to go in such icy conditions.

2 **Add a negative prefix to the underlined words in sentences 1–6.**

1 One <u>advantage</u> of winter is how much we spend on heating our homes.

2 I <u>read</u> how severe the weather conditions would be so was not prepared.

3 It's <u>likely</u> that we'll be able to have a barbecue unless it gets much warmer.

4 I've noticed that people get <u>patient</u> when they're driving during hot weather.

5 It was a great job despite the <u>regular</u> working hours.

6 I'd be <u>capable</u> of surviving in low temperatures even if I had the right equipment.

3 **Work in pairs. Discuss something**

1 which is unusual about you.

2 incredible that has happened to you.

3 that makes you impatient.

Word formation (Part 3)

▶ **EXAM** FOCUS p.203

4 **Look at the photo and the title of the article. What kind of place do you think Death Valley is? How do you think it got its name?**

5 **Look at each gap and decide what part of speech is missing.**

6 Use the word given in capitals at the end of some of the lines to form a word that fits in the gap in the same line. Which words need a negative prefix?

EXAM TIP

You may need to add a prefix or a suffix to change the word to another part of speech e.g. *happy* → *happi**ness***.

DEATH VALLEY

The **(0)** *hottest* place in North America got its name when a very **(1)** .... group of miners crossed it on their way to California in 1849. They had no idea that temperatures could get above 120 degrees Fahrenheit and nearly **(2)** .... there as a result. This is why they gave it the name that it still has today.

Despite its name, more than 1.3 million **(3)** .... still go there every year. It is likely, however, that many of them have absolutely no idea how **(4)** .... being in such a hot, dry climate can be. Also, **(5)** .... walkers often do not drink nearly enough water or wear **(6)** .... clothes, which this extreme heat requires.

Heatstroke often occurs when the body is unable to control its temperature. **(7)** .... signs of this are high body temperature, red, dry skin, very bad headaches and feeling dizzy. All this is also often accompanied by **(8)** .... If heatstroke is **(9)** .... , it is necessary to get the person out of the sun at once and get urgent medical **(10)** ...., otherwise they have only a 20 percent chance of surviving.

HEAT
LUCK
DEATH
VISIT
DANGER
EXPERIENCE
SENSE
WARN
SICK
SUSPECT
ASSIST

7 **What advice would you give to someone going to a very hot or cold climate?**

Examples:
You should (drink)... Make sure you (wear)... Avoid (sitting in the sun). Don't (ignore) warning signs.

Reading

1 Read the story. Don't worry about the gaps yet. Why was it a bad day for Josh?

STORY

A disastrous day

Saturday didn't start off too badly. In fact, **(1)** .... it seemed as if it was going to be a <u>nice</u> sunny day so **(2)** .... he'd had his breakfast, Josh texted his friends and said he was on his way to pick them up. However, **(3)** .... he was driving into town he <u>remembered</u> that he'd left his phone at home and **(4)** .... decided to go back to get it. <u>However</u>, he got stuck in a traffic jam and couldn't move for <u>a long time</u>. **(5)** .... he arrived and <u>went</u> into the house but couldn't find his phone anywhere. **(6)** .... , as got back into his car again his elderly neighbour tapped at his window. 'I've locked myself out of my house' she said. Josh had to go back inside to get her spare key **(7)** .... he could set off again. **(8)** .... he was on his way. He drove straight there but **(9)** .... he got there, his friends had already <u>gone</u>. And **(10)** .... he found his phone on the floor of his car.

2 Complete gaps 1–10 with these time expressions.

as soon as	at first	at last	before
by the time	eventually	immediately	
later	then	while	

EXAM TIP

Try to include some time expressions, narrative forms and other expressions which add interest.

Story (Part 2)

▶**WRITING** REFERENCE p.184

3 Divide the story into four paragraphs.

Paragraph 1: set the scene

Paragraphs 2 and 3: the body of the story should say what happened and how the writer felt

Paragraph 4: say what happened in the end – and include a 'twist'

4 Look at the story again and underline examples of narrative verb forms.

5 Replace the words and phrases underlined in Activity 1 with words from the box below to add interest.

absolutely ages	disappeared	perfect
rushed	suddenly realised	unfortunately

6 Look at the exam task. Then read the example of how the first paragraph might continue. Think of two other ideas.

> You have been asked to write a story for your student magazine which must begin with the following words.
>
> *When Lucy woke up in hospital it took her a while to piece together where she was and why she was there.*

When Lucy woke up in hospital it took her a while to piece together where she was and why she was there.
Then, as she tried moving her leg, which seemed to be broken, it all came flooding back to her. She'd been skiing down the mountain when the fog had come down suddenly.

7 Work with a partner and plan your story.

1 Discuss how the story might continue. Plan what will be in each of the four paragraphs, including an element of suspense to keep the reader's attention.

2 Think about how the story might end. Try to think of an unusual twist which will surprise the reader.

8 Now write your story, beginning with the sentence in Activity 6. Try to include some of the time expressions from Activity 2. Write 120–180 words.

1 Complete the gaps in the article with *a/an*, *the* or (-) for no article.

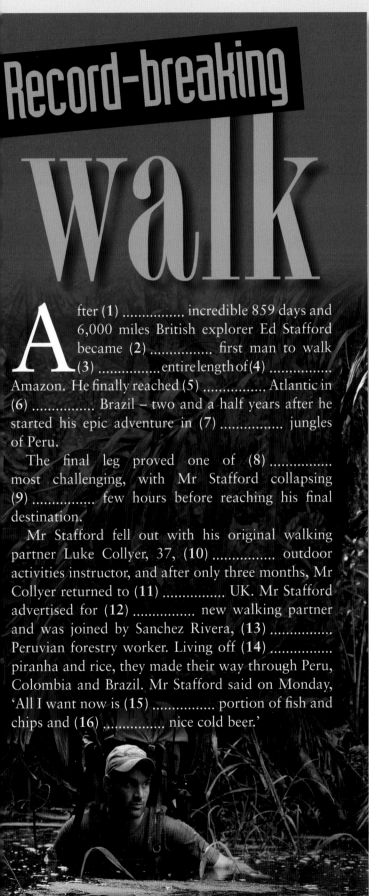

Record-breaking walk

After **(1)** .... incredible 859 days and 6,000 miles British explorer Ed Stafford became **(2)** .... first man to walk **(3)** .... entire length of **(4)** .... Amazon. He finally reached **(5)** .... Atlantic in **(6)** .... Brazil – two and a half years after he started his epic adventure in **(7)** .... jungles of Peru.

The final leg proved one of **(8)** .... most challenging, with Mr Stafford collapsing **(9)** .... few hours before reaching his final destination.

Mr Stafford fell out with his original walking partner Luke Collyer, 37, **(10)** .... outdoor activities instructor, and after only three months, Mr Collyer returned to **(11)** .... UK. Mr Stafford advertised for **(12)** .... new walking partner and was joined by Sanchez Rivera, **(13)** .... Peruvian forestry worker. Living off **(14)** .... piranha and rice, they made their way through Peru, Colombia and Brazil. Mr Stafford said on Monday, 'All I want now is **(15)** .... portion of fish and chips and **(16)** .... nice cold beer.'

2 Use the word given in capitals at the end of the sentence to form a word that fits the space.

1 I am .... of skiing. I'm too scared. **CAPABLE**

2 I .... his explanation and went the wrong way. **UNDERSTANDING**

3 He is a very .... worker. He never arrives on time. **RELY**

4 My mother is .... with my younger brother. She never explains things properly. **PATIENCE**

5 That is an extremely .... way to behave. You should be trying to set a good example. **RESPONSIBILITY**

6 If you're ...., speak to the manager and I'm sure he'll be able to help. **SATISFACTION**

3 Match the first part of sentences 1–5 to their endings A–F.

1 I always *put my foot in it* when I'm nervous and

2 I can never *keep a straight face* so

3 I'm *getting cold feet* about the cycling race because

4 Tom and I don't *see eye to eye* about many issues so

5 My parents want me to *keep an eye* on my brother so

6 If something in a shop window *catches my eye*

A I'm useless at telling jokes.

B I say really embarrassing things.

C I won't be able to go out tonight.

D I can't resist going in to look at it.

E I don't think I've trained enough.

F I can't see our relationship lasting.

4 Complete the second sentence so that it has a similar meaning to the first sentence. Use between two and five words, including the word given.

1 I lived in London until I got married last year.
BEEN
I .... in London until I got married last year.

2 It took three days for us to walk there.
WERE
We .... three days.

3 I couldn't remember the way there so I got a taxi.
FORGOTTEN
I .... get there so I got a taxi.

4 It was three years since I'd visited Peru.
NOT
I .... to Peru for three years.

Eat your heart out!

Sumo wrestler, Japan

Speaking and vocabulary

1 **Work with a partner. Look at the photos, which show daily diets from around the world, and discuss the questions.**

1 How similar do these diets look to each other?

2 Which diet looks most similar to your own?

3 What can we tell about the countries by looking at these people's diets?

2 **Find out if your partner**

1 snacks between meals.

2 eats fast food regularly.

3 drinks a lot of tea and coffee.

4 has plenty of fresh fruit.

5 prefers organic food.

6 is allergic to any food.

3 **Complete the phrases with the words in the box.**

| fat | free | vegetarian | balanced | vitamins | low |

1 a high- .... diet

2 a strict .... diet

3 a diet rich in ....

4 a well- .... diet

5 a .... salt diet

6 a dairy- .... diet

4 **Use the phrases in Activities 2 and 3 to describe the diet most people have in your country. How healthy is it?**

Maasai farmer, Kenya

Student, Venezuela

LANGUAGE TIP

Rice is uncountable in English but countable in many other languages. For example, in English we say *There are **many different types of rice*** (NOT *rices*). Other English words like this include *advice, information, health, news, luggage, knowledge.*

Countable and uncountable nouns

▶ **GRAMMAR** REFERENCE p.167

5 **Match the nouns to the options A, B and C.**

salt	meat	egg	vegetable	chocolate	cheese	honey
curry	fat	fruit	coffee	cake	rice	chicken

A always uncountable

B always countable

C can be countable or uncountable

6 **What's the difference in meaning between the countable and uncountable forms of the nouns in these examples?**

1 **A** Is there a lot of cake left?
   B Are there a lot of cakes left?

2 **A** I like chicken.
   B I like chickens.

Expressions of quantity

LANGUAGE TIP

Don't get confused between *a few* and *few*
- *The party was OK; there were **a few** people I knew there.* (*a few = some*)
- *The party wasn't a success; **few** people turned up.* (*few = hardly any*). *Hardly any* is more natural in spoken English.

▶ **GRAMMAR** REFERENCE p.168

7 **Turn to page 160 for more practice with countable and uncountable nouns.**

8 **What's the difference in meaning between these examples?**

1 **A** The shop sells a few cakes.
   B The shop sells very few cakes.

2 **A** There's a little cheese left.
   B There's very little cheese left.

9 **Work in pairs. Ask and answer questions based on the sentences in Activity 7.**

Open cloze (Part 2)

▶ **EXAM** FOCUS p.202

1 **Work in pairs and discuss whether you agree with the following statements.**

1 I can't stand the taste of chilli. It's too hot.

2 I love food which has lots of spices and different flavours.

2 **Read the text quickly, and choose the correct words in these statements.**

1 The writer *likes/doesn't like* chilli.

2 Chilli *can be/isn't* very addictive.

3 Children generally *like/don't like* chilli.

3 **Look at the gaps in the text. In which four gaps should you put an expression of quantity?**

EXAM TIP

In Part 2 you need to use a variety of grammatical forms, such as
• pronouns (*he, them*)
• prepositions (*at, about*)
• articles (*a, the*)
• auxiliaries (*do, are*)
• linking expressions (*despite, next*)
• comparisons (*than, as*)
• quantifiers (*any, many*)

4 **Now think of the word which best fits each gap. Use one word in each gap. There is an example at the beginning.**

5 **Work in pairs and discuss the questions.**

1 How far do you agree with the writer's opinion of chilli?

2 What other foods do you think are an acquired taste?

6 **Underline all the prepositions in the text. Then find one example of**

1 a phrasal verb

2 an adjective + preposition

3 a verb + preposition

4 a fixed expression

Why do people love chilli?

People don't wash their eyes in lemon juice or pour boiling hot tea **(0)** ....*over*.... themselves, so why are we prepared to go through so much pain **(1)** .... the sake of chilli? Chillies burn our tongues, make our eyes water and bring **(2)** .... out in a sweat.

Chillies are one of the few foods that we simply should not enjoy and not just because of the way they taste. Not **(3)** .... people like the bitter taste of coffee to begin with but soon most of us **(4)** .... used to it. But coffee contains caffeine which has some addictive qualities, and this explains **(5)** .... it is so popular. Capsaicin, the ingredient **(6)** .... makes chillies hot, does not seem to have **(7)** .... addictive qualities whatsoever, and it also has very **(8)** .... health benefits. And yet it has **(9)** .... used in cooking in almost **(10)** .... culture for thousands of years.

Few young children, even from cultures known **(11)** .... their spicy recipes, actually like chilli **(12)** .... first. So it seems chilli is an acquired taste. It takes time to get to like the burning sensation. I'm still waiting! ∎

Sentence completion (Part 2)

▶ **EXAM** FOCUS p.204

1 What have people always eaten in your culture? What have they started eating only recently?

2 You are going to listen to part of a radio programme about the history of cooking. Look at the gapped sentences and say how many of the missing words are

A nouns
B numbers
C adjectives
D verbs

3 Underline the key words and make sure you understand what each sentence means.

EXAM TIP
You may hear more than one number/noun/adjective that will fit grammatically. But only one of these will fit the meaning.

4 ▶ 1.18 For questions 1–10, listen and complete the sentences.

5 Read through your answers to check they make sense.

6 Discuss these questions.

1 How much raw food do you eat?
2 Do you think people should eat less meat?
3 What would you like to eat more or less of?

The history of cooking

About _____ **1** percent of the chimpanzee's diet is fruit.

A chimpanzee diet is difficult to digest and has a _____ **2** taste.

Humans can't survive for long on fruit because they have a small _____ **3** .

Before they discovered cooking, people spent almost as much time eating food as they did _____ **4** it.

One benefit of cooking was that it helped to _____ **5** food.

Some scientists think cooking resulted in an increase in the size of the _____ **6** .

The idea of sharing a _____ **7** probably started when people began to cook.

Waiting until food was cooked meant there was a risk that it could be _____ **8** .

New evidence in Africa shows that early humans used _____ **9** for cooking over one million years ago.

The earliest real evidence of cooking in Europe dates back to the _____ **10** .

Speaking

1 **Discuss the following questions.**

1 How common is it in your country to eat out in restaurants?

2 What kind of restaurants do different age groups tend to eat in?

3 What kind of food do you enjoy eating most when you go out?

Multiple choice (Part 1)

▶ **EXAM** FOCUS p.200

2 **Read the article about a restaurant food critic and say in what ways David is unusual.**

3 **Read the questions (don't read the options yet) and underline the part of the text each one refers to. Then underline the key words in the options.**

4 **For questions 1–8, choose the answer (A, B, C or D) which you think fits best according to the text.**

EXAM TIP

The questions will follow the order of the text, apart from the last one, which may test global understanding of the whole text.

1 David wanted to go to the new restaurant because

A he prefers Italian food to Greek food.

B he was attracted by its appearance.

C he wanted to write his first food review for publication.

D he prefers eating in a restaurant to having takeout food.

2 Why was David lucky to get a table at the Salumeria Rosi?

A The restaurant wasn't keen to serve a child on his own.

B Most tables were reserved for celebrities.

C The restaurant was completely booked up.

D He couldn't afford a proper meal.

3 How did the customers react to David?

A They were worried about him.

B They were interested in him.

C They wanted to hear his opinions on the food.

D They felt they should talk to him in case he was lonely.

4 What did David appreciate about the restaurant?

A the fuss they made of him

B the unusual food he was given to try free

C the fact that they explained how the food was made

D the fact that they didn't treat him like a child

Food and drink

The most famous restaurant critic in America

Apparently it's never too soon to start being a restaurant food critic.

That's why David Fishman (pictured), a New York City native who had just turned twelve, decided to take himself out for dinner one night. His parents had called him at home to say they were running late, suggesting that he grab some hummus from his usual Greek takeout restaurant. David thought he could do better than that. He had recently passed by the Salumeria Rosi, a newly-opened Italian restaurant a few blocks from his home, and had been fascinated by the reflective black wall, the dried pork hanging from the ceiling, the little jars of olives and artichokes on the walls. If it was OK with his mom (and it turned out it was), he wanted to try that instead.

That night turned out to be one of the first that the restaurant was open to the public. David requested a menu, which the waitress handed to him and decided that it was within his budget. Then he asked for a table for one and waited to see what she'd say. A year before, he had been turned away from a half-empty restaurant and told that it did not serve children unaccompanied by adults. Grown-up or not, tables were hard to come by that evening – every seat was reserved, mostly by friends of the Italian chef and owner, Cesare Casella. Even TV actor Tony Danza turned up. But the waitress decided to squeeze in the Salumeria's first unaccompanied customer under 1.4 metres, as long as he promised to be out by 8 p.m. It was a deal.

Nobody at the restaurant seemed terribly impressed by Tony Danza, but David Fishman – now that was something. People tried not to stare, but couldn't help themselves. Where were his parents? Was he enjoying the food? Cash or credit? An Australian couple seated beside him struck up a conversation and a young couple on the other side of his table insisted on buying him a chocolate mousse. In turn, he recommended that they try the arugula salad.

David had ordered a speciality of the restaurant, as well as salad leaves with Parmesan cheese. 'Good variety,' he wrote in the leather-bound notebook he brought along, restaurant-critic-like. 'Softish jazz music. Seem to enjoy kids but not overly.' In other words, no sickly-sweet smiles or insulting offer of grilled cheese.

The kitchen workers were so fascinated by the young adventurous eater that they sent out a bowl of complimentary tripe stew, which he enjoyed, although, he admits, 'It wasn't my favorite.' He was a little surprised to learn later that tripe was prepared with intestines. His eyes went wide. 'The intestines of what?' he asked. (Somehow, that seemed to matter.)

line 52

But the young foodie has got a new fan in Chef Casella, who came over to extend a greeting. Though David was disappointed that the restaurant did not serve Italian ice cream, he got points with Mr Casella for knowing a little something about Italian cuisine. 'He reminded me of me, when I was younger,' said Mr Casella, who used to drive all over Europe by himself to try the best restaurants. 'He is so cool, though – more confident than I am when I eat out by myself. His taste comes from inside him. It is like a brilliant violinist – he does not get this talent by learning.'

An only child, David grew up in a family where eating well and imaginatively at home was important. His mother encouraged him to make notes about what he liked, and it developed from there. But little did he know how dramatically his life would change after he wandered into the Salumeria Rosi. During dinner, while he was chatting with customers and taking notes, he was noticed by a woman who has a friend at the *New York Times*. The article she wrote about him led to the kind of media attention that contestants on Pop Idol dream will be theirs. Despite his tender years, he is now reviewing more of the city's top restaurants, making television appearances, touring Europe, and there is even a possible film under discussion.

line 78

5 What does *that* refer to in line 52?
A which part of an animal tripe was
B why he had been given tripe
C how the intestines were prepared
D the kind of animal the intestines came from

6 What do we learn about David from the last two paragraphs?
A He is a very talented musician.
B He has eaten in a lot of restaurants.
C He is very sure of himself as far as food is concerned.
D He has always been encouraged to cook a lot at home.

7 The expression *tender years* in line 78 refers to David's
A sweet nature.
B extreme youth.
C child-like behaviour.
D lack of qualifications.

8 In this article the writer suggests that David's main ambition is
A to try out a variety of new food.
B to have his reviews published.
C to be a media celebrity.
D to become a famous chef.

Speaking

5 Work in pairs. Do you think people reading David's reviews would take them seriously? Why/Why not?

Vocabulary

phrasal verbs with *turn*

6 Match definitions 1–6 with the phrasal verbs with *turn* from the wordpool. Some of the verbs are underlined in the text.

| turn off | turn down | turn away |
| turn up | turn out | turn on |

1 refuse an invitation
2 arrive somewhere, especially unexpectedly
3 suddenly attack someone, physically or with words
4 have a particular or unexpected result
5 make somebody decide they don't like something
6 refuse someone permission to enter a place

7 Work in pairs. Choose four of the phrasal verbs in Activity 6. Write a paragraph which includes them all.

Passive forms

1 Read the extract from an article. What is unusual about this celebration?

On the last weekend in November, a feast <u>will be organised</u> in Lopburi, Thailand. A huge amount of fruit and vegetables <u>will be provided</u> by local people, and chefs <u>have been invited</u> to prepare a wonderful meal. Not so unusual, perhaps, except that the 3,000 guests are all monkeys! Monkeys <u>can be seen</u> everywhere in this jungle town, and the feast <u>is being held</u>, as it is every year, to say thank you to them. In this town at least, monkeys <u>are believed to bring</u> wealth, in the form of tourism.

2 Look at the passive forms underlined in Activity 1 and make them active.

Example: People will organise a feast on the last weekend in November.

LANGUAGE TIP
- We use the passive form when we don't know/it doesn't matter/it's obvious who does the action.
- Use a form of *to be* + past participle.

▶ **GRAMMAR** REFERENCE p.172

3 Complete the sentences about other celebrations, using the appropriate form of the passive.

1 At the wedding I went to in Italy last week, sugared almonds .... (*give away*) to all the guests.

2 Since 1368, moon cakes .... (*eat*) in China to celebrate the Harvest Festival.

3 Some people hate .... (*give*) surprise parties on their birthdays.

4 A decision must .... (*make*) about which restaurant we are going to book for Mum and Dad's wedding anniversary.

5 I hope that noodles are .... (*serve*) at my Korean friend's wedding tomorrow.

6 I was really thrilled .... (*ask*) to give a speech at the wedding reception.

4 Work in pairs. Think of popular celebrations in your country. What food is typically eaten there and how is it made?

Passive reporting verbs

5 Look at sentences A, B and C. Which sentence(s) avoid saying *who* believes? What is the difference in form?

A Thai people believe that monkeys bring wealth.

B Monkeys are believed to bring wealth.

C It is believed that monkeys bring wealth.

LANGUAGE TIP
We can report what people say or believe with verbs such as *think*, *believe* and two structures:
- *It* + passive reporting verb + *that* clause
- subject + passive reporting verb + present/perfect infinitive

6 Complete the second sentence so that it has a similar meaning to the first sentence, using 2–5 words including the word given.

1 People expect tourists to carry sticks to protect themselves from curious monkeys.
ARE
Tourists .... sticks to protect themselves from curious monkeys.

2 Thai people know that the monkeys are a huge tourist attraction.
BE
Monkeys .... a huge tourist attraction.

3 Reports claim that twenty top chefs have been invited to prepare the meal.
THAT
It .... twenty top chefs have been invited to prepare the meal.

4 Locals believe that 2,000 kilos of food were consumed at the last feast.
HAVE
2,000 kilos of food .... consumed at the last feast.

5 The tourist office has estimated that over 10,000 visitors watch the feast.
BEEN
It .... that over 10,000 visitors watch the feast.

6 Some people think monkeys get very aggressive around food.
TO
Monkeys .... very aggressive around food.

7 Work in pairs. Discuss stories which have been reported recently on TV or in the newspapers.

Long turn (Part 2)
comparing and giving a reaction

▶ **EXAM** FOCUS p.206

> Both these photos show people eating out in restaurants. I'd like you to compare the photos and say why the people might choose to eat in places like these.

1 Look at the photos and the exam task, and tick the statements you agree with. Can you think of any other points of comparison between the photos?

1 Although the food in an expensive restaurant may be wonderful, the atmosphere isn't as friendly as in fast food restaurants.

2 In expensive restaurants you often have to have full meals, whereas you can usually just get a snack in fast food places.

3 While fast food restaurants are quick and cheap, they usually serve unhealthy junk food.

4 Both formal restaurants and fast food cafés are popular with young people.

2 Underline the linking expressions which are used to compare and contrast.

▶ **GRAMMAR** REFERENCE p.165

3 Work in pairs. Match the sentences 1–6 with the types of restaurants in photos A and B.

1 You *don't have to* dress up.

2 You *can't* hear yourself speak.

3 It's *overpriced*.

4 They're good for *special occasions*.

5 The atmosphere is more *casual*.

6 The food's a bit *basic*.

Listening

4 ▶ **1.19** Listen to Danuta doing the task and answer the questions.

1 What differences does she mention between the photos?

2 How does she respond to the second part of the question?

Speaking

5 Work with a partner. Turn to page 152.

Student A: do the task.

Student B: listen and answer the follow-up question.

Then turn to page 154 and swap roles.

EXAM TIP

Make sure you allow enough time to answer the second part of the question or you will miss the focus of the task. You have only one minute to do both.

Reading

1 Read the restaurant review and tick the things that are mentioned.

staff	writer's expectations	location
décor	other diners	atmosphere
prices	food	service

2 Work in pairs and discuss the questions.

1 Would you go to the Hard Rock Café in London after reading this review?

2 Have you ever been disappointed or pleasantly surprised by a meal in a restaurant?

3 Copy and complete the table with words/phrases from the review.

food	staff	atmosphere
poor quality		*full of tourists*

4 Underline examples of where the writer uses structures 1–4. Say why they are used.

1 phrases containing negatives which have positive meanings

2 adverbs

3 the passive

4 the past perfect

5 In which paragraph does the writer

A give details about the food?

B say who she recommends the restaurant for?

C give some basic information about the restaurant?

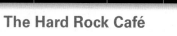

🏠 Home | Restaurants | Diners | Cafés | Bars | ⭐ Star reviews

The Hard Rock Café

EXCELLENT ★★★★★

I'd always avoided visiting the legendary Hard Rock Café in London's Piccadilly, as I thought it would be full of tourists and the food would be poor quality and overpriced. But I have to say I was pleasantly surprised. The food was outstanding, the staff extremely welcoming and the atmosphere certainly didn't disappoint.

As a vegetarian, I thought there wouldn't be much to tempt me on the menu. I decided to try the veggie burger, even though these are quite often stodgy and bland. But this one wasn't. It was perfectly cooked and far from bland. I'd heard that you sometimes have to wait a long time for your food but mine was served in just twelve minutes.

The only downside was the fact it got so busy; literally the place was already packed by 7p.m. And when I needed to pay the bill I had to wait a while. But the staff are so friendly and helpful it almost seems mean to mention it. On the whole I'd really recommend going there. It's a great place for a fun night out with friends.

Review (Part 2)

▶ **WRITING** REFERENCE p.190

6 Read the exam task and write a review, using some of the ideas and language from the review of the Hard Rock Café. You should write 120–180 words.

You recently saw this advertisement in the local paper.

Wanted: Restaurant Critics!

Have you tried any of the restaurants in the area recently? If so, send us a review and you could win a free meal at the restaurant of your choice. We'd like to know your opinion, not only of the food, but also the staff, the atmosphere and the prices. Remember to tell us what you didn't like, as well as what you liked.

Write your **review**.

1 Complete the sentences with the correct preposition. You may need to use them more than once.

after away off up on down out over

1 I wasn't expecting him to arrive. He just turned .... with no warning.

2 I had to turn .... the invitation to dinner because I was working late.

3 The restaurant is so popular that people are often turned .... at the door.

4 Getting food poisoning from shellfish really turned me .... eating it again.

5 The play turned .... to be a disappointment after a great start.

6 The chef turned .... me and blamed me for burning the meal.

7 When I have more time, I'm going to take .... tennis.

8 I had to leave work at five but a friend took .... for the last hour.

9 The band have completely taken .... in America: everyone loves them.

10 I think he must take .... his mother. She's really clever, too.

2 Choose the best answer A, B, C or D.

1 He snacks a lot .... meals.
   A besides   B on   C between   D from

2 It's important to eat a diet .... in vitamins.
   A rich   B high   C full   D plenty

3 People would be healthier if they ate less .... food.
   A fast   B quick   C hurried   D speedy

4 Never add salt to any dish without .... it first to see if it's needed.
   A tasting   B cooking   C flavouring D pouring

5 Some cultures are known .... their spicy food.
   A by   B for   C about   D with

6 What .... are needed to make that dish?
   A parts   B items   C ingredients D pieces

3 Complete these sentences with one word.

1 We've got very .... cheese left. Can you go to the shops for me?

2 I don't eat .... eggs these days; just two a week.

3 There's .... milk left in the fridge. Who's drunk it all?

4 She eats .... any chocolate these days.

5 I think I am .... followed by someone.

6 A lot of excellent work .... been done today.

7 The onions must .... fried until they are soft.

8 Those chefs .... said to be extremely talented.

4 There is a mistake in each of the following sentences. Underline the mistakes and correct them. There may be more than one possibility.

1 They live there for more than twenty years.

2 I run more fastly than he does.

3 My friend isn't having much money at the moment.

4 The team tried very hardly to win the match.

5 I'm afraid there are a very few tickets left for that performance.

6 That was by far the more expensive holiday we've ever had.

7 He has run, which is why he's tired.

8 That band gets really popular these days.

9 He works like a waiter during his holidays.

10 During the storm, lot of roofs were blown off.

11 We were all absolutely frightened by that film.

12 She is used to travel long distances for her job now.

13 I tried to get in touch with him but he already left.

14 He was playing the golf when it started raining.

15 Did you promise taking her to the shops?

5 Choose the correct alternative in each of these sentences.

1 While I was tidying my room, I came *over/across* a story I had written.

2 My *taste/feeling* in music has changed a lot over the years.

3 My sister's favourite band have just *brought/released* a new album.

4 My maths teacher's mood is rather *unpredicted/unpredictable*.

5 What is the *different/difference* between these two words?

6 Some actors are out of work for years before they finally *do/make* it.

7 I get really annoyed *of/by* my brother's behaviour.

8 I am a bit *short/low* of money at the moment.

9 Suddenly, a movement *caught/attracted* my eye.

10 We decided not to go because of the *hard/strong* wind.

11 The boss was very *freezing/icy* towards us when we returned late.

12 It's a pity that you had to be so *impatient/unpatient* with him.

13 Tom is not very good at *taking/doing* responsibility.

14 It looks *though/like* it's going to rain later on.

15 The situation is extremely *embarrassed/embarrassing*.

PROGRESS TEST 1

Multiple-choice cloze (Part 1)

6 For questions 1–12, read the text below and decide which answer (A, B, C or D) best fits each gap. There is an example at the beginning.

Happy families

It came as no surprise to me when a newspaper article I read **(0)** _B_ claimed to prove that the happiest children tend to be **(1)** .... children.

When I was younger, I used to **(2)** .... having a brother because I thought that parents with just one child were bound to **(3)** .... them more attention and love them more. And you wouldn't have to share your toys **(4)** ....! Friends of mine who were in this enviable position **(5)** .... me as confident, more mature and … well, lucky!

My most unhappy childhood memories involve my older brother Thomas. I didn't get **(6)** .... with him at all and, because he was much bigger than me, he would always **(7)** .... any fights we had. My parents took the view that they should not interfere in our arguments, and made us sort them **(8)** .... ourselves. Which meant that Thomas could do whatever he wanted.

(9) .... , the good news about siblings is that as they get older they seem to start valuing each other more. In fact, nowadays Thomas and I are quite **(10)** .... I suppose this is not surprising, since we share a **(11)** .... that goes back a long way, and no one else knows much about it or is very interested **(12)** .... it.

0	**A** lately	**B** recently	**C** currently	**D** presently
1	**A** only	**B** single	**C** unique	**D** individual
2	**A** miss	**B** hope	**C** wish	**D** regret
3	**A** pay	**B** make	**C** allow	**D** provide
4	**A** too	**B** either	**C** neither	**D** as well
5	**A** hit	**B** struck	**C** seemed	**D** appeared
6	**A** on	**B** by	**C** round	**D** away
7	**A** win	**B** beat	**C** succeed	**D** overcome
8	**A** of	**B** over	**C** out	**D** through
9	**A** Even	**B** Despite	**C** Although	**D** However
10	**A** near	**B** close	**C** familiar	**D** attached
11	**A** story	**B** record	**C** history	**D** narrative
12	**A** of	**B** in	**C** by	**D** about

Open cloze (Part 2)

7 For questions 13–24, read the text below and think of the word that best fits each gap. Use only one word in each gap. There is an example at the beginning.

The coldest city on earth

Yakutsk is extremely big, remote and cold, **(0)** _even_ by Siberian standards. Although the region covers more than a million square miles, it is home to **(13)** .... than one million people and has **(14)** .... any large towns. In January the temperatures are -45°C, causing the metal on people's spectacles to stick to **(15)** .... cheeks.

Locals claim there are **(16)** .... lakes and rivers in the region for each inhabitant to have one. According **(17)** .... legend, when the god of creation arrived in Yakutsk he got **(18)** .... cold that his hands were frozen and he dropped all the natural resources there.

The capital of the region, also called Yakutsk, is six time zones away from Moscow, and 200 years ago **(19)** .... would take more than three months to travel between the two places. Now you can get there **(20)** .... six hours by plane, although tickets cost twice the average monthly salary.

There's no railway, so travellers have the option of a 1,000-mile boat ride up the Lena river during **(21)** .... few months of the year when it isn't frozen, or they have to use the 'Road of Bones', **(22)** .... was built by prisoners and can only be used in winter, when the rivers freeze over. Truck-drivers bringing supplies to remote villages go in pairs and never turn their engines **(23)** .... during the two-week drive. **(24)** .... they break down on the little-used road, it means almost certain death.

Word formation (Part 3)

8 For questions 25–34, read the text below. Use the word given in capitals at the end of some of the lines to form a word that fits the gap in the same line. There is an example at the beginning.

Anyone for bugs?

In the kitchen of the Archipelago restaurant in London, the head chef is making final

(0) ..*preparations*.. to one of the salads that has helped to make his restaurant so (25) .... Taking a wok off the stove, he spoons a (26) .... red sauce on to a bed of salad leaves. At first (27) .... this could be any other Thai salad, with its chilli, garlic and many other (28) .... ingredients.

But it's not long before you can recognise the shape of an insect – the thin legs, huge eyes and a long tail of a locust. The less (29) .... among us would not be too keen on eating insects such as locusts and crickets, but apparently, if you are able to get over your initial fear, they are in fact (30) .... tasty.

Restaurants like this (31) .... people who are (32) .... with eating the same food day in and day out. For around 2.5 billion of the world's population however, insects like these form part of their (33) .... diet. As well as being energy efficient, insects are low in fat, high in protein and full of vitamins, but (34) .... the consumption of insects seems to be declining in some parts of the world.

	PREPARE
	FAME
	SPICE
	SEE
	COLOUR
	ADVENTURE
	SURPRISE
	FASCINATING
	BORE
	DAY
	FORTUNE

Key word transformations (Part 4)

9 For questions 35–42, complete the second sentence so that it has a similar meaning to the first sentence, using the word given. Do not change the word given. You must use between two and five words, including the word given. Here is an example.

Example:
I don't think John has got his father's musical talent.
AFTER
John doesn't appear ..*to take after*.. *his father as far as musical talent is concerned.*

35 Julia can sing better than me.
   WELL
   I .... as Julia.

36 A fast food chain has taken over two of our local restaurants.
   BY
   Two of our local restaurants ....
   a fast food chain.

37 Nearly all the shops in this town are expensive.
   HARDLY
   There .... shops in this town.

38 It's ages since I've seen him.
   NOT
   I .... ages.

39 I think I forgot to lock the door.
   REMEMBER
   I .... the door.

40 I prefer watching TV to going out.
   RATHER
   I .... go out.

41 Before I got my car, I walked to the station every day.
   USED
   Before I got my car, I .... to the station every day.

42 My brother often arrives unexpectedly.
   TURNING
   My brother is .... unexpectedly.

On camera

6

Speaking

1 **Work in pairs and discuss the questions.**

1 What kind of live performances do you enjoy?

2 Do you ever give money to street performers? Why/Why not?

2 **Choose the word which does NOT fit in phrases 1–3.**

1 The *main/most obvious/highest/key* (dis)advantage of (being a street performer) is…

2 *Another/One further/One different/An additional* (dis)advantage of (working in) is…

3 …is a *huge/considerable/major/large* (dis)advantage.

3 **Work in pairs. What might the advantages and disadvantages of being a circus performer and a street performer be? Use the phrases in Activity 2 and the ideas in the box to help you.**

pay   fun   working hours   travel   practice
the risk of injury   the stress of performing

Discussion (Part 4)

▶ **EXAM** FOCUS p.207

4 ▶ 1.20 **Read the Part 4 questions and listen to two students, Roberto and Beata, answering question 1. Do you agree with their opinions?**

1 Which do you think you need more of, luck or talent, to succeed in the arts?

2 How important do you think it is for schools to offer art, dance and drama classes to all students?

3 What do you think of people who take part in TV talent shows like *The X Factor*?

5 **What language did Roberto/Beata use to**

1 ask his/her partner a question?

2 summarise his/her partner's opinion?

3 accept his/her partner's argument?

6 Do you think they answered the question well?

7 Work in pairs. Discuss the questions from Activity 4.

Vocabulary
the arts

8 Complete the sentences with one of the words in the box.

critics	production	script	set

1 The .... took months to make.
2 The play received good reviews from the ....
3 This .... was first performed in 1922.
4 The .... was difficult for the actors to learn.

9 Look at the paintings. Do you recognise them? Which one do you like the most? Match the words with one of the pictures.

landscape	graffiti	still life	abstract	portrait

10 Work in pairs. Take turns to describe a favourite painting or photograph. Find out as much information as you can about your partner's favourite artist or photographer.

It was painted by…
It's on display in…
It makes me feel…
It shows…

Multiple choice (Part 1)

▶ **EXAM** FOCUS p.204

1 ▶ 1.21 **You will hear people talking in eight different situations. First, underline the key words for question 1. Then listen and choose the best answer A, B or C.**

1 On the radio, you hear a woman talking about a play. What did she dislike about the play?

  A the lighting

  B the music

  C the costumes

2 **Check with a partner and answer these questions. Then listen to question 1 again.**

1 Was the information in the recording in the same order as options A, B and C?

2 Did you hear any of the key words in options A, B or C?

3 Does the woman make negative comments about all the options, A, B or C?

4 Which words did you hear that refer to lighting, music and costumes?

5 Which words signal what the woman disliked about the play?

3 ▶ 1.22 **Listen to questions 2–8 and choose the best answer, A, B or C.**

> **EXAM TIP**
>
> Don't worry if you don't understand every word. Just focus on choosing the best option to answer the question.

2 You overhear a man and a woman talking about a visit to the theatre. Why do they decide to meet at 6p.m.?

  A The show starts earlier than they had thought.

  B They want to eat before the performance

  C They need to get tickets.

3 You hear someone talking about a famous actor. Where will fans be able to see the actor next week?

  A on the set of his new film

  B performing on stage

  C on a TV chat show

4 You hear a woman giving some information on the radio about a comedy festival. Why is the festival going to be different this year?

  A The tickets will be more expensive.

  B It will be held in a smaller venue.

  C It will be on different dates.

5 You hear a man interviewing a ballet dancer on the radio. Why is she going to retire later this year?

  A She is worried about getting injured.

  B She no longer enjoys performing.

  C She wants to see more of her family.

6 You hear a man and a woman talking on the radio about a new art exhibition. What is special about it?

  A its content

  B its location

  C its size

7 You hear an actress being interviewed on the radio. What is the actress doing?

  A giving her opinion

  B describing future events

  C stating an intention

8 You hear two friends talking in a café. What are they talking about?

  A a play they're going to see

  B their favourite actress

  C a college production

4 **Work in pairs and discuss the questions.**

1 How often do you go to the theatre/the cinema/art galleries?

2 What do you like seeing?

Future forms

▶ **GRAMMAR** REFERENCE p.177

1 **Look at the underlined verbs. Which ones are examples of present continuous, present simple, *will*, *going to* and modal verbs?**

A: Who do you think will get the main part?

B: I expect **(1)** it'll be Zoe. She's a good singer and dancer. But it **(2)** could be Molly. I thought she did a good audition too. Mr Paton says **(3)** he's going to tell us in class this week.

A: When **(4)** are you starting rehearsals?

B: On Friday. **(5)** It's going to be really hard work because performances **(6)** start in three weeks.

A: **(7)** I'll help you learn your lines, if you like.

B: Thanks. That would be very helpful

2 **Match the numbered future forms in the dialogue with their uses A–G.**

A an offer

B a fixed arrangement

C a timetabled event in the future

D an intention – something that someone has decided to do in the future

E a prediction based on a belief or opinion

F a prediction – based on fact

G a future possibility

3 **What words can you use instead of *could* for example 2 in Activity 1?**

4 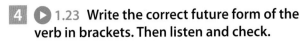 1.23 **Write the correct future form of the verb in brackets. Then listen and check.**

1 *will / present simple / present continuous*

A: What **(1)** .... (*do*) this weekend?

B: I **(2)** .... (*go*) to the dance festival in the park. It's on all weekend.

A: Oh I'd really like to go but my brother **(3)** .... (*move*) house on Saturday and I have to help him.

B: That's a shame!

A: Never mind. I'm sure you **(4)** .... (*enjoy*) it.

2 *going to / will / present simple*

A: Hi Ben! Are you going to the film festival at the weekend?

B: Yes, on Saturday. I **(5)** .... (*buy*) the tickets online today.

A: How much are they?

B: Only £15. I **(6)** .... (*get*) you one if you like.

A: That would be great. What time **(7)** .... (*start*)?

B: At 7.30. But I **(8)** .... (*leave*) home early, at six o'clock because of the traffic. I'll pick you up on my way if you like.

5 **Listen again and underline the stressed words in each sentence.**

Example: What are you <u>doing</u> this <u>weekend?</u>

6 **Practise the dialogues in pairs, paying attention to contractions, weak forms and the main stress in each sentence.**

LANGUAGE TIP

Future time expressions: *as soon as, when, before, after*, are used with the present simple.

As soon as *the film **ends** we'll call a taxi.*

*We'll have dinner **when** she **arrives**.*

Before *you see the film, you must read the book.*

*She's hoping to become an actress **after** she **leaves** school.*

Speaking

7 **Tell your partner one hope, arrangement, intention or prediction for**

1 later today.

2 next weekend.

3 your next holiday.

4 next year.

Speaking

1 Work in pairs and discuss the questions.

1 Why do you think people still go to the cinema rather than watching films at home?

2 Which are more popular in your country: international blockbusters or independent films made in your own country?

Gapped text (Part 2)

▶ **EXAM** FOCUS p.201

2 Read the title and sub-heading carefully. Then read the article quickly. Why are blockbusters and 'niche' products doing so well these days?

3 Seven sentences have been removed from the text. Look at the text around the first gap and answer the questions.

1 What does *that* refer back to?

2 How does the information after the gap relate to the information before the gap?

3 What kind of information do you think is missing?

4 What kind of linking word or expression would you expect to find in the missing sentence?

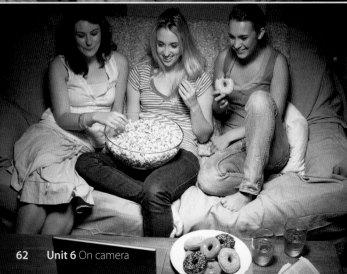

4 Look at the options A–H and choose the one that fits the first gap. Then do the same for the rest of the gaps (2–7). There is one extra sentence which you do not need to use.

> **EXAM TIP**
>
> Try to predict what kind of information will be in the gap before looking at the options.

Speaking

5 Discuss the questions in pairs.

1 Which 'niche' or small independent films have been successful in your country?

2 How do you choose what films to see or books to read?

3 What effect has digital technology had on the film industry so far? What do you think the future of the cinema and entertainment in general will be?

Vocabulary

word formation: adjectives from nouns; nouns from verbs

6 Work in pairs to form the words in questions 1 and 2. Then check with the words underlined in the article.

1 What are the adjectives from these nouns?

| access | anxiety | romance | succeed |

2 What are the nouns from these verbs?

| choose | entertain | grow | live |
| produce | separate | supply | |

7 Tick the statements you agree with. Then discuss your opinions in groups, giving reasons and examples.

The films I enjoy the most

A tend to have a happy ending.

B are usually romantic comedies.

C generally have amazing special effects.

D always have a great soundtrack.

E are often blockbusters.

The future of entertainment

More than ever, media is separating into mass market blockbusters on the one hand and 'niche' products – attracting small groups of people with similar interests – on the other. Everything else is struggling to compete.

Joe Swanberg makes films about the <u>romantic</u> lives of young people in the city. He shoots quickly with a digital camera and asks actors to wear their own clothes. His low-budget films are hardly ever shown in cinemas. By keeping his costs down and distributing digitally, Mr Swanberg is making a <u>living</u>.

Technology was expected to help young people like him. A few years ago it was predicted that the internet would vastly increase the <u>supply</u> of small independent films and other niche media <u>products</u> and increase their audiences. That has certainly happened. [1] Blockbusters are also tightening their grip on audiences, whether it's in the area of film, music, television or books. The <u>growth</u> of both niche products and huge sell-out successes has been at the expense of the things in the middle which are just quite popular – the near misses.

[2] As in the past, people still want to have something to talk about with their friends. Which is why talent shows such as *American Idol* do pretty much as well as they did ten years ago, and why the latest blockbuster still breaks new records at the box office. Research shows that people still choose blockbusters more often than less well-known books and films. This is probably because people tend to try only things they have heard of – which for many people means only media-hyped blockbusters.

Furthermore, all the technology that has made niche content so much more <u>accessible</u> has also proved handy for pushing blockbusters. Missed the last popular film? [3]

Blockbusters are doing well not in spite of the fact that people have more <u>choice</u> in entertainment, but because of it. Imagine walking into a music shop which has more than 10 million songs, as iTunes does, all of them arranged alphabetically. Making up your mind would be impossible! [4]

Is this increasingly more common <u>separation</u> into blockbusters and niches good or bad? It certainly makes life harder for media companies. In a world where <u>entertainment</u> choices are growing, it is more important than ever to make a big impact with your product. [5] The possibility of failing can make people <u>anxious</u> and more conservative. Television programmes must be <u>successful</u> quickly or they will be cancelled. It is becoming even harder to talk the decision-makers in the movie industry into approving films if they are not confident there is a demand for them.

[6] In the past, these powerful business people could get away with supplying content that was not that good to people who did not have much to choose from. These days, with so many options, there is rarely nothing good on television. So the media industry must raise its game.

Intelligent people naturally wish that more money were available to produce the kind of music, films and television programmes they like. [7] Some may love watching a programme about the history of dance; others may want to spend an hour being told how to look after pet snakes. But not many want to do either of these things, which explains why such programmes are niche products. There are only a few things that can be guaranteed to delight large numbers of people. They are known as blockbusters.

A Don't worry, because there will be other chances to see it, in a wide variety of formats.
B The problem is that everybody has different ideas about exactly what they want to watch.
C If it isn't a hit, it will have to fight for attention together with thousands – perhaps millions – of other offerings.
D State broadcasters like the BBC have some protection from the poor economic climate.
E Yet this can be a big advantage for consumers.
F However, so has the opposite.
G So, rather than having to decide, it's much easier to just grab what everybody is talking about.
H There are several reasons why big hits still do so well.

Future perfect and continuous

▶ **GRAMMAR** REFERENCE p.177

1 **Do you agree with these predictions?**

> By 2020, we'll be watching TV programmes in 3D. They might even have found a way to project our faces on to the screen by then.

> In twenty-five years, people will have learned how to monitor the electronic activity of your brain and when you play video games, your thoughts will be controlling your avatar.

2 **Look at the sentences again.**

1 Write down the time linkers connected to the future.
2 Underline two actions which began before a specific time in the future and will continue after it.
3 Circle two actions which are already over before a specific time in the future.

3 **Complete the notes.**

- future continuous: *will/may/might* + ... + *-ing*
- future perfect: *will/may/might* + ... + ...
  participle

LANGUAGE TIP

You can also use future continuous to talk about things you expect will happen because they usually do.

*Do you think **you'll be going** to Spain again for your holidays?*

4 **Choose the correct alternative to complete the sentences.**

By 2050…

1 most cinemas will *be closing down/have closed* down.
2 everybody will *be using/have used* surround sound systems with their TVs.
3 we'll *be choosing/have chosen* from a huge cyber library whatever television programme we want to watch.
4 we will not *be interacting/have interacted* with the screen when we move and speak.
5 they will *be inventing/have invented* contact lenses with a chip inside so that we can watch the screen in 3D.
6 holographic TV screens will *be projecting/have projected* images around our rooms at home.

5 **Tick the sentences you agree with in Activity 4. Then discuss your opinions in pairs.**

6 **Work in pairs. What do you think the world will be like in fifty years' time? What will have changed, and what will be happening? Use the ideas in the box to help you.**

leisure time	the environment	the family
food	work	travel
medicine and technology		

Vocabulary

expressions with *get*

1 *Get* has lots of different meanings. Replace *get* in questions 1–6 with one of the verbs in the box. Then ask each other the questions in pairs.

become	have	move/travel	persuade
receive	understand		

1 Was there a subject at school that you really didn't get?
2 What techniques do you use to get people to do what you want?
3 When do you normally get the time to relax?
4 In which situations do you get angry?
5 How do you get from one place to another?
6 How many texts do you get in an average day?

Multiple-choice cloze (Part 1)

▶ **EXAM** FOCUS p.202

2 Read the text quickly. What did science fiction get right and wrong when it predicted the future? What did it not predict?

EXAM TIP

Part 1 tests language (focusing on vocabulary) such as
- phrasal verbs (*get away*)
- collocations (*do your homework*)
- words with similar meanings (*travel, trip, journey*)
- linking words (*although*)
- set phrases (*on purpose*)

0	**A** say	**B** call	**C** tell	**D** name
1	**A** true	**B** right	**C** exact	**D** correct
2	**A** get	**B** arrive	**C** reach	**D** appear
3	**A** on	**B** by	**C** with	**D** at
4	**A** drive	**B** travel	**C** voyage	**D** journey
5	**A** told	**B** claimed	**C** advised	**D** informed
6	**A** free	**B** ready	**C** vacant	**D** available
7	**A** unable	**B** unused	**C** helpless	**D** hopeless
8	**A** for	**B** to	**C** in	**D** against
9	**A** up	**B** off	**C** over	**D** down
10	**A** hand	**B** way	**C** side	**D** place
11	**A** make	**B** do	**C** get	**D** take
12	**A** end	**B** effect	**C** result	**D** solution

3 Read the text again and decide which answer (A, B, C or D) best fits each gap.

4 Do you agree with the writer about the importance of the computer? What other inventions do you think have had a huge impact on our lives?

From fiction to reality

Science fiction films have promised us many exciting gadgets. We have seen hoverboards, domestic robots and flying cars to **(0)** *D name* just a few, but most of these predictions have not come **(1)** .... yet. For example, this morning I did not **(2)** .... to the office on a hoverboard, I came **(3)** .... bike instead. The bicycle was invented in the nineteenth century. Almost the whole **(4)** .... was on a form of tarmac, also invented that same century. Instead of a pill for breakfast I had a bacon roll. Science has not **(5)** .... us the truth. Although robotic vacuum cleaners, for example, are commercially **(6)** .... , they are fairly **(7)** .... and we are still doing a lot of housework ourselves. And **(8)** .... some people's surprise, robots haven't taken **(9)** .... the workplace yet either.

On the other **(10)** .... , in 1987, Star Trek predicted we would be using touchscreen technology. So perhaps fiction doesn't always **(11)** .... it wrong after all. But maybe the most astonishing development has been the microchip and its place in computers. The **(12)** .... on our lives has been more amazing than anything else, and this was never really predicted.

Report (Part 2)

▶ **WRITING** REFERENCE p.186

1 **Read the report which a teacher was asked to write for the director of her language college. Answer the questions in pairs.**

1 What was the purpose of her report?

2 What is her recommendation?

3 Is it written in an informal or semi-formal style? Give examples.

Report on suggestion for a college cinema

(1) ....

The aim of this report is to outline the advantages and potential problems of investing money in a small cinema, and make recommendations. In order to do this, both students and staff were consulted.

(2) ....

A cinema was felt to be an ideal venue for students and teachers to meet socially. It was suggested that films in other languages as well as English could be shown, which would widen the appeal, and that the cinema might also be used for conversation classes.

(3) ....

The main concerns that were raised are as follows:

1 It would be expensive to set up and run.

2 Since many students watch DVDs on their laptops, they might not be prepared to pay to watch films.

3 Only big cinemas have access to blockbusters when they first come out.

(4) ....

I am concerned that the cinema may not pay its way at first. However, all things considered, the benefits outweigh the disadvantages. I would therefore recommend going ahead with the project.

2 **Give each of the four sections of the report a heading, so that it is easier to read.**

| Advantages | Potential problems |
| Introduction | Recommendation |

3 **Look at the underlined phrases in the text. Find examples of the following and discuss why they are commonly used in reports.**

1 passive forms/reporting verbs

2 linking words

3 clauses of purpose

4 **Read the exam task below and underline the key words.**

The director of your college wants to invest money in a self-study centre and has asked you, as student representative, to visit a college which has one and speak to both students and teachers.

You should say how successful that self-study centre has been, and recommend whether or not your college should have one.

Write your **report** to the director. Write your answer in **120–180 words** in an appropriate style.

5 **Divide these points into the advantages and disadvantages of the study centre you saw.**

1 It is under-used at weekends.

2 People from the community use the facilities, which helps to fund it.

3 Many students still prefer to study in their own rooms.

4 The worksheets provided give extra practice of classroom work.

5 A full-time assistant has to be on duty, even if the centre is empty.

6 The facility helps to attract potential students to the college.

7 It cost a lot to set up because of all the computers etc.

8 Writing materials for the centre is time-consuming for the teachers.

6 **Write your report. Use some of the points above and any others you can think of.**

EXAM TIP

Make your report impersonal and only give your recommendation at the end.

1 Complete the following sentences, using the correct form of the word in capitals.

1 Comedy stand-up has been my favourite form of .... since I was a teenager. **ENTERTAIN**

2 The rapid .... of our national film industry has been very welcome. **GROW**

3 Although I wasn't .... in the audition, I was glad I'd taken part. **SUCCEED**

4 The theatre has invested money so that the building is .... to people in wheelchairs. **ACCESS**

5 He wants to be an actor but he is .... about getting a job. **ANXIETY**

6 We wanted to see a film, but there wasn't much .... **CHOOSE**

2 Choose the correct option, A, B or C.

1 Sorry, I can't come on Saturday. I .... an old school friend for lunch.

   A meet   **B** am meeting   **C** will meet

2 As soon as she ...., will you text me?

   A phones   **B** will phone   **C** will be phoning

3 I .... my drama course by the end of next year.

   A will be completing   **B** will have completed
   C am completing

4 This time tomorrow, I .... in front of hundreds of people.

   A will dance   **B** will be dancing   **C** dance

5 Don't worry, I haven't forgotten. I .... to him later.

   A speak   **B** will have spoken
   C am going to speak

6 I'll meet you after I .... work.

   A finish   **B** am finishing   **C** will finish

7 Don't be nervous. I'm sure you .... really well tomorrow.

   A do   **B** are doing   **C** will do

8 Let's hurry! They .... the theatre doors at 7.30 and then you have to wait until the interval to go in.

   A close   **B** are going to close   **C** are closing

3 Choose the correct word in the box to complete the sentences.

away	down	into
over	round	through

1 The only way I can get .... to my cousin is by talking about dance.

2 *City Lights* is on TV tonight. I never got .... to seeing that in the cinema.

3 It took him ages to get .... the disappointment of not being in the play.

4 If I stay in every night watching TV, it gets me ....

5 Comedians can't get .... with simply repeating the same jokes at every performance.

6 Everyone says it's a really good series. I just can't get .... it.

4 Make sentences using the future continuous form or the future perfect form of the verbs in brackets.

1 I think I'll still .... (*learn*) my lines until just before the play starts.

2 The film may already .... (*start*) by the time we get there.

3 I hope they'll .... (*show*) his still lifes at the exhibition.

4 We might .... (*use*) the same costumes in our next production.

5 People will probably still .... (*watch*) live theatre in fifty years time.

6 I think people will .... (*lose*) interest in computer games a long time before 2020.

A home from home

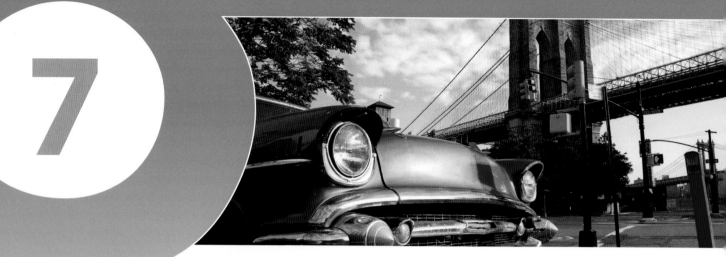

Speaking

1 You are going to read an extract from a novel about Eilis, a young girl in the 1950s, who is about to leave her home in Ireland to go and live in America. Work in pairs and discuss how you would feel about leaving your family, town and country to emigrate.

Library ☰   AA Q

line 1   Until now, Eilis had always presumed that she would live in the town all her life, as her mother had done, knowing everyone, having the same friends and neighbours, the same routines in the same streets. She had expected that she would find a job in the town, and then
line 3   marry someone and give up the job and have children. Now, she felt that she was being singled out for something for which she was not in any way prepared, and this, despite the fear it carried with it, gave her a feeling, or more a set of feelings, she thought she might experience in the days before her wedding, days in which everyone looked at her in the rush of arrangements with light in their eyes, days in which she herself was fizzy with excitement but careful not to think too precisely about what the next few weeks would be like
line 7   in case she lost her nerve.

    There was no day that passed without an event. … Father Flood wrote with more details, of where she would stay when she arrived and how close it would be to her place of work; her ticket arrived for the ship to New York, which would leave from Liverpool. … The house was, she thought, unusually, almost unnaturally happy, and the meals they shared were full of too much talk and laughter. It reminded her of the weeks before Jack had left for Birmingham when they would do anything to distract themselves from the thought that they were losing him.

    One day, when a neighbour called and sat in the kitchen with them having tea, Eilis realized that her mother and Rose were doing everything to hide their feelings. The neighbour, almost casually, as a way of making conversation, said: 'You'll miss her when she's gone, I'd say.'

    'Oh, it'll kill me when she goes,' her mother said. Her face wore a dark strained look that Eilis had not seen since the months after
line 17   their father died. Then, in the moments that followed, the neighbour appearing to have been taken aback by her mother's tone, her mother's expression became almost darker and she had to stand up and walk quietly out of the room. It was clear to Eilis that she was
line 19   going to cry. Eilis was so surprised that, instead of following her mother into the hallway or the dining room, she made small talk with
line 20   their neighbour, hoping her mother would soon return and they could resume what had seemed like an ordinary conversation.

    Even when she woke in the night and thought about it, she did not allow herself to conclude that she did not want to go. … It struck her on one of those nights, as she lay awake, that the next time she would open the suitcase it would be in a different room in a
line 23   different country, and then the thought came unbidden into her mind that she would be happier if it were opened by another person who could keep the clothes and shoes and wear them every day. She would prefer to stay at home, sleep in this room, live in this house, do without the clothes and shoes. The arrangements being made, all the bustle and talk, would be better if they were for someone else, she thought, someone like her, someone the same age and size, who maybe even looked the same as she did, as long as she, the person who was thinking now, could wake in this bed every morning and move as the day went on in these familiar streets and come home to the kitchen, to her mother and Rose.

line 29   Even though she let these thoughts run as fast as they would, she still stopped when her mind moved towards real fear or dread, or worse, towards the thought that she was going to lose this world for ever, that she would never have an ordinary day again in this ordinary place, that the rest of her life would be a struggle with the unfamiliar. Downstairs, once Rose and her mother were there, she talked about practical things and remained bright.

Reading for detail (Part 1)

▶ **EXAM** FOCUS p.200

2 Read the extract quickly. Does Eilis feel positive about the move?

3 Read the extract again and answer questions 1–3. Choose the answer which you think fits best according to the text.

1 From the first paragraph we understand that Eilis is

  A worried about adjusting to the new plans for her future.

  B anxious that she won't be ready in time for her departure.

  C disappointed about not being able to get married in Ireland.

  D upset that she might lose touch with everyone she cares about.

2 What impression do you get of Eilis's family?

  A They don't pay much attention to each other's lives.

  B They have not yet got over the death of Eilis's father.

  C They are used to family members leaving to go abroad.

  D They tend to avoid talking to each other about their emotions.

3 What did Eilis worry about in bed at night?

  A whether the clothes she had packed were appropriate

  B whether she would ever feel at home anywhere again

  C whether she would like the place where she was going

  D whether her mother would be lonely when she had gone

4 Work in pairs and discuss why you chose the answers you did, and why the other ones weren't possible.

5 In what ways do you think emigrating in the 1950s would have been a more life-changing experience than it is these days?

Vocabulary deducing meaning

6 Work in pairs. For each question, which option is correct? How did you guess?

1 In line 19 *small talk* means

  A talked very little.

  B talked very quietly.

  C talked about unimportant things.

  D talked about childish things.

2 In line 20 *resume* means

  A start doing something again.

  B make a summary of something.

  C discuss the meaning of something.

  D try to understand why something happened.

7 In pairs, try to work out the meanings of these words and expressions from the context.

1 *presumed* (line 1)   **3** *lost her nerve* (line 7)   **5** *unbidden* (line 23)

2 *singled out* (line 3)   **4** *taken aback* (line 17)   **6** *dread* (line 29)

8 Work in groups and discuss the questions.

1 What would you miss most about your home town if you had to emigrate?

2 Are you happiest in familiar places and with people you know or are you always looking for new experiences?

EXAM TIP

The other options may seem tempting, but there is only evidence for one answer in the text.

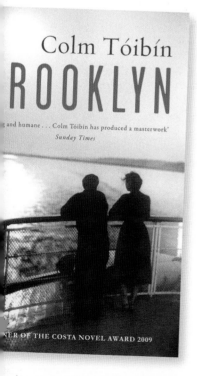

Colm Tóibín

ROOKLYN

g and humane . . . Colm Tóibín has produced a masterwork'
Sunday Times

ER OF THE COSTA NOVEL AWARD 2009

Modal verbs

possibility and certainty

▶ **GRAMMAR** REFERENCE p.170

1 **Agree or disagree with opinions 1–5 about the novel extract on page 68. Give reasons.**

Example: Father Flood must be a relation of Eilis.
No, he could be a family friend.

1 Jack could be Eilis's father.
2 Rose might be Eilis's sister.
3 Father Flood can't be living in New York.
4 Eilis couldn't have realised how her mother was feeling about her leaving.
5 Father Flood may have found Eilis the job in America.

2 **Look at sentences 1–5 again and underline a modal verb in each one. Then complete the gaps in rules A–C with the modal verbs.**

A When we are sure something is true we use ....
B When we are sure something is not true we use .... or ....
C When we think something is possibly true we use ...., ... or ....

3 **Answer the questions.**

1 Which sentences in Activity 1 refer to the present? Which refer to the past?
2 What verb form do we use after the modal in a) the present? b) the past?

> **LANGUAGE TIP**
>
> Use the weak form of *have* /əv/ in past modals.
> *She must have* /məstəv/ *missed the bus.*

4 **Choose the best alternative in the following sentences.**

1 He *might/must* be here somewhere because he promised to meet me.
2 The boat for New York *can't/could* be leaving already. It's too early.
3 She *must have decided/ must be deciding* to stay in the US. I haven't seen her for ages.
4 Surely they *can't be playing/must be playing* football. It's snowing!
5 Sam *couldn't be/can't have been* driving the car. He was at home with me.
6 He *may have seen/might be seeing* a ghost. But I never really believed him.

5 **Work in pairs. Take turns to use the cues in brackets to make responses to the statements. Remember to use the weak form of *have* for past forms.**

1 A James looks very relaxed these days.
  B .... (*must/give up/work*)
2 A I think that's Alfie who's running towards us.
  B ....(*can't/never take/any exercise*)
3 A Florence keeps checking her phone.
  B .... (*may/expect/a message*)
4 A It's unusual for Amy not to come out clubbing.
  B .... (*might/run out/of money*)
5 A It's strange that we haven't seen Jo and Rebecca for ages.
  B .... (*may/go/on holiday*)
6 A Jess isn't wearing her glasses, but she's as blind as a bat without them.
  B .... (*may/wear/contact lenses*)
7 A Do you like their new car?
  B .... (*must/spend/a fortune on it*)
8 A I can't understand where the cat is in all this rain.
  B .... (*may/hide/in the shed*)

6 **Look at the picture below. What do you think might be happening?**

Speculating (Part 2)

▶ **EXAM** FOCUS p.206

1 **Work in pairs and compare the photographs. Use some of these expressions of certainty, probability and doubt.**

They seem/appear (to be)…

It looks like/as if (they are)…

It must/could/may/can't (be/have done)…

I'd imagine (that they are)…

I'm fairly/absolutely certain (they are)…

As far as I can see, (they are)…

I suppose (they are)…

They are definitely…

Listening

2 ▶ 1.24 **Read the exam task. Then listen to a student doing it. Which place did he choose?**

> Look at the photos, which show unusual places to stay. Compare the photographs and say which of the places you think would be more enjoyable to stay at.

3 **Complete these sentences, which focus on expressions of speculation. Then listen again and check.**

1 I'm not absolutely .... what the place on the left is.

2 It .... be an underwater hotel.

3 The other one .... to have been built in the trees.

4 The underwater hotel .... quite luxurious.

5 The treehouse .... to be more basic.

6 It would .... be less expensive to stay at.

7 It .... be an interesting experience to stay at both of them.

8 I'd .... the treehouse might not be such fun in bad weather.

4 ▶ 1.25 **Listen again to the sentences from Activity 3 and underline the words which are stressed. Practise saying them with the same 'certain' or 'uncertain' intonation.**

EXAM TIP

In the first part, summarise the main similarity and difference. Mention any other similarities and differences if you have time. Don't describe one picture in detail.

5 **Work in pairs.**

Turn to page 153 and complete Task 1.

Then turn to page 155 and swap roles for Task 2.

Vocabulary
describing places

1 Look at the photo of the monastery in Tibet. Which of these adjectives do you think you could use to describe it?

breathtaking	inspirational	luxurious
magnificent	mysterious	peaceful
remote	spiritual	

2 ▶ 1.26 Underline the stressed syllable in each adjective and then listen and check. Practise saying the words.

3 Look at the dictionary entry and answer the questions.

Shangri-la /ʃæŋgri ˈlɑː/ *n*
1 An imaginary remote paradise on earth; utopia
2 A distant beautiful imaginary place where everyone is happy

from the Longman Dictionary of Contemporary English

1 What do you know about Shangri-la?

2 What's your idea of paradise on earth? How do you imagine: the landscape, the people, the way of life?

The classic tale of Shangri-La
LOST HORIZON
JAMES HILTON

Multiple choice (Part 4)

▶ **EXAM** FOCUS p.205

4 ▶ **1.27** You will hear a woman called Olivia Rees, talking on a travel programme about a place called Shangri-la. First read the questions and options and underline the key words. Then listen and choose the best answer, A, B or C.

> **EXAM TIP**
>
> If you can't answer a question during the first listening, continue answering the other questions and wait until the second listening before deciding on an answer. Guess if you are not sure.

1 Why does Olivia say the novel *Lost Horizon* was so popular in the 1930s?
   A People needed to escape from reality.
   B People believed Shangri-la was a real place.
   C People were interested in finding out about Tibet.

2 How did the travellers in *Lost Horizon* get to Shangri-la?
   A Guides took them there.
   B Their plane crashed there.
   C They found it using an old map.

3 What was special about the people of Shangri-la?
   A They were very wise.
   B They lived a very long time.
   C They could speak every language.

4 What does Olivia say about the author, James Hilton?
   A He became a Buddhist.
   B He only made one trip to Tibet.
   C He got his ideas from books and magazines.

5 Olivia says the similarities between the stories of Shambhala and Shangri-la show that Hilton
   A was interested in Tibetan culture.
   B believed such a society could really exist.
   C was unable to think of original ideas.

6 What information is given about the county of Zhongdian?
   A It was originally called Shangri-la.
   B It has a large number of monasteries.
   C It has found a new source of income.

7 Olivia says people who visit modern-day Shangri-la may be
   A shocked.
   B confused.
   C disappointed.

5 Listen again and check your answers to question 1 in Activity 4.

1 Which words from options A, B and C are mentioned in the recording?

2 Which words are a paraphrase of the correct answer?

3 Which words show why the wrong options are wrong?

6 What places in the world

1 have a relaxed pace of life?

2 have/haven't lived up to your expectations?

3 are cut off from the outside world?

Vocabulary

travel and expressions with *world*

7 Choose the word which does NOT collocate with the noun.

1 a *domestic/direct/long distance/seasonal* flight

2 a *season/direct/one way/open/return* ticket

3 a *sightseeing/package/round/guided* tour

4 a *package/camping/shopping/tourist* expedition

5 a *tourist/weekend/long distance/sightseeing* excursion

6 a *business/coach/day/round/direct* trip

8 Complete the expressions with the correct preposition.

1 It's very remote, completely *cut* .... *from* the outside world.

2 He travels *all* .... *the world* with his job.

3 It's the most magical place, quite .... *of this world*.

4 *There's a world* .... *difference between* the north and south of the country.

5 He has no idea what's going on. He's .... *a world of his own*.

6 They've got *the world* .... *their feet*. There's nothing they can't achieve.

7 I wouldn't live anywhere else. This house *means the world* .... *me*.

8 I'm so lucky. I've got the best job .... *the world*.

9 Which of the expressions in Activity 8 are similar to expressions in your language?

10 Think of somewhere that's special to you and use some of the expressions to describe it and how it makes you feel.

Relative clauses

▶ **GRAMMAR** REFERENCE p.172

1 **Read the text (right) and guess which place is being described.**

2 **Decide which lines contain**

A a defining relative clause (provides essential information)?

B a non-defining relative clause (adds extra information)?

3 **In which line(s) could the relative pronoun**

A be replaced by *that*?

B be left out?

C be replaced by *where?*

LANGUAGE TIP

that • can't be used in non-defining relative clauses.
• can be used instead of *which* or *who* in defining relative clauses.
• can be used for both people and things.

---

4 **Join these pairs of sentences with relative clauses. Add commas where necessary.**

1 The nearest town doesn't have a train station. It's 5km from here.

2 The local people now work in tourism. They used to work in the fishing industry.

3 Where's the bus? It goes to the beach.

4 This hotel belongs to a woman. She's not here at the moment.

5 In summer the water is warm. You can go swimming.

6 That man is a tour guide. I met him yesterday.

7 The road takes you to the top of the mountain. It's very steep.

8 It's a very beautiful place. We stayed there last summer.

5 **Describe one of the most popular places in your country and why people go there. Use these phrases:**

It's a place which…

It's somewhere that…

The people who live there…

One reason why people like it is…

The land of ice and fire

1 The island, which is bigger than Ireland, has a population of only 370,000. Around two thirds of people live in the southwest of the country, where the capital Reykjavík 5 is situated. In recent years the island, whose main attraction is its abundance of volcanoes and geysers, has become increasingly dependent on tourism. It's easy to understand why most tourists 10 who come to the island choose to come in summer, when there are over twenty hours of daylight. But although it's known as 'the land of ice and fire', winter temperatures, which average about –1°C, are not as 15 cold as you might expect. One of the places which tourists most want to visit is the Blue Lagoon, a naturally heated pool of seawater in the middle of a lava field, in which you can bathe all year round.

so, such, too, very, enough

1 **Choose the correct words to complete the sentences.**

1 It rains *so/such* a lot that no one bothers to carry an umbrella because they're *so/enough* used to getting wet.

2 Going by taxi is *very/too* expensive but it takes *too/very* long to walk.

3 The hotel is a *very/such* relaxing place because it's *so/too* near the beach.

4 There are *too/very* many cars on the road and not *enough/such* bicycles.

5 He's done *so/too* much travelling recently that he's tired *too/enough* to sleep for a week!

6 *Very/Such* few people have visited it because the location is *so/such* remote.

2 **Look at the examples in Activity 1 and complete the rules with *so, such, too, enough* or *very*.**

1 ...., ... and .... are used before an adjective.

2 .... is used after an adjective.

3 .... is used before countable and uncountable nouns.

4 ...., ... and .... are used before the determiner *much*.

5 .... is used to show that there is an excessive amount of something.

6 .... and .... are used before the determiner *few*.

▶ **GRAMMAR** REFERENCE p.175

Speaking

3 **Complete the sentences so they are true about you. Then compare with a partner.**

1 I haven't got enough time to…

2 It's such a long time since I've…

3 I'm feeling so excited about…

4 I don't think I'm old enough to…

5 I don't think I have enough…

6 I find it too expensive…

Sentence transformation (Part 4)

▶ **EXAM** FOCUS p.203

4 **Complete the second sentence so that it has a similar meaning to the first sentence, using the word given. Do not change the word given. You must use between two and five words, including the word given.**

EXAM TIP

Don't write more than five words – remember contractions, e.g. *isn't*, count as two words.

Example: It was the most depressing story I have ever heard.

NEVER

I have *never heard such a* depressing story.

1 It was too foggy for us to ski.
SO
It was .... not ski.

2 He couldn't afford a taxi so he went by bus.
ENOUGH
He .... for a taxi, so he went by bus.

3 She wanted to stay at home that winter because of all the travelling she'd been doing.
TOO
She wanted to stay at home that winter because she .... travelling.

4 I knew it was a terrible idea for us to go by train.
SHOULD
We .... by train.

5 There was so much traffic that we missed the show.
SUCH
There was .... that we missed the show.

6 It's possible that you saw a ghost, but I'm not convinced.
COULD
You .... a ghost, but I'm not convinced.

7 She is definitely lying.
BE
She .... the truth.

8 This is probably where the photograph was taken.
MAY
The photograph .... here.

A memorable journey

The journey itself wasn't memorable. The scenery was dull and anyway I'd seen it dozens of times before. I'd anticipated a quiet journey with only my book for company and I hadn't bothered to put on any make-up. So imagine my panic and shock when I got on and saw who was sitting next to me on the only free seat on the train – the captain of our college rugby team and the coolest guy on the planet.

3 Underline examples where the writer

A contrasts expectations with reality.

B uses exaggeration for emphasis.

C involves the reader.

4 Complete the sentences in an interesting way.

1 The train was so crowded that ....

2 I was hoping that I would be sitting next to ...., but instead ....

3 I had imagined that the scenery would be ...., but to my amazement ....

4 Imagine how happy you'd feel if ....

5 Match the two halves of the sentences.

1 I arrived at work ten minutes late for work and *to make matters worse*

2 *Not only had I* left my train ticket at home, *but*

3 The flight was delayed, there were no rooms left at the airport hotel, and *on top of that*

4 We were stuck in traffic on the motorway for seven hours, and *what's more*

A all the restaurants were full.

B we ran out of petrol.

C my boss saw me running into the building.

D I forgot to get off at the right station.

6 Now write your article. You should write 120–180 words. Try to use some of the language from Activities 3, 4 and 5 to make your writing more interesting.

Speaking

1 **Tell your partner about a time when you**

1 travelled in style.

2 got lost.

3 met someone unexpected on a journey.

4 got on the wrong bus/train.

5 were very late for something important.

Article (Part 2)

adding interest and more information

▶ **WRITING** REFERENCE p.187

2 **Look at the exam task and Paragraph 1 of a model answer. How do you think the article continues?**

You see this advertisement in a travel magazine.

A memorable journey

Write an article about a memorable journey you've had. It can be any kind of journey but you should describe why it was memorable and how you felt. We will publish the best articles in the June edition of *Traveller's World*.

EXAM TIP

Try to grab the reader's attention with your introductory paragraph.

7 **Check your article for spelling, punctuation and grammar mistakes.**

1 Complete this story about Mothman, using the correct form of the modals in brackets.

Mothman

Many years ago a strange creature was spotted in West Virginia in the USA. It looked like a man with wings and most witnesses claim it (**1**) .... (*must/be*) nearly two metres tall; others say it (**2**) .... (*may/have*) eyes in its chest. Nobody is very sure what this creature (**3**) ....(*could/be*). Some people today think these witnesses (**4**) .... (*might/mistake*) big owls flying around for the creature. Others feel it (**5**) .... (*must/be*) a UFO because there were also strange lights around it. And even people who think there (**6**) ....(*can/be*) such things as a Mothman enjoy watching the films about it or visiting the four-metre sculpture in West Virginia.

The Mothman

2 Complete the text by putting the correct relative pronoun in each gap.

Cape Cod

Cape Cod, (**1**) .... is referred to locally as 'the Cape', is famous around the world as a summer playground for the rich and powerful, (**2**) .... own charming seafront summer houses there. But it is also the destination of choice for many East-Coast middle-class families (**3**) .... come to enjoy the relaxing pace of life. It's a place (**4**) .... people come to fish, sail, and generally get in tune with nature. It is hard to overestimate the Cape's stunning beauty. The coast, (**5**) .... faces the Atlantic, amounts to one long, awesome beach, (**6**) .... is backed by giant sand dunes and protected from development. The towns and villages are very attractive, with pretty cottages and clapboard houses, (**7**) .... were built by sea captains 200 years ago.

However, unlike other US beach destinations such as Florida or California, (**8**) .... it is consistently hot, Cape Cod can be misty and even chilly occasionally during the summer season.

3 Decide which answer A, B, C or D best fits each space.

1 We went on an interesting guided .... of a fishing village.
   A journey   **B** expedition
   C tour   **D** visit

2 I need to get a .... ticket because I am coming back this evening.
   A round   **B** return
   C package   **D** direct

3 We had to .... the car and walk home when it broke down.
   A cut   **B** miss
   C abandon   **D** lose

4 She was sure she must have been there before as the place seemed so ....
   A routine   **B** ordinary
   C usual   **D** familiar

5 It's a very remote location, completely cut .... from the outside world.
   A by   **B** out
   C off   **D** down

6 The first time people try sky-diving they sometimes lose their .... and can't jump out of the plane.
   A fear   **B** nerve
   C dread   **D** worry

Moving on

8

Multiple matching (Part 3)

▶ **EXAM** FOCUS p.205

1 **You will hear five different people talking about the future of their profession. What do you think these jobs involve?**

social-networking counsellor	vertical farmer	robotics engineer
virtual lawyer	spaceship pilot	

EXAM TIP

Hearing exactly the same word on the recording as in one of the options doesn't necessarily mean that option is the correct answer.

2 ▶ **2.01** **Listen and choose from the list A–F what each speaker says. Use the letters only once. There is one extra letter which you do not need to use.**

A	My job will involve working with new employees.	Speaker 1 ☐
B	My job will involve getting new qualifications.	Speaker 2 ☐
C	My job will involve helping a wide range of people.	Speaker 3 ☐
D	My job will involve providing a service that costs less than today.	Speaker 4 ☐
E	My job will involve being available on demand.	Speaker 5 ☐
F	My job will involve providing a fast and efficient service.	

3 **Check your answer for Speaker 1 by looking at the tapescript on page 160. Underline the part of the text that gives the correct answer.**

4 **Now listen to Speakers 2–5 again. Identify the key phrases that give the answers.**

Speaking

5 **Discuss the questions in pairs.**

1 Which job would you most like to have? Why?
2 Which of the jobs wouldn't you consider doing? Why?
3 Which of these jobs do you think is the most: worthwhile? highly-skilled? stressful? physically demanding?

Vocabulary

collocations and phrasal verbs with *work*

6 **Choose the correct word.**

1 Helping people gives me a lot of *work/job/employment* satisfaction.
2 I expect there isn't much *job/work/career* security in counselling.
3 Until quite recently, engineering used to be seen as a male *employment/career/occupation*.
4 When I leave university, I hope to join the medical *profession/career/occupation*.
5 The *work/profession/employment* agency found me my first job in sales.
6 It's important to look for a job that offers good *work/career/profession* opportunities.

7 **Match the phrasal verbs with one of the definitions A–F.**

1 We finally *worked out* how much tax we would have to pay.
2 Things *worked out* really *well* for him after he moved abroad for his job.
3 I *get worked up* about things too easily at work; especially if a customer is rude or difficult.
4 I *work out* at the gym three or four times a week during my lunch hour.
5 We need to *work out* who would be the best person to talk to the boss.
6 If the meeting is cancelled, we'll just have to *work around* it and sort the problem out ourselves.

A do exercise
B become angry or upset
C have a (good/bad) result
D calculate
E deal with
F plan/decide

8 **Discuss the questions with a partner.**

1 What do you get worked up about?
2 Do you think working out at the gym is the best way to keep fit?
3 Have you had to work around any obstacles recently?
4 How easy is it for you to work out solutions to problems?

LANGUAGE TIP

Some phrasal verbs have more than one meaning. But they are not all used in the same way. For example *work out* (solve) takes a direct object
I **worked out** the problem.
I **worked** the problem **out**.

But *work out* (take exercise at the gym) does not
I **work out** every day.

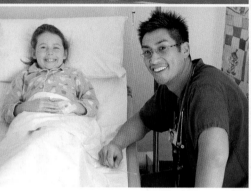

Collaborative task and discussion (Parts 3 and 4)

agreeing and disagreeing

▶ **EXAM** FOCUS p.207

1 **Look at the speaking task and underline the key words.**

The local government in your area wants to find out what people think of public services. Look at the pictures and discuss how useful the jobs are. Then decide which job is the most important.

2 **Look at the statements made by some students. For each one, mark whether you agree (✓) disagree (✗) or are not sure (?).**

> **1** The government shouldn't waste money on street cleaners; people should learn not to drop litter.

> **2** Everyone should have training in how to deal with a fire, and then we wouldn't need so many firefighters.

> **3** If there are lots of security cameras around, you don't need so many police officers on the street to catch criminals.

> **4** They should make unemployed people do things like street cleaning and gardening.

3 ▶ **2.02** **Listen and copy the intonation patterns in these phrases for agreeing and disagreeing.**

1 Actually, I'm not sure about that.
2 I agree up to a point but…
3 I suppose so.
4 That's just what I was going to say!

4 **Work in pairs. Take turns reading out the statements in Activity 2 and using the phrases in Activity 3 to agree and disagree with them.**

5 **Do the speaking task in Activity 1.**

EXAM TIP

Make sure that you talk about all the pictures before you try to come to some kind of decision, but avoid spending too long on one picture.

6 **Discuss the Part 4 questions.**

1 Do you think people should be paid more for doing a dangerous job?
2 Would you want to have the same job/career for your whole life?
3 Do you think it's possible for anyone to become a police officer?

Listening

1 ▶ **2.03 You will hear people talking in three different situations. For each question, choose the best answer, A, B or C.**

1 You hear a manager talking to an employee. What is the manager doing?

   A requesting some information

   B advising the employee about a problem

   C explaining how to do something

2 You hear someone talking about job interviews on the radio. What does the presenter recommend?

   A doing research about the company

   B asking lots of questions

   C appearing very confident

3 You hear a discussion between two colleagues. What is the woman doing?

   A reminding the man to do something

   B accusing the man of not telling her something

   C apologising for forgetting something

Reporting verbs

▶ **GRAMMAR** REFERENCE p.173

2 **Use the verbs in the box to report the information from Activity 1. More than one verb may be possible.**

accused	advised	asked	denied
explained	offered	recommended	
reminded	suggested	told	warned

1 The manager .... Amy to keep the report brief.

2 The manager .... that she should keep the report brief.

3 The presenter .... finding out as much as you can about your prospective employer.

4 The woman .... Mike of forgetting to give her a message.

5 Mike .... taking any calls from the customer.

6 Mike .... to find out what had gone wrong.

> **LANGUAGE TIP**
>
> *recommend* and *suggest* do not take a direct object:
> He **recommended** *something* **to me.**
> NOT
> ~~He recommended me something~~.

3 **Look at the examples in Activity 2 and match the reporting verbs from the box to the patterns. For some verbs more than one pattern is possible.**

A verb + object + infinitive, e.g. *advise, ask, remind*

B verb + infinitive

C verb + *-ing*

D verb + object + *of* + *-ing*

E verb + *that* + clause

Speaking

4 **Work in groups. Prepare four pieces of advice about what to do at a job/college interview. Exchange advice with another group. Then use the verbs in Activity 2 to report the recommendations you have been given.**

Speaking

1 **You are going to read an article about five people whose work involves them living abroad. Work in pairs and answer the questions.**

1 Why do some people choose to go and work in another country?

2 What do you think the disadvantages of living abroad would be?

Multiple matching (Part 3)

▶ **EXAM** FOCUS p.201

2 **Read questions 1–15 and underline the key words. This will make it easier to locate the information that you're looking for. The first one is done for you.**

> **EXAM TIP**
>
> The information in the text may not come in the same order as the questions.

3 **For questions 2–15, choose the best answer from the people A–E.**

Which person

has always had a <u>passion to see the world</u>?	1	B
wanted more of a challenge in their work?	2	
decided to live abroad because it was less expensive?	3	
had not expected to be starting a new life abroad?	4	
took a while to adapt to their new way of living?	5	
has been in some risky situations at work?	6	
found their ideal job by accident?	7	
discovered unexpected things about the place they went to?	8	
regularly travels long distances to do a specific job?	9	
sacrificed career opportunities in order to live abroad?	10	
appreciates the long holidays which their job makes possible?	11	
got advice before they decided to go and live abroad?	12	
lives in a very primitive environment?	13	
needs to have a flexible attitude to work?	14	
is now glad that they decided to make their relationship a priority?	15	

To the ends of the earth

Five people tell us how they've found succe living and working in exotic locations.

A **Emma** <u>While</u> I enjoyed my job at a busy surgery in Oxford, checking people's blood pressure wasn't really stretching me enough, <u>so</u> I applied for and got a job with the Flying Doctor service in Australia. Practising medicine over an area covering 800 miles means you have to be good at dealing with uncertainty and multi-tasking. We doctors are dropped off by plane at remote houses in the bush, which we use as clinics. Common problems we have to treat are injuries after falls from horses, farm accidents, snake bites, <u>as well as</u> road accidents in the middle of nowhere. I wanted a job which would enable me to experience extraordinary places and people, and this job certainly does that.

B **Heather** I've had the travel bug ever since I was very young. As soon as I left university, where I studied journalism, I got myself an administrative job and saved up enough money to go backpacking to New Zealand. When I got back, I started job-hunting <u>so that</u> I could save money for another big trip, which is when I stumbled across an advert for a job with a publisher of travel guides. When I was offered the job and sent to South Africa <u>to</u> write a blog, I could have burst with excitement. I spend a lot of time in Southeast Asia but I'm still based in the UK and the best part of my job is being able to take time off to go travelling for a couple of months. <u>Although</u> I travel for work, it's not the same as a holiday, when I can switch off and don't have deadlines. <u>Still</u>, I can't think of any job I'd rather be doing.

C **Jonathan** I'm a graphic designer, and when I was made redundant I decided to set up my own business with my wife. The only problem was meeting the same standard of living – apartment, car, meals out. <u>That's why</u> I hit on the idea of moving somewhere in the world where you can enjoy the same lifestyle for far less. <u>In order to</u> help us make the decision, we made contact through Facebook and Twitter with other people who have done the same thing. Moving around the world can be unsettling but there are high points <u>too</u>, such as living in the Caribbean and being able to swim in the warm sea every day.

Annie I was on a business trip to Buenos Aires for a couple of weeks when I met an Italian who became the love of my life. <u>Since</u> I was freelance and he was a TV producer in Argentina it made sense that I would be the one to move. <u>Despite</u> this, the decision was agonising <u>as</u> I was building a career as a newspaper correspondent and all my contacts were in London. There was <u>also</u> the issue of leaving my family, friends and home but I knew if I didn't give it a try I'd regret it forever. Fede took time off to help me settle in, but then I began to realise the enormity of what I'd done. <u>Whereas</u> previously my independence had defined my life, now my world consisted entirely of Fede and myself. <u>Because</u> I didn't speak Spanish very well, I felt frustrated and stupid but four months on I don't regret a thing.

Phil As an engineer, I happily accepted an invitation to build a scientific research centre in Antarctica. Everything is different here, and we have only the basic requirements for human survival. From the moment you arrive you are faced with danger, whether it is landing in a plane on an ice runway or travelling across sea ice. <u>However</u>, seeing giant icebergs for the first time blew my mind. There are lots of surprises <u>as well</u>, such as suffering from sunburn and the twenty-four hours of sunlight a day which makes it difficult to sleep <u>even though</u> you are exhausted. The main challenge is being away from loved ones, although you don't get lonely <u>as</u> you are living very near to other people.

Speaking

4 **Discuss the questions in pairs.**

1 Which of these jobs would you find most interesting? Why?

2 Which do you think is more important: the job you do or the place that you live in?

Vocabulary

linking words and expressions

5 **Look at the linking expressions underlined in the text. Which are used to**

1 give extra information?

2 express reason/result?

3 express a purpose for doing something?

4 contrast information?

6 **Look carefully at how the linking expressions are used in context, including the punctuation. Complete these sentences with one of these linking words or phrases.**

although	as well as	despite	however
in order to	so	that's why	too

1 I applied for the job. .... , I didn't get it, unfortunately.

2 I didn't even get an interview, ... I am more than qualified for the job.

3 I love travelling. .... the work was perfect for me.

4 I think the reason I didn't get the job was my poor Spanish, ... I have enrolled on a beginners' course.

5 .... learning Spanish, I am trying to improve my French.

6 I am watching French films .... improve my vocabulary.

7 .... the high salary I was offered, I decided to turn down the job.

8 I enjoyed my time at the law firm. I made a lot of friends there ....

Listening

1 ▶ **2.04** You'll hear part of a job interview with Lauren. Listen and underline eight mistakes in Lauren's email to her mum.

2 Work in pairs. Correct the incorrect details. Then listen again and check your answers.

Example: She told her she'd spotted the advert on the internet.

Hi Mum,

The interview for the job in Greece went well, I think. First the interviewer asked me how I'd heard about it. I told her I'd spotted the advert in a local newspaper and thought it was something I'd enjoy doing.

Then she said the job would involve looking after young teenagers and asked me whether I'd had any experience of doing this. So I told her that I look after Sandra and Davy now and again and that I was taking them camping the next day. She said I might be unlucky, as she'd heard it was going to snow. Then she told me to enjoy the weekend and said she'd phone soon. She told me not to worry if I didn't hear anything for a few weeks.

Fingers crossed,

Lx

Reported statements

▶ **GRAMMAR** REFERENCE p.173

3 Turn to page 159 and follow the instructions.

4 Complete the table to show how direct speech changes to reported statements. Use the tapescript on page 159 to help you.

Direct speech	Reported statements
past simple	*past perfect*
present perfect	
present simple	
will	
present continuous	
be going to	
would, *might*	

LANGUAGE TIP

You don't need to change the verb if the situation remains the same and it is clear from the context. *She said **she looks after** Sandra and Davy* (and she still does).

Reported questions and imperatives

▶ **GRAMMAR** REFERENCE p.174

5 How did the interviewer say sentences A–D in direct speech?

A She asked me how I'd heard about the job.

B She asked me whether I'd had any experience of this.

C She told me to enjoy my weekend

D She told me not to worry.

6 Look at the things that Lauren's friend Jack asked or said after she started the job. Change them to reported speech, using *tell, ask,* etc. or a reporting verb.

1 'Do you get paid well?'

2 'Let me know if there are any more job vacancies!'

3 'Who are you going to be working with next week?'

4 'What did you do yesterday?'

5 'Don't forget to take some photos.'

6 'We'll email you if we come over to Greece.'

LANGUAGE TIP

- Remember to change pronouns, e.g. *I* → *she; me* → *her.*
- Time expressions may change (*yesterday* → *the day before*)

7 Work in pairs and follow the instructions.

1 Tell your partner four things about yourself. One of them should be false.

2 Join up with another pair. Tell the others what your partner told you.

3 Guess which of the four things they tell you is untrue.

Vocabulary
concrete and abstract nouns

1 Which word in each pair is a concrete noun such as a person and which is an abstract noun?

engineering/engineer   journalist/journalism
music/musician   visitor/visit

2 What suffixes do you often add to a word to make a concrete noun? Complete the table.

	Abstract noun	Concrete noun
1	creation	*creator*
2	advice	
3		employer/ee
4	tourism	
5		applicant
6		representative
7	childhood	
8		politician

3 Divide these words into verbs and adjectives. What is the abstract noun for each?

angry   arrive   behave   confide
difficult   friendly   know   permit
progress   sad   short   strong

4 Change the word in brackets to a noun. Add *a/an* if necessary.

1 The school won't give us .... (*permit*) to take a week off during term time.

2 I'm finally beginning to make .... (*progress*) with my maths and science.

3 She had .... (*difficult*) understanding what I wanted her to do.

4 We're going on .... (*visit*) to Rome next week.

5 I can't carry this any further, I haven't got the .... (*strong*)!

6 Cara and I have .... (*friend*) built on respect and trust.

Word formation (Part 3)

▶ **EXAM** FOCUS p.203

5 Use the word given in capitals at the end of each line to form a word that fits the gap in the same line.

The video game designer

Time is running out on the **(0)** *production* of this video game. A huge clock is ticking loudly on the wall and everyone has their heads down. The game's **(1)**........... team must be feeling the pressure. The licence for the game cost millions of dollars – so there's no room for any **(2)**........... . However, everyone seems calm and there is no obvious panic yet.
When I meet Tim, who has **(3)**........... for the design, he explains why it takes over 100 people to make just one video game. Apparently it's because of the complex **(4)**........... which is involved. He himself is not actually personally involved in doing the diagrams. That job is done by the team of **(5)**........... which he employs to work for him. And the code that makes everything work is done by the many computer **(6)**........... that I can see all around the office. However, what he has to do is to make all the plans and **(7)**...........
One would imagine this is not always totally straightforward!
Despite the time pressures, he claims to find his work **(8)**........... and appears to welcome the **(9)**........... challenges he must have to face on a **(10)**........... basis.

PRODUCE

CREATE

FLEXIBLE

RESPONSIBLE

TECHNICIAN

ART

PROGRAMME

DECIDE

ENJOY

VARY

DAY

6 Would you like to do this job? Why/Why not?

Reading

1 Read the letter of application. What job is Magda applying for?

Dear Sir/Madam.

Following your recent advertisement in *The Traveller*, I would like to apply for the **(1)** *job/ position* of hotel receptionist.

(2) *Right now/At present* I am completing my second year at Poznan University, where I have been studying Spanish. I would now like to spend some time developing my confidence in spoken Spanish.

As well as Polish and Spanish, I also speak fluent English. I **(3)** *got/obtained* the diploma you **(4)** *require/want* three years ago and I have worked in hotels **(5)** *on a number of occasions/ lots of times*. **(6)** *In addition/Also*, **(7)** *I possess/ I've got* the energy and good communication skills which you are looking for.

I would be grateful if you could send me further details of the job, including the salary. I enclose my CV and I **(8)** *look forward/am looking forward* to hearing from you **(9)** *soon/in the near future*.

Yours faithfully.

Magda Koblewska

2 Look at the options in italics in the letter and underline the most appropriate one.

3 In which paragraph is Magda

A giving her qualifications and experience?

B giving a reason for writing?

C saying why she wants the job?

D asking for information

4 Look at the letter again and find fixed phrases for 1–5.

1 to say where you heard about the job

2 to say which job you're interested in

3 to give details of your qualifications

4 to ask for further information

5 to explain what you are sending with the letter

Letter of application (Part 1)

▶ **WRITING** REFERENCE p.188

5 Read the exam task and the advertisement. Underline the important information in the advertisement.

> You have seen a job advertisement on the internet and have decided to apply for the job. Read the advertisement and the notes you have made. Then write a letter of application, using all your notes.

| Home | About us | Activities | Jobs |

Temporary summer employment available with SGP International

Activity instructors: Share your love of sports and the outdoors with our young guests as well as helping to organise and participate in evening entertainments.

say what sports you could do

Minimum age: 18 years

Languages:
English essential; others an advantage

describe your level

Qualifications:
none required as we offer a training course to give you the skills to do your job.

ask about the course

We are looking for applicants who can demonstrate energy, enthusiasm and the ability to relate to young people.

give examples of experience

Please apply in writing to:

Mr Andrew Eames
SGP International
6 Woodland Avenue
Sheffield SK11 8AY

6 Read the exam task again. Make a detailed plan about what will be in each paragraph of your letter. Follow the structure of Magda's letter.

EXAM TIP

If you begin the letter with the name of the person you are writing to, end the letter *Yours sincerely*. If you start with *Dear Sir/ Madam*, end with *Yours faithfully*.

7 Write your letter. When you have finished check your work, using the checklist on page 179 to help you.

1 Choose the correct option to complete these sentences.

1 I'm happy at my place of work, but there aren't many .... opportunities.

A profession   B work   C career

2 Have you managed to work .... how much overtime we've earned this week?

A out   B in   C up

3 I enjoy working there, ... there's a lot of pressure at times.

A although   B despite   C however

4 I have an interview next week .... I'm going to get something smart to wear.

A that's why   B so   C in order to

5 Can I borrow your computer .... I can do my CV?

A so that   B to   C in order

6 There is a problem with staffing at the moment but we'll have to work .... it.

A for   B around   C over

2 Use the word in capitals to form a word that fits the gap in the same line.

1 .... from ten different companies will give talks at the Careers Fair. **REPRESENT**

2 Because of the economic crisis, there is a lot of .... in the area. **EMPLOY**

3 I need to send in an .... for a summer job. **APPLY**

4 Unfortunately, there is a job .... at the moment. **SHORT**

5 When she resigned, there was a lot of .... **SAD**

6 .... usually appreciate being met at the airport. **TOUR**

7 On .... , most holidaymakers are taken to their hotel by coach. **ARRIVE**

8 It's useful to employ people who have some .... of the local area. **KNOW**

3 Complete the second sentence so that it has a similar meaning to the first sentence, using no more than five words, including the word given.

1 'Make sure you lock up when you leave the office tonight.' Jake told his colleagues.
REMINDED
Jake .... lock up when they left the office that night.

2 'Carol, why not take a break, while things are quiet?' the manager said.
SUGGESTED
The manager .... take a break while things were quiet.

3 'It was Anna who lost the contract.' said Jon.
ACCUSED
Jon .... losing the contract.

4 'You mustn't talk to the press about the incident,' the boss said to us.
WARNED
The boss .... talk to anyone from the press about the incident.

5 'I'm really sorry that I didn't meet the deadline,' said Joanna.
APOLOGISED
Joanna .... meeting the deadline.

6 'I'm going to hand in my notice tomorrow.' said Alfie.
THE
Alfie decided to hand in .... day.

7 'If I were you, I would look for another job,' said Max.
RECOMMENDED
Max .... for another job.

8 'I didn't break the photocopier,' said Maria.
DENIED
Maria .... the photocopier.

Lucky break?

9

Speaking

1 Discuss the questions.

1 Who is your role model or hero from the sports world?
2 What qualities do you think a great sprinter must have?

Gapped text (Part 2)

▶ **EXAM** FOCUS p.201

2 Quickly read the article about Usain Bolt and compare it with your ideas in Activity 1.

3 Seven sentences have been removed from the article. Choose from the sentences A–H the one which fits each gap 1–7. There is one extra sentence which you do not need to use.

EXAM TIP

Make sure you read the text for gist before focusing on the missing sentences.

A It took a lot of persuasion because Bolt had been running the distance for less than a year and was surviving on a diet of junk food.

B But before that he has more to achieve on the track.

C This condition should have made it impossible for him to have a career in sport.

D I ask him what's it like to run so fast, to race the wind.

E 'I try not to let them, but they do.'

F Having fun on the track helps him to relax.

G His manager says he runs like a cheetah.

H Winning that race changed his whole life, but for much of the next three years he was injured.

Speaking

4 Discuss these questions.

1 How is Bolt different from most sportspeople?
2 How easy is it for a very successful person to stay grounded?
3 When does a successful person become a legend, and why? Give some examples.

Usain Bolt:
Fast and loose

When Usain Bolt was a young boy growing up in Jamaica, his parents took him to the doctor because he couldn't keep still. He was gifted at cricket, his first love. 'But I just happened to run fast. They said, try track and field, and I continued because it was easy and I was winning. And my dad said I should concentrate on running because it's an individual sport and, if you do good, you do good for yourself.'

Nobody can hold a light to Usain Bolt – he is a one-off. There's the size, for a start: 1.96 metres. (ideal sprinters are thought to be no more than 1.85 metres) Then there's the scoliosis, a curved spine which means one leg is shorter than the other. [1] And the attitude – at warm-up his rivals look as if they will explode with tension, but Bolt smiles, even dances. And, of course, Bolt is said to be the fastest man ever, although he wasn't even giving his all when he broke the 100 and 200 metre records.

Bolt maintains that he isn't quite as cool and laid-back as he appears to be. There are things that bother him. [2] For example, he says he was so uptight before the Junior World Championships final – where he became the youngest gold medallist at the age of fifteen – that he put his shoes on the wrong feet. 'I've never been so nervous in my whole life. I was shaking because everyone was expecting me to get a medal.'

[3] That's when Jamaica turned on him. His own people said he was undisciplined, he partied too much. And yes, he did; but the truth was he was suffering with his spine.

People, he says, are quick to criticise. Even now. 'People say I'm always partying. Well, I do party. I work hard and I'm going to enjoy myself. I'm not going to let people hold me back. That's when the stress comes in and when you get stressed you start to lose it.'

Bolt arrived in athletics at a time when the profession had lost a lot of respect over drug-taking. Here was a man who looked and acted differently. In 2008, though, he had to beg his coach to let him run the 100 metres at the Beijing Olympics. [4] Despite that, not only did he win gold but he broke the 100 metre world record.

His team say that he can break his own record if he tries. 'He's lazy,' says his manager. 'But when he trains, he trains very hard. The image on the track is that he just turns up and runs but it isn't true. He's very competitive.' And the thing is, says Bolt, if he weren't easy-going, he wouldn't run so fast. [5] 'If you're tense, you'll make mistakes.'

He looks a little blank when I ask him what makes him such a good runner. Perhaps his height helps, and those huge strides, he suggests. [6] 'The way his feet move, the way the mechanics are so perfect. And the strength he can generate from his hips and his hamstrings, everything is perfect for running.'

I've never met a sportsman quite like Bolt. While so many are uncommunicative, conventional and self-important, he is opinionated, funny and grounded. I ask him about his ambitions. Eventually, he says, he'd like to make a go of playing football professionally. [7] 'People say I'm a legend but I'm not until I've fulfilled my potential.'

Vocabulary
collocations: success and failure

5 Complete the sentences with one of the verbs. They may be used more than once.

be   fulfil   have   make   overcome   set

1 To be successful, sportspeople need to .... a strong competitive streak.
2 They often have to .... setbacks, so it's important for them to .... motivated and determined.
3 Sportspeople often .... themselves goals or deadlines.
4 A lot of young athletes don't .... their potential.
5 If you want to .... a go of a career in sport, you need to .... a lot of stamina.
6 Winners are usually single-minded and .... a lot of commitment.

6 Use one of the words to complete the phrases.

down   in   for   on   with   up

1 cope .... pressure
2 focus .... achieving their goal
3 aim .... the top
4 take .... new rivals
5 give .... to pressure
6 face .... to problems
7 let your team ....
8 succeed .... your career

7 Work in pairs. Use some of the language from Activities 5 and 6. Compare your attitudes to success and failure.

1 How well do you think you cope with success and failure?
2 Do you have a drive to succeed or are you more laid-back?

Listening

1 Work in pairs. What do you think makes some people more successful than other people?

2 ▶ 2.05 Listen to two students answering a similar question. Which of these factors do they mention?

ambition	dedication	family support
good health	money	personality	talent

Compensation strategies

3 Match strategies A–C to examples 1–3. Then listen again and tick the language the students use.

A correcting yourself/explaining something in other words
B giving yourself time to think
C checking you understand

1 Do you mean…?
   I'm sorry, did you say…?
   So, what you're saying is…?

2 OK, let me see
   Well, it's difficult to say, of course, but…
   As far as I know, …
   Right, …

3 I mean…
   What I meant was…
   What I'm trying to say is…
   … or rather, …

4 ▶ 2.06 Listen to someone saying the expressions in Activity 3. Then practise saying them in pairs.

Discussion (Part 4)

▶ **EXAM** FOCUS p.207

5 Work in pairs. Take turns to ask and answer the questions. Use some of the expressions from Activity 3.

1 What sports do you most enjoy playing or watching?
2 Do you think anyone can become good at sport if they practise?
3 How important is sport for good health?
4 What are the advantages and disadvantages of team sports over individual sports?
5 Would you say you were a competitive person?

EXAM TIP

Try to keep talking. If you have no ideas, you could ask your partner what they think.

Conditional forms

▶ **GRAMMAR** REFERENCE p.166

1 **Look at the sentences. In which one is the situation: a) unlikely/imaginary? b) generally true? c) possible/likely?**

zero conditional:	When you get stressed, you start to lose it.
first conditional:	If you're tense, you'll make mistakes.
second conditional:	If he weren't so easy-going, he wouldn't run so fast.

2 **Underline the verb forms in the sentences in Activity 1. Then answer questions 1–3 about the form of conditional sentences.**

1 In which type of conditional can *when* be used instead of *if*?

2 In first conditional, which modals and verb forms can be used instead of *will*?

3 In second conditional, which other modals can be used instead of *would*?

LANGUAGE TIP

Continuous forms can be used instead of simple forms.

If you're driving, will you give me a lift?

If you were thinking of taking up a new sport, which one would you choose?

---

3 **Decide how likely these sentences are, and use the words in brackets to make questions. Then work in pairs and ask each other the questions.**

1 If (*you/become*) a famous film star, who (*you/want*) to act with?

2 If (*you/win*) a lot of money, what (*you/spend*) it on?

3 If (*you/learn*) another language, which one (*you/choose*)?

4 If (*you/have*) the money to go to any place in the world, where (*you/go*)?

5 If (*you/have*) the chance to do anything this evening, what (*you/do*)?

6 If (*the weather/be*) good this weekend, what (*you/do*)?

7 if (*you/get married*) next year, what kind of ceremony (*you/have*)?

8 If (*someone/follow*) you down the street, what (*you/do*)?

4 **Complete the sentences so they are true for you.**

1 If I didn't live in .... , I…

2 If I could change one thing in the world…

3 If I found some money in the street…

4 If I could meet three people, …

Speaking

5 **If you could live twenty-four hours in the life of anyone in history, who would you choose and why?**

Example:

If I could, I'd be Neil Armstrong in 1969. I'd love to be able to walk on the moon.

Multiple choice (Part 4)

▶ **EXAM** FOCUS p.205

1 **Discuss the questions.**

1 Do you think that some people are born lucky?

2 Talk about a time in your own life when you were lucky/unlucky?

2 ▶ 2.07 **You're going to listen to a radio programme about luck in sport. Look at question 1 in Activity 3 and think of paraphrases for the options. Then listen to the text for question 1. What paraphrases did you hear?**

3 ▶ 2.08 **Listen to the whole text and, for questions 1–7, choose the best answer, A, B or C.**

1 The presenter says that top sportspeople usually believe their success is due to
   A good fortune.
   B hard work.
   C natural skill.

2 What do the examples of recent sporting achievements prove?
   A that people in general have become stronger and fitter
   B that standards are getting higher
   C that technology is responsible for improved performance

3 What does the presenter say about very talented young children?
   A It's easy to tell which will be the top performers.
   B They will succeed without special training.
   C As they get older their development may be slower.

4 Matthew believes he had a greater chance of success because of
   A his parents' love of table tennis.
   B his competitive brother.
   C his own ambition.

5 What was the advantage of the Omega club when Matthew joined?
   A It was open all the time.
   B It had a lot of good players.
   C It had great facilities.

6 Matthew thinks the success of the Omega Club members was
   A hard to explain.
   B easy to predict.
   C a happy accident.

7 The presenter says that a ten-year investigation has shown that lucky people
   A believe they will succeed.
   B look for good opportunities.
   C depend less on talent.

4 **Check your answers. What paraphrases did you notice?**

EXAM TIP

Check your answers carefully the second time you listen.

5 **Discuss whether it's too easy to blame bad luck when things go wrong.**

Vocabulary

1 **Use the word given to form a word that fits the gap in the following sentences.**

COMPETE

1 It is argued that encouraging children to be .... puts them under too much pressure.

2 There was disagreement between the .... teams about who should be the referee.

PERFECTION

3 Many athletes are .... and insist on getting it right every single time.

4 There are always slight .... in every gymnast's performance.

ATHLETICS

5 He's one of the best .... of his generation.

6 It requires more .... to be a ballet dancer than a footballer.

2 **How are the words you completed in Activity 1 pronounced? Mark the main stress.**

Word formation (Part 3)

▶ **EXAM** FOCUS p.203

3 **Read the text and decide which is the best summary. Don't worry about the gaps yet.**

A superstitious athletes are the most successful

B reasons why athletes are superstitious

C the most common superstitions among athletes

EXAM TIP

Look carefully at the text around the gaps to see what part of speech the word should be.

4 **Use the word given in capitals at the end of some of the lines to form a word that fits in the gap in the same line. There is an example at the beginning (0).**

5 **Underline three examples of negative prefixes in the completed text.**

6 **Find out if your partner has any lucky charms or rituals to bring good luck/keep them safe.**

Sport

Superstitious athletes

Superstitions usually come about because athletes **(0)** _mistakenly_ associate some unrelated thing or behaviour with good **(1)** .... If, for example, they happen to have a red wristband on the day they score three goals, they might **(2)** .... to continue wearing the same one every match. It becomes a lucky charm, even if it doesn't always bring good luck.   **MISTAKE** / **PERFORM** / **DECISION**

Because superstitions help athletes to feel less stressed, it's not **(3)** .... to argue that they do help to increase their **(4)** .... Often the difference between winning and losing is a question of **(5)** .... However, these little superstitions could also be potentially **(6)** .... to their mental health. At an extreme level they could be **(7)** .... as obsessive compulsive disorders where somebody feels that if they do the same thing over and over again, things will go **(8)** ....   **POSSIBILITY** / **ATHLETIC** / **CONFIDENT** / **DANGER** / **DESCRIPTION** / **PERFECTION**

Often the superstition presents itself in the form of a ritual. For example, many athletes insist on eating exactly the same food or listening to a particular song before they compete. During the event itself, some **(9)** .... indulge in irrational **(10)** .... , like kissing the ground after winning a race or, very oddly, talking to the ball or even the goalposts. ■   **COMPETE** / **BEHAVE**

Speaking

1 **Complete the superstitions with a word from the box. Are they lucky or unlucky?**

knife	ladder	umbrella	cat	wood
mirror				

According to superstition it's lucky/unlucky

1 to walk under a ....

2 to see a black .... in front of you.

3 to break a ....

4 to touch ....

5 to give someone a ....

6 to open your .... in the house.

2 **Discuss the questions with a partner.**

1 Do you have the same superstitions in your country? Do you know any others?

2 What do you think superstitions are based on?

3 How lucky or unlucky are your favourite teams/sports heroes? Why?

Collocations with *luck*

3 **Choose the correct word.**

1 They had an amazing *piece/slice* of luck. The ref sent off the other team's best player.

2 With a *bit/little* of luck our team should win the Cup.

3 She's *had/got* nothing but bad luck since she was injured last year.

4 They *wished/told* me the best of luck before the match.

5 I couldn't *accept/believe* my luck. I'd been picked to play on the first team.

6 They'd been winning every match, but their luck *ran/went* out last week.

4 **Which of the verbs in the box do nouns 1–5 go with?**

achieve	beat	give up	lose	miss
reach	waste	win		

1 an opportunity

2 an ambition

3 a competition

4 an opponent

5 a target

5 **Complete the sentences with the correct form of one of the verbs from Activity 4. There may be more than one possible answer.**

1 Great players never .... a chance to score a goal.

2 We were disappointed that we were knocked out before we .... the second round.

3 Well done everyone. You deserved to .... that match.

4 It's a pity she played so badly. She .... the opportunity to show everyone just how talented she is.

5 Only a lucky few ever .... their dream of becoming an Olympic medallist.

6 I don't mind .... to an opponent if I know he played better than me.

7 It was frustrating being .... so easily. I thought we had a good chance of winning.

8 She's the most competitive person I've ever met. She never .... even when she's losing badly.

Speaking

6 **Find out what ambitions your partner has achieved/given up.**

Third conditional

▶ **GRAMMAR** REFERENCE p.166

1 Read the text at the bottom of the page and tick the sentence, A or B, which best summarises Tom's feelings.

A If Tom hadn't had his monkey with him at the Olympic Games, he would have felt something was missing.

B If Tom had thought his monkey wasn't lucky, he wouldn't have taken him to the Olympic Games.

2 Which of these statements do you agree with?

1 If Tom Daley hadn't had a lucky monkey, he might not have won so many medals.

2 If Matthew Syed had lived in a different street, he wouldn't have become a table tennis champion.

3 Usain Bolt couldn't have been the world's fastest man if he hadn't grown up in Jamaica.

4 Serena Williams might have won fewer championships if her sister hadn't also been a tennis champion.

3 Look at the rules below and choose the correct words.

1 The third conditional is used to speculate about things in the *past/present*.

2 The 'if' clause *always comes first/can come first or second*.

3 *If* is always followed by the *past perfect/would have*.

4 *Might, could/may* and *will* can be used instead of *would*.

4 Complete these sentences using the third conditional.

1 Michael Johnson didn't win a fifth gold Olympic medal because he was injured.
Michael Johnson could have won ....

2 Ellie didn't train properly for the marathon so she wasn't able to finish the race.
If Ellie had ....

3 Lola and Marc met while they were doing a scuba diving course in Thailand.
Lola and Marc wouldn't ....

4 I went out jogging and fell over and broke my ankle on the ice.
If I hadn't ....

5 Complete the sentences so that they are true about you.

1 If I hadn't met ....

2 If I hadn't decided to ....

3 I'd have been very disappointed if
....

4 Things might have turned out differently if I
....

6 Compare your answers in pairs. Did you learn anything new about your partner?

Tom's monkey

Olympic diver Tom Daley, who won a gold medal at the European Championships at the age of 13, has always had a lucky orange monkey. The monkey goes with him to all his events and sits on the poolside, and was even at the Olympic Games. Tom has had a few setbacks during his career so he admits the monkey doesn't always bring good luck, but Tom would feel something was missing if his monkey wasn't there.

Essay (Part 2)
organising paragraphs and arguments

▶ **WRITING** REFERENCE p.189

1 Read the writing task. Then look at the the student's introduction and say whether sentences A and B are true or false.

> You have been discussing in class how to be a successful person. Now your teacher has asked you to write an essay, giving your opinion on the following statement.
>
> *Without failure there can be no success.*

> Without failure there can be no success.
> It's often said that it's impossible to succeed the first time you do something, and that the most successful people in life have many failures behind them.

A The introduction repeats the statement in the title but in different words.

B The writer states his/her opinion in the introduction.

2 Look at the student's second paragraph. Answer the questions and put sentences A, B and C in the correct order.

> ᴬIn the world of sport, failure is part of success because not everyone wins all the time. ᴮThere are examples in many areas which show that failure is important. ᶜFor the top athletes, losing a race or not scoring a goal can make them more determined to succeed the next time.

1 Which sentence introduces the main point and should come first?

2 Which sentence gives the main point and should come second?

3 Which sentence supports the main point and should come last?

3 Now look at the third paragraph and conclusion. Which phrase(s)

1 highlights a well-known fact or opinion?

2 supports a point ?

3 gives a possible point of view?

4 introduces a contrasting point?

5 is used to summarise ideas?

> On the other hand, it's clear that there are many people who achieve almost instant success at a very young age. This is true of many athletes and musicians. However, because so many of these people find it very difficult to deal with huge success and the money and fame that come with at such a young age, you could say that instant success without failure first is a bad thing.
>
> To sum up, it is possible to have success without failure but, in my opinion, it is better to fail first.

EXAM TIP

It's important to give your opinion in the conclusion.

4 Read the exam task and write your own essay, using Activities 1–3 to help you.

> You have been discussing in class how to be a successful person. Now your teacher has asked you to write an essay, giving your opinion on the following statement.
>
> *Sporting heroes should try to be good role models.*
>
> You should write between **120** and **180** words.

5 Check your work for spelling, grammar and punctuation mistakes.

1 Choose the correct word to fit in each space, A, B, C or D.

1 To be successful you often need to overcome ....

   A goals   **B** setbacks

   C motivation   **D** deadlines

2 It's important to try and .... your potential.

   A succeed   **B** aim

   C fulfil   **D** commit

3 In order to achieve things you need to .... yourself goals.

   A set   **B** find

   C make   **D** expect

4 To perform well in sports you need to be able to cope .... pressure.

   A in   **B** on

   C for   **D** with

5 You should always try to focus .... achieving your goals.

   A with   **B** to

   C on   **D** in

6 Listen to good advice if you want to succeed .... life.

   A in   **B** on

   C for   **D** with

2 Correct the mistakes with the verb forms.

1 If I met Usain Bolt, I take a photograph of him.

2 We can get tickets for the match if we would book them today.

3 If you will practise harder, you could be a good player.

4 If you helped me more, I didn't have so many problems.

5 He can become world champion if he'd had a different coach.

6 He might have decided to join another team if the club wouldn't have offered him so much money.

7 She didn't become a world champion if she hadn't taken her trainer's advice.

8 They would have travelled to South Africa to see the final if they could afford it.

3 Use the word given in capitals at the end of some lines to form a word that fits in the space in the same line. There is an example at the beginning (0).

Imagine your success

Mental imagery involves the **(0)** _athletes_ imagining themselves in a specific environment or **(1)**............ a specific activity. The images have to involve the athlete doing these activities very **(2)**............ .

       ATHLETIC

       PERFORM

       SUCCESS

You should imagine that you find the activity **(3)**............ and are satisfied with your skills. You should attempt to enter fully into the image with all your senses. Sight, hearing, taste, touch, smell are all important in helping you to **(4)**............ doing something to the best of your **(5)**............ .

       ENJOY

       IMAGINATION

       ABLE

To make the most of this technique, you have to **(6)**............ it every day, on your way to training, during training, after training, and in the evenings before sleeping. If you want to **(7)**............ and use mental imagery to your fullest advantage, you can start by doing two things. In every training session, before you try out any skill or combination of skills, first do it in your mind as precisely as possible. See, feel, and experience yourself moving through the **(8)**............ in your mind, as you would like them to happen in real life. In **(9)**............ , before the event starts, mentally recall your preparation, goals and **(10)**............ , or any feelings that you want to carry into the event.

       PRACTICAL

       PERFECTLY

       ACT

       COMPETE

       ACHIEVE

Virtual friends

10

Speaking

1 Discuss the questions in pairs.

1 How easy is it to be a good friend?
2 Why do people sometimes lose touch with friends?

2 Do the quiz. Then add up your score.

LIFESTYLE

What kind of friend are you?

1 How many close friends would you say you have?
   A 1–3   **B** 4–8   **C** more than 8

2 Which of these things is the most damaging to friendship?
   A favouritism   **B** selfishness   **C** dishonesty

3 Do you think the best test of a close friend is
   A always being there to have fun with?
   B always being ready to do a favour?
   C always being able to pick up where you left off last time?

4 Where would you place friendship in relation to career and family?
   A more important than career and family
   B more important than career, less important than family
   C important, but less important than either career and family

5 Do you have someone you could call a best friend?
   A I used to
   B definitely
   C no – I have lots of friends

6 When you haven't seen a close friend for a long time, do you
   A not worry about it?
   B contact them via social networking?
   C feel guilty?

7 Which do you most value in a friendship?
   A loyalty   **B** generosity   **C** trust

8 The most important quality you need to be a good friend is to be
   A self-aware.
   B content with your own life.
   C lively and outgoing.

3 Look at the results on page 158. Discuss in groups whether the results describe you accurately or not.

Vocabulary

4 Are these adjectives positive or negative? Work in pairs and use at least four to describe people you know. Give examples of their behaviour.

self-aware	self-centred	self-confident	self-conscious	self-important
selfless	self-satisfied	self-sufficient		

5 Put the following features of friendship in order of importance.

- [ ] having a lot in common
- [ ] having a laugh together
- [ ] seeing eye to eye about things
- [ ] having the same tastes in music and films, etc.
- [ ] having shared experiences/memories
- [ ] being there for each other

6 Work in groups. Compare your lists and find someone who agrees with your order. What other features are important?

Multiple matching (Part 3)

▶ **EXAM** FOCUS p.205

7 You will hear five different people talking about their closest friend. Look at options A–F and think of paraphrases for each of the options.

8 ▶ 2.09 Listen and choose from the list (A–F) what each speaker says about their relationship with their closest friend. Use the letters only once. There is one extra letter which you do not need to use.

EXAM TIP

Check that the option you have chosen summarises each speaker's main idea or opinion.

A We always try to help each other.
B We disagree about a lot of things.
C We have very different personalities.
D We have only known each other for a short time.
E We enjoy doing the same things.
F We don't see each other often enough.

Speaker 1 [ ]
Speaker 2 [ ]
Speaker 3 [ ]
Speaker 4 [ ]
Speaker 5 [ ]

9 Listen again and note down the matching paraphrases for options A–F. Did you predict any of the paraphrases correctly?

10 Describe your closest friend(s). Say

1 how you met.
2 what you do together.
3 why you like him/her.
4 what kind of person she/he is.

Conditionals

alternatives to *if*

1 Look at the examples from the listening text and answer the questions.

> Unless we're very organised, it's hard to arrange to go out.

1 Do they need to be organised in order to see each other?

> Even if we haven't seen each other for a while, we can catch up really easily.

2 Does it matter if they don't see each other often?

> As long as we plan ahead, it's fine.

3 Is it essential for them to plan ahead?

> We don't go to football matches together. Otherwise, we'd end up arguing.

4 Would they argue if they went to a football match together?

2 Choose the correct word or phrase.

1 *Unless/As long as* you make an effort, it's too easy to lose touch with old friends.

2 I text my boyfriend every day. *Otherwise/Provided that* he gets upset.

3 I want to invite all my friends to the party, *even if/whether* they can't all come.

4 *Provided that/Unless* I know some people who are going, I don't mind going to parties on my own.

5 I don't know *whether/if* or not to talk to him about the problem.

3 Which word or phrase from Activity 2

1 means *if not*?

2 is used instead of *if* before infinitives?

3 means *despite the fact that something may/may not happen*?

4 is quite formal?

5 means *in a different situation*?

6 means the same as *as long as*?

▶ **GRAMMAR** REFERENCE p.166

Use of English

key word transformations (Part 4)

▶ **EXAM** FOCUS p.203

EXAM TIP

A range of grammatical structures and vocabulary may be tested. There will usually be two things you have to change in your answer.

4 For questions 1–6, complete the second sentence so that it has a similar meaning to the first sentence, using the word given. Do not change the word given. You must use between two and five words, including the word given.

1 I'll phone you tonight if it isn't too late when I get home.
   UNLESS
   I'll phone you tonight .... too late.

2 He will do anything for you, whether he likes you or not.
   EVEN
   He will do anything for you .... like you.

3 Unless it's raining, I'll wait for you outside the cinema.
   LONG
   As .... raining, I'll wait for you outside the cinema.

4 We couldn't go to the party because of the snow.
   HAVE
   If it hadn't been snowing, we .... to the party.

5 We should finish by four o'clock but it means we can't take a break for lunch.
   PROVIDED
   We should finish by four o'clock .... take a break for lunch.

6 Depending on the traffic, I might be a bit late.
   WHETHER
   I might be a bit late .... any traffic.

Vocabulary

easily confused adjectives

1 Decide which adjective(s) can be used in the examples. More than one may be possible.

actual	present	current

1 We have no more information at the .... time.

2 I know she's in her early twenties but I don't know her .... age.

3 He's very interested in .... affairs.

typical	common	usual

4 He's not as lively as ....

5 On a .... Saturday night we would stay up late and watch a movie.

6 It's very .... to meet your future husband or wife at work.

particular	individual	unique

7 She doesn't get much .... attention from the teacher on the art course she's doing.

8 We decided to drive to the coast for no .... reason.

9 It's a .... opportunity to make new friends.

Multiple-choice cloze (Part 1)

▶ **EXAM** FOCUS p.202

2 For questions 1–12, decide which answer (A, B, C or D) best fits each gap. There is an example at the beginning (0).

EXAM TIP

Before filling in any of the gaps, always read the title and text quickly to get an idea of what it is about.

3 Work in pairs. Do you agree with what Andy says about making friends?

Speaking

4 Discuss which activities it's best to do with friends and which it's best to do alone, and why. Use the ideas in the box to help you.

going to the gym	playing computer games
shopping	watching TV

Need a friend?

I meet my friend Andy in a café. **(0)** _B Over_ a coffee we chat about music, **(1)** .... affairs and the ups and downs of our working lives. We don't **(2)** .... a lot of time talking about our feelings or our relationship, or the past. It's just not that kind of friendship. I **(3)** .... it that way, and I know Andy doesn't mind because I'm paying him to be my friend for a few hours.

Not so long ago, a friend was one **(4)** .... that money couldn't buy. Friendships were **(5)** .... But no more. You can hire someone to show you around town, or hang out at the gym, or **(6)** .... you company while you shop.

My friend Andy is an actor. He has never been paid to be someone's friend before, but he understands why someone might **(7)** .... buying companionship. When he first came to London from Scotland a year and a half ago, he **(8)** .... socialising difficult. 'It actually took a long time to make some kind of contact **(9)** .... people other than workmates,' he says.

Andy thinks it could be the desire **(10)** .... undemanding companionship, rather than loneliness, that is driving the growth in friend-hire. 'The **(11)** .... person doesn't want to have loads of **(12)** .... friends because it makes life too complicated.'

101 SUPPLEMENT

	A	B	C	D
0	Beside	Over	Across	Through
1	common	usual	current	actual
2	have	take	lose	spend
3	choose	wish	select	prefer
4	fact	matter	thing	point
5	special	unique	individual	particular
6	stay	keep	life	face
7	decide	think	consider	encourage
8	experienced	realised	discovered	found
9	with	in	to	off
10	from	for	of	on
11	usual	typical	common	average
12	present	right	real	certain

Speaking

1 **Discuss the questions in groups.**

1 Where did you first meet most of your friends?

2 What proportion of your friends are
   A close friends
   B acquaintances
   C colleagues
   D people you only communicate with online?

3 How important is social networking to you as a way of making friends?

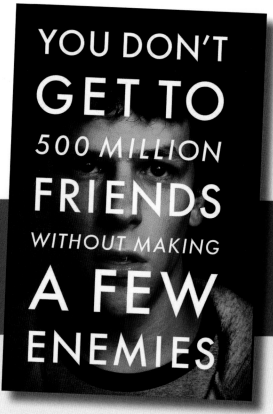

YOU DON'T GET TO 500 MILLION FRIENDS WITHOUT MAKING A FEW ENEMIES

VIRTUAL PEOPLE REAL FRIENDS

The benefits of forming friendships with those we meet online are obvious, so why do people still make fun of the idea?

ANOTHER WEEK, another survey claiming to reveal great truths about ourselves. This one says that (shock horror!) people are increasingly turning 'online friends' into people they'd think worthy of calling real-life friends. Well, that's stating the obvious, I would have thought! If there's a more perfect place for making friends, I have yet to find it. However, when surveys like this are reported in the media, it's always with a slight air of 'It's a crazy, crazy world!' And whenever the subject crops up in conversation, it's clear that people look down on friends like these. In fact some members of my family still refer to my partner of six years as my 'Internet Boyfriend.'

It's the shocked reaction that surprises me, as if people on the internet were not 'real' at all. Certainly, people play a character online quite often – they may be a more confident or more argumentative version of their real selves – but what's the alternative? Is meeting people at work so much better than making friends in a virtual world? Perhaps, but for some a professional distance between their 'work' selves and their 'social' selves is necessary, especially if they tend to let their guard down and might say or do something they will later regret. And are people really much more themselves at a party than online?

Those people disapproving of online friendships argue that the concept of 'friendship' is used loosely in a world driven by technology, in which you might have a thousand online friends. They make a distinction between 'social connections' – acquaintances who are only a click away – and meaningful human interaction, which they say requires time and effort. They note that for many Facebook 'friends', conversation is a way of exchanging information quickly and efficiently rather than being a social activity. With its short sharp updates on what you're thinking 'right now', Facebook has been criticised for encouraging rushed and therefore shallow friendships.

This may all have an element of truth. However, I've found that far from being the home of oddballs and potential serial killers, the internet is full of like-minded people. For the first time in history, we're lucky enough to choose friends not by location or luck, but by those who have similar interests and senses of humour, or passionate feelings about the same things. The friends I've made online might be spread wide geographically, but I'm closer to them than anyone I went to school with, by a million miles. They are the best friends I have.

And for people like me who might be a little shy – and there are plenty of us about – moving conversations from the net to a coffee shop is a much more natural process than people might expect. After having already made friends online, you can get rid of the social awkwardness that comes with trying to make a friend out of someone you don't know at all. You can enjoy their company when you eventually meet, knowing that you have enough in common to sustain the friendship. The benefit is clear – you cut out all the boring small talk. What could be better?

Obviously, there will always be concerns about the dangers of online friendship. There are always stories buzzing around such as 'man runs off with the woman he met on Second Life' or people who meet their 'soulmate' online and are never seen again. But people are people are people, whether online or not. As for 'real' friendship dying out, surely social networking is simply redefining our notion of what this is in the twenty-first century? The figures – half a billion Facebook users worldwide – speak for themselves. And technology has allowed countless numbers of these people to keep in close contact with their loved ones, however far away they are. Without it, many disabled or housebound people might go without social contact at all. Call me naive, call me a social misfit, I don't care. Virtual people make the best real friends. ■

line 11

line 22

Multiple choice (Part 1)

▶ **EXAM** FOCUS p.200

2 **Read the article about making friends online. For questions 1–8, choose the answer (A, B, C or D) which you think fits best according to the text.**

1 The writer thinks the findings of the survey described in the first paragraph are

   A amusing.　　　C predictable.

   B ridiculous.　　D impressive.

2 What does *the subject* refer to in line 11?

   A surveys　　　C real friends

   B the media　　D online friends

3 What does the writer say about 'real' and 'virtual' friendships in the second paragraph?

   A There is more chance of making friends online than at a party.

   B The first impression is rarely accurate in either kind of friendship.

   C There is less pressure to impress 'virtual' friends than 'real' friends.

   D People should avoid spending free time with their work colleagues.

4 What does the phrase *let their guard down* mean in line 22?

   A like being on their own

   B show dislike towards their colleagues

   C prefer to spend time away from their work colleagues

   D speak or act without worrying about the consequences

5 According to the third paragraph, online friendships are often criticised because

   A their purpose is functional rather than social.

   B the people have no shared history to hold them together.

   C the more friends people have, the less each one is valued.

   D the friendship can't be genuine until people meet face to face.

6 According to the fourth paragraph, what are the advantages of online friendships?

   A It's better to have friends that don't live nearby.

   B It's likely that these relationships will last a long time.

   C It's valuable for those who don't have any old schoolfriends.

   D It's possible to find people with whom you have a lot in common.

7 How does the writer feel about meeting up with her online friends?

   A It's a waste of time.

   B It can be difficult to arrange.

   C It's easier than meeting complete strangers.

   D It can often lead to even stronger friendships.

8 What is the writer's reaction to fears and warnings about online friendships?

   A She accepts there will always be dangers however you make friends.

   B She is nervous about the risks but thinks the benefits make it worthwhile.

   C She believes that online relationships are safer than face to face friendships.

   D She recommends online friendships only for people who can look after themselves.

> **EXAM TIP**
>
> The words or phrases in the text will be paraphrases or summaries of the option, NOT the exact words.

Speaking

3 **Work in pairs. Do you agree with the writer's opinions of online friendships? Why/Why not?**

Vocabulary

compound adjectives: personality

4 **Use words from the box to make compound adjectives which describe people's characters.**

kind	level	like	old	quick	strong

1 We enjoy the same kind of things; we're very ....-minded.

2 My brother hardly ever argues but my sister's always been ....-tempered.

3 As a child, he always got what he wanted; he was very ....-willed.

4 I have my head in the clouds, whereas my husband is very ....-headed.

5 Although he is so young, he has some ....-fashioned ideas.

6 I'm sure Jessica will help you. She's a ....-hearted person.

5 **Work in pairs. Think of a friend who has one of these characteristics and describe their behaviour. Can you guess which characteristic your partner is describing?**

Participles (-*ing* and -*ed*)

participle clauses

▶ **GRAMMAR** REFERENCE p.171

1 **Look at extracts A–C and underline a present participle or past participle in each sentence. Which participles have an active meaning? Which have a passive meaning?**

A Another week, another survey claiming to reveal great truths…

B Those people disapproving of online friendships…

C …in a world driven by technology…

2 **Look at the extracts rewritten with relative pronouns. Which words are missed out with participles? Which words change?**

A Another week, another survey which claims to reveal…

B Those people who disapprove of online friendships…

C …in a world which is driven by technology…

3 **Replace the words in italics to make participle clauses.**

Example:

The woman <u>who lives</u> next door is my best friend.
The woman <u>living</u> next door…

1 She is a kind-hearted woman, *who bursts* with energy.

2 Her sense of style, *which was developed* during her stay in France, is famous.

3 She recently twisted her ankle *while we were playing* tennis.

4 She has blonde hair, *which is cut* very short.

5 She gave me a fantastic picture, *which was painted* by her brother.

6 Everyone *who speaks* to her is impressed by her charm.

7 She has a job *in which she designs* clothes.

other uses of participles

4 **Match extracts 1–4 from the text with other uses of participles A–D.**

1 It's easy to criticise Facebook for *encouraging* rushed and therefore shallow friendships.

2 …which involves *sharing* your authentic self.

3 It's the *shocked* reaction that surprises me.

4 After *having* already *made* friends online.

A after certain verbs

B after conjunctions

C after prepositions

D as an adjective

5 **Read the text quickly. Why are Ewan and Charlie such good friends?**

6 **Complete the text using a present or past participle form of one of the verbs in the box.**

amaze	become	content	go
hate	have	say	talk

My best friend

Charley Boorman, actor, talks about his famous friend Ewan McGregor

I first met Ewan while we were filming *The Serpent's Kiss*. I remember (**1**) .... up to him and introducing myself, by (**2**) .... 'Hi, I'm Charley. I hear you're into motorbikes.' After that we didn't stop (**3**) .... for the rest of the evening. Well, in fact, we haven't stopped for the last ten years!

After both (**4**) .... fathers for the first time, we had even more in common. When we decided to ride our motorbikes round the world, people said it would go one of two ways. Luckily for us, it went the good way and we had an (**5**) .... experience. People said we might end up (**6**) .... each other but we were able to help each other especially because we missed (**7**) .... our children around so much. We are both similar because we are happy and (**8**) .... with our lives and our families, and that has created a deep bond between us.

7 **Talk about the friend or friends you have got a deep bond with. What creates bonds between friends of different ages?**

Listening

1 ▶ **2.10 Listen to two students doing the speaking task below. Which age group did they choose?**

Talk about how important friends are at different ages. Then decide which of these age groups needs friends the most.

2 Listen again and complete the extracts.

1 OK, ... we begin?
2 We .... start .... looking at…
3 .... you think?
4 .... …oh, sorry!
5 No, that's OK. ....
6 I was .... to say…
7 Would you .... that?
8 Anyway, I think we .... up our .... which one to choose.

3 Which of the conversational strategies (A–D) do sentences 1–8 fit into?

A starting a discussion
B interrupting someone when you want a turn
C encouraging the other person to say something
D bringing the discussion to an end

Grammar

emphasis with *what*

▶ **GRAMMAR** REFERENCE p.168

4 Write the sentences in another way, without using *what*. Start with the words in italics.

1 What's really important to young kids is their *friends*.
2 What *you need* to have at that age is friends to go out with.

5 How could you say sentences 1–4, using *what* for emphasis?

1 I used to love going to theme parks.
2 It must be difficult staying at home all day with a baby.
3 It's interesting that men often take up sport as a way of making friends.
4 People need friends for every stage of their life.

Collaborative task (Part 3)

turn-taking

▶ **EXAM** FOCUS p.207

6 Work in pairs and do the exam task in Activity 1.

EXAM TIP

Take turns to speak and don't dominate. If you feel your partner is talking too much, interrupt politely by saying *Can I say something here?*

Reading

1 **Read Carlo's email. What is the main focus of each paragraph?**

2 **Work in pairs. Underline examples of language and punctuation typical of informal email-writing.**

Hi,

Great to hear you're in the area – hope the meetings go OK.

If you're around tomorrow, a friend and I are going to see that new Cohen Brothers film. It's on at the Odeon at 7p.m. If you fancy it, we'll be in Pizza Palace first. Meeting at six should give us loads of time.

When you come out of the tube station, turn right and go straight along King Street. Cross the road when you get to the supermarket – you'll see Pizza Palace on your left. The cinema's just round the corner.

If I'm not there, keep an eye out for Luc! I know you haven't met him. He's tall, well-built, with fairly long dark curly hair. He always wears jeans and a hoodie – usually looks as if he's just got out of bed!

Can't wait to catch up!

Carlo

3 **Choose the correct option in the sentences below. Both may be possible.**

1 I walked *along/down* the street *to/at* the cinema.

2 When I was *in/at* the restaurant, I sat *at/on* a table in the corner.

3 I saw Tim *in/at* Oxford Street *at/on* six o'clock.

4 Is there anything good *on/in* this evening *at/to* the cinema?

5 I'll see you *at/on* the bus stop, which is *at/in* the end of the road.

6 Take the first turning *at/on* the right *by/at* the garage.

Informal email (Part 1)

▶ **WRITING** REFERENCE p.185

4 **Read the email from your sister and the notes you have made, then write a reply. Remember to**

1 divide it into paragraphs, each with a topic.

2 refer to her email.

3 include all the necessary information.

EXAM TIP

Check you are using an appropriate style of writing for your target reader.

1 of 1

Hi,

Great to hear you've settled down well at university. Is your flat as good as you'd hoped? — *Yes! give information*

Life here is just as usual. I'm taking Mum and Dad out for a meal next week for their wedding anniversary, so could you remind me how to get to that Italian restaurant we went to in the summer? I can get as far as the market square but then I don't know what to do next! — *give directions*

I got in contact with Sam online the other day – the Sam who we were friendly with at primary school! We've arranged to meet for coffee in town – she's visiting a cousin near here. But now I can't remember what she looks like and it'll be embarrassing if I don't recognise her. Can you remind me? — *give description*

Anyway, really looking forward to seeing you at the end of term. It's very quiet here without you! — *invite her to come and stay*

Love,

Big Sis XXXX

5 **Use the checklist on page 179 to check your work.**

1 Choose the correct word/phrase to complete the sentences.

1 *As long as/Even if* he doesn't turn up, we can still go to the cinema.

2 *Provided that/Unless* the train's on time, I'll meet you at six outside the restaurant.

3 I still think he should apologise *whether/if* it's his fault or not.

4 Let's agree to disagree, *otherwise/even if* we'll have a big argument.

5 *As long as/Unless* it doesn't rain, I'll invite everyone for a barbecue in the evening.

6 We would never have met *if/whether* you hadn't got lost on your first day at university.

2 Choose the best answer A, B, C or D.

1 I don't like people who are .... They're only interested in themselves.
   A self-aware B self-centred
   C selfless D self-confident

2 We don't .... a lot in common.
   A have B get C see D make

3 She's late again. That's .... of her.
   A usual B common C particular D typical

4 At the .... time there are nearly a billion users of Facebook worldwide.
   A actual B present C current D typical

5 Let's meet for a coffee at our .... place.
   A usual B typical C individual D unique

6 She's very level- .... and good at making decisions.
   A minded B willed C headed D hearted

7 There's a world .... difference between travelling by train and by plane.
   A from B of C in D to

8 My garden means the world .... me.
   A for B by C off D to

3 Join these sentences using an *-ing* or an *-ed* participle.

Example:
My favourite possession is this book. It was signed by the author.
My favourite possession is this book, signed by the author.

1 That woman is waving to us. She's one of my work colleagues.

2 That's the path. It leads to the sea.

3 I saw your brother. He was waiting for a train.

4 I found the money. It was hidden under my bed.

5 I'm living in a flat. It's owned by an old friend.

6 Shall we book the flight to Rome? It leaves at 6 p.m. from Heathrow.

4 There is a mistake in each of these sentences Underline the mistakes and correct them.

1 He must have gone to France because I saw him a few minutes ago.

2 Tom has done so a lot of cycling that he is very fit.

3 We were warned driving slowly because of the icy roads.

4 I'm sure he'll phone as soon as he'll get there.

5 I ordered a fish risotto, that was delicious.

6 The boss wanted to know why was I resigning.

7 Next Sunday at midday, my daughter will get married.

8 I might go with him if I hadn't been so busy at work.

9 If we don't make a decision soon, they will be selling all the tickets.

10 My father suggested her that she went to work for him.

11 Here's the article I told you about, wrote by my sister.

12 I asked them don't speak in the library.

13 Louise may leave already, but I'll check if you like.

14 I'll come, whether I have enough money.

15 If I weren't a teacher, I'll want to be a doctor.

5 Choose the correct alternatives in these sentences.

1 I started to climb the mountain but after an hour, I *forgot/lost* my nerve.

2 His job takes him all *over/through* the world.

3 How do you *get/reach* to work every day?

4 *Work/Job* security is very important to think about.

5 Young people seem to be getting more *competing/competitive* at sports.

6 Shall we have a coffee and work *out/up* what to do?

7 One of the many strengths of the play is the amusingly written *set/script*.

8 The *growing/growth* in production seems to have slowed down in many places.

9 *Applications/Applicants* are all expected to have some previous experience.

10 Tom has decided to give up swimming in order to focus *on/in* athletics.

11 What are the chances of getting a direct *trip/flight* to Singapore next Tuesday?

12 I'm working overtime *in order to/that's why* save money for my holidays.

13 Digital technology appears to have taken *over/up* the world in the past five years.

14 I am not convinced that the government is *telling/informing* us the whole truth.

15 My son has just gone on a package *expedition/tour* with his two best friends.

Multiple-choice cloze (Part 1)

6 For questions 1–12, read the text below and decide which answer (A, B, C or D) best fits each gap. There is an example at the beginning.

Journey into space

The day Neil Armstrong **(0)** ..._landed_.. on the Moon, twelve-year-old Claudie Haigneré was on holiday on a French campsite. The first Frenchwoman in space recalls that day; 'My father was an engineer who was always **(1)** .... about the world and he **(2)** .... us that something really extraordinary would happen. It was a beautiful evening so we sat under the stars and watched TV. To see a man climb down a ladder onto the **(3)** .... of the moon and **(4)** .... the same time to see a thing in the sky which seemed so **(5)** .... was just incredible.' After the moon landing Haigneré read and watched whatever she could about space. **(6)** .... there herself seemed unimaginable. Much later when she was working as a medical researcher, she saw a message on the hospital noticeboard. France's space centre was **(7)** .... for astronauts. It was an opportunity that Haigneré couldn't **(8)** .... Of 1,000 candidates, seven were chosen: six men and Haigneré.
Seven years after applying, Haigneré started training and eventually went into space twice. What was it like being **(9)** .... from life on earth? 'I only made two short flights and I had a packed work programme but once I decided to **(10)** .... some time to enjoy the spectacle. I watched the Earth turn and I saw darkness fall as the sun went **(11)** .... It was a moment of **(12)** .... extraordinary joy.'

0	**A** went	**B** came	**C** landed	**D** travelled
1	**A** curious	**B** surprised	**C** interested	**D** fascinated
2	**A** said	**B** told	**C** explained	**D** suggested
3	**A** top	**B** side	**C** level	**D** surface
4	**A** at	**B** on	**C** in	**D** by
5	**A** far	**B** long	**C** remote	**D** outside
6	**A** Making	**B** Finding	**C** Reaching	**D** Travelling
7	**A** asking	**B** looking	**C** offering	**D** requesting
8	A miss	**B** lose	**C** wait	**D** avoid
9	**A** put off	**B** cut off	**C** set out	**D** got away
10	**A** do	**B** get	**C** take	**D** spend
11	**A** up	**B** off	**C** into	**D** down
12	**A** so	**B** too	**C** such	**D** very

Open cloze (Part 2)

7 For questions 13–24, read the text below and think of the word that best fits each gap. Use only one word in each gap. There is an example at the beginning.

Success

I have **(0)** ....._never_.. met anyone successful who didn't know what they wanted to do. Knowing what you want to **(13)** .... achieved in ten years time, **(14)** .... if it doesn't seem a realistic goal for today, will give you the passion and drive needed to reach your ultimate goals. If you wake up in the morning and are **(15)** .... to answer the simple question 'What do I want to do?', then don't expect to go very far. People want to work **(16)** .... those who are passionate about what they do, and **(17)** .... knowing this means you can't have the ambition and determination that it takes to succeed. **(18)** .... you can answer the question 'What do I want to do?' clearly and confidently, then you don't have much chance of success. Don't forget you'll **(19)** .... spending the rest of your life working **(20)** .... it's incredibly important to identify what it is you really want to aim **(21)** ...., and to set targets.

On the **(22)** .... hand, just because you're passionate about what you want to do, doesn't necessarily **(23)** .... you'll be any good at it. You need to recognise your capabilities and accept your limitations. There are certain skills you can learn, but real talent is **(24)** .... people are born with and it's impossible to learn this.

Word formation (Part 4)

8 **For questions 25–34, read the text below. Use the word given in capitals at the end of some of the lines to form a word that fits the gap in the same line. There is an example at the beginning.**

Tired of waiting

Although Simon is going to university this autumn to study **(0)** _journalism_ , he has been working as a waiter for six months to pay for a holiday.   **JOURNALIST**

At first, he says, he was absolutely **(25)** .... at the job. It took him far longer than he'd expected to be able to do it **(26)** ...., and he was given no formal **(27)** .... at all. It would not, he says, have been his first choice but it was the only job he could find. He'd been shocked by how difficult it was to find any kind of temporary **(28)** .... at all. At every interview he went to, there were dozens of other **(29)** .... applicants.   **USE**

SUCCESS
TRAIN

EMPLOY

HOPE

The salary is not good, either, especially in view of the number of hours he works. Waiters can't rely on being given a share of the **(30)** .... charges because this is often not passed on by **(31)** ...., so he just has to hope for generous tips.   **SERVE**

MANAGE

He explains that this influences the way waiters treat different customers, since some **(32)** .... are much more likely to tip better than others. He would never consider working in a restaurant again, mainly because of the rude and **(33)** .... attitude of many chefs towards waiters and other helpers. However, he admits there were very few **(34)** .... about the food.   **NATION**

PLEASE

COMPLAIN

Key word transformations (Part 4)

9 **For questions 35–42, complete the second sentence so that it has a similar meaning to the first sentence, using the word given. Do not change the word given. You must use between two and five words, including the word given. Here is an example.**

Example:
We're going to camp whether or not it's raining.
EVEN
We're going to camp .._even if it's_.. raining.

35 He'll be there at six unless he's held up at work.
PROVIDED
He'll be there at six, ... held up at work.

36 I'm not sure if I should invite Rob to the gig.
NOT
I'm not sure .... I should invite Rob to the gig.

37 There were so many people at the station that I lost my friend.
SUCH
There were .... people at the station that I lost my friend.

38 I probably saw this film before on a plane.
MAY
I .... this film before on a plane.

39 The cinema was too far to walk to so we went by bus.
ENOUGH
The cinema .... to walk to so we went by bus.

40 'I'm really sorry I broke your camera, Mum', Ellie said.
APOLOGISED
Ellie .... mum's camera.

41 'Why don't we go camping in Greece?' said Micky.
SUGGESTED
Micky .... camping in Greece.

42 'You shouldn't swim here,' the instructor told us.
WARNED
The instructor .... here.

Living on the edge

Gapped text (Part 2)

▶ **EXAM** FOCUS p.201

1 **Look at the photo. What is your opinion about young people going on adventures like this? What are the risks and benefits for them?**

2 **Read the title and introduction to this article about a young mountaineer.**

1 What kind of person do you think he is?

2 Read the main text quickly. Was there anything that surprised you about Jordan?

3 **Seven sentences have been removed from the article. Choose from the sentences A–H the one which fits each gap (1–7). There is one extra sentence which you do not need to use.**

Speaking

4 **Work in pairs and discuss the questions.**

1 What do you think about Jordan's achievement? Do you think his father was right to encourage him?

2 Do parents always encourage their children to achieve for the right reasons?

3 At what age do you think young people are ready to take decisions about their lives?

Vocabulary

using prefixes to work out meaning

5 **Look at the words in the box, which are also underlined in the text, and match the prefixes to meanings 1–6.**

international	pre-schoolers	tricycle	disorder
immobility	hyper-competitive	overtime	re-occur

1	*not*	3	*before*	5	*three*
2	*again*	4	*more than usual/too much*	6	*involving two or more different things*

6 **Work in pairs. Choose three prefixes and ask each other questions using them.** *Example: Have you ever done a triathlon?*

the kid who climbed Everest

When 13-year-old Jordan Romero became the youngest climber to conquer Everest, he became an inspiration to his peers and sparked a debate on whether teenagers should be allowed to take grown-up risks.

Jordan Romero's mother drops him off at his father's house in Big Bear, California, and everyone assembles for their morning meeting. Team Jordan – which is how they refer to themselves, comprises father Paul, stepmother Karen and the climbing wonderchild – who is on track to become the youngest person to climb all the highest mountains on the world's seven continents.

Jordan leads a bit of a double life. **(1)** .... When he's staying at what Paul calls 'base camp,' things are considerably more intense. When training for a climb, Jordan often sleeps in a special tent to get his body used to lower oxygen levels. He has spent hundreds of hours wearing a weighted backpack, dragging a tyre up and down the driveway.

The place is littered with adventure gear. This is not just for Jordan; Paul, 42, and Karen, 46, have been professional adventure racers for a decade. 'As soon as the sun rises, we have a coffee and just go hard until dark,' Paul says with obvious pride. He makes it seem like a kind of paradise. **(2)** ....

The international media reception of their successful Everest attempt has been divided. As Team Jordan was still doing interviews, sixteen-year-old Abby Sunderland, who was attempting to become the youngest solo sailor to sail around the globe, had to be rescued from the middle of the Indian Ocean. **(3)** .... Abby and Jordan's adventures started a controversy about pushing kids too hard too young.

(4) .... At the age of three, he was beating fellow pre-schoolers in neighbourhood tricycle events. At six he graduated to BMX racing. He was one of the best riders in the nation until one day, at about Jordan's age, he was diagnosed with a rare knee disorder and the doctors warned that even walking might be painful. Luckily, Paul's knees recovered. However, the months of immobility seem to have encouraged him to make adventure sports into a lifestyle.

When he was little, Jordan didn't appear to have Paul's hyper-competitive gene. **(5)** .... That's because Paul was pretty busy training for races or working overtime to pay the bills. What does a nine-year-old do to bond with a father who loves adventure? In Jordan's case, he pointed at a picture of the highest summits on each continent and said, 'Hey Dad, I want to climb these mountains.' Pretty much any other dad would have mouthed some vague agreement. Paul said, 'Well, we'd better start training.'

Of course, it is not unusual for fathers to pass on their passions to their sons like this. **(6)** .... What's more, for Paul, there's the memory of all the things the doctor told him when he was Jordan's age – the 'maybes' and 'possiblys' about whether his bone disease would re-occur.

(7) .... It's because, in his driven philosophy of life, it is always better to seize the day. And so, once Paul realised his son was willing to put in the hard work, they began to climb.

Driving home, after dropping his son off, Paul is bursting with pride. 'We're just surfing the big wave of life. I just want him to grab life and ride it.'

A The public's opinion of young record-breakers quickly soured.

B However, whereas there's usually lots of opportunity to play golf or go fishing, for extreme sports there's not a big window of time when father and son will be in top physical shape.

C In fact, although he was close to his father, he saw very little of him.

D To understand why Paul encouraged his son to climb one of the world's deadliest mountains, you have to understand his background.

E At his mother's house, he's a normal sporty teen, with homework and strict bedtimes.

F When Paul and Karen competed in their first wilderness race in 1999, Paul finally felt like he had found his true calling.

G Which is why, for Paul Romero, all the questions about risk and responsible parenting completely miss the more personal justification for climbing Everest with Jordan even before he could legally drive.

H Paul is clearly trying to emphasise what a positive environment he creates for his son.

Mixed conditionals

▶ **GRAMMAR** REFERENCE p.167

1 **Look at these pairs of sentences. In each sentence, underline the verb forms in both the *if* clause and the conditional clause.**

1 **A** If Paul hadn't had a bone disease, he wouldn't be so driven today.

 B If Paul hadn't had a bone disease, he wouldn't have been so driven.

2 **A** If Paul hadn't been an extreme athlete, Jordan might not have climbed Everest.

 B If Paul weren't an extreme athlete, Jordan might not have climbed Everest.

3 **A** Paul might still be cycle racing if he hadn't had the knee disorder.

 B Paul might have raced cycles if he hadn't had the knee disorder.

2 **Which sentence in each pair is a 'mixed' conditional, where one clause refers to past time and one part refers to present time?**

3 **In which sentence is something which is true now caused by an event in the past?**

4 **Complete the following sentences, using the correct form of the verbs in brackets. If there is more than one possibility, say why.**

1 What a shame. If we .... (*see*) the advert, we could have gone to that show.

2 If I'd left the party earlier, I .... (*not/feel*) so tired today.

3 I would have got that job if I .... (*speak*) fluent French.

4 If you'd let me drive, we .... (*not/be*) lost now.

5 I'd be much happier if I .... (*speak*) to Tom yesterday.

6 I would have gone on holiday with Alex if I .... (*enjoy*) skiing, but I don't.

7 I .... (*might/earn*) more now if I'd gone to university.

8 If I'd started taking lessons earlier, I .... (*play*) the piano much better than I do.

5 **Change these sentences, using mixed conditional forms.**

1 My car broke down because it's so old.
 If ....

2 I spent too much money in the sales, which is why I'm broke.
 If ....

3 He plays football all the time ever since I took him to that Liverpool match.
 If ....

4 The only reason I learned Russian is because my aunt lives in Moscow.
 If ....

5 The reason I know so many people is that Paula introduced me to them.
 If ....

6 I went to live abroad because I couldn't get a job at home.
 If ....

Speaking

6 **Work in pairs and discuss these questions.**

1 If you could have chosen your nationality, which one would you want to be?

2 If you had had the choice at birth, which famous person would you want to look like?

3 If a machine allowed you to go back in time, what would you have done differently?

4 If you were a different sex, how do you think it would have affected your life?

Vocabulary

verbs, nouns and adjectives

1 Look at the underlined verbs. Which part of speech are they related to?

1 The public's opinion of young record-breakers quickly <u>soured</u>.

2 Pretty much any other dad would have <u>mouthed</u> some vague agreement.

3 The place is <u>littered</u> with adventure gear.

2 Complete the table and underline the prefixes or suffixes in the verb column.

Verb	Noun	Adjective
educate		
terrify		terrifying
		strong
	critic	
	danger	

3 Circle the nouns and underline the adjectives. Which words don't change for the verb form? How do you form verbs from the other words?

blood   cheat   dry   experience   frozen
hot   just   length   low   memory
modern   separate   sure   threat

Word formation (Part 3)

▶ **EXAM** FOCUS p.203

4 Read the article below quickly. Why was Simone's walk the 'walk of a lifetime'?

5 Use the word in capitals to form a word that fits the gap in that line. There is an example at the beginning (0).

EXAM TIP

Read the text again when you have finished to make sure your answers make sense and the words are spelt correctly.

6 Which achievement are you most proud of?

Walk of a lifetime

When Simone Powell told her parents about her **(0)** _decision_ to join a team which was   **DECIDE**
walking to the North Pole in aid of charity, they tried to **(1)** .... her to change her   **PERSUASION**
mind. However, as soon as they realised she was absolutely **(2)** .... to do it, their   **DETERMINATION**
next reaction was to **(3)** .... that their only daughter was well-prepared and had   **SURE**
all the equipment necessary for her long and dangerous expedition. For them, their
daughter's well-being and **(4)** .... was their first concern.   **SAFE**

At the beginning of her trip Simone got flu, but she stayed calm and waited for it to
pass. She had absolutely no **(5)** .... of giving up, she said, after she had got so   **INTEND**
far. Although she knew she was **(6)** .... compared to the other members of the   **EXPERIENCE**
team, she also felt she had trained long and hard and was ready to be put to the test.

Simone has now **(7)** .... completed the expedition, which makes her the   **SUCCEED**
youngest person ever to have done it. Simone says that her parents have been very
(8) .... , even though they were against the idea at first. They are also very proud   **SUPPORT**
of her, but the fact that she is now home is a huge **(9)** .... off their shoulders after   **WEIGH**
so many months of worrying. Simone is now planning to go to university, where her new
challenge is to study **(10)** ....   **ENGINE**

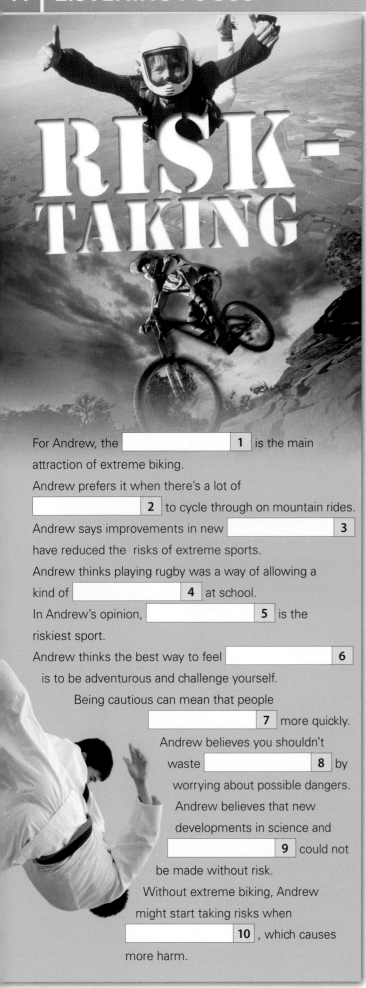

For Andrew, the [_____] **1** is the main attraction of extreme biking.

Andrew prefers it when there's a lot of [_____] **2** to cycle through on mountain rides.

Andrew says improvements in new [_____] **3** have reduced the risks of extreme sports.

Andrew thinks playing rugby was a way of allowing a kind of [_____] **4** at school.

In Andrew's opinion, [_____] **5** is the riskiest sport.

Andrew thinks the best way to feel [_____] **6** is to be adventurous and challenge yourself.

Being cautious can mean that people [_____] **7** more quickly.

Andrew believes you shouldn't waste [_____] **8** by worrying about possible dangers.

Andrew believes that new developments in science and [_____] **9** could not be made without risk.

Without extreme biking, Andrew might start taking risks when [_____] **10**, which causes more harm.

Speaking and vocabulary

1 Look at the photos around the text and discuss the questions.

1 Which of these sports do you think is the riskiest?

2 *It's better to be safe than sorry.* What does this mean? Do you agree?

3 How is extreme mountain biking different from normal cycling? How risky do you think it is?

2 Which adjectives refer to the sport and which to the person who does them?

adventurous	brave	breathtaking
demanding	determined	exciting
exhausting	irresponsible	skilful
terrifying	worthwhile	

Sentence completion (Part 2)

▶ **EXAM** FOCUS p.204

3 You will hear a man called Andrew talking about extreme mountain biking. First, read sentences 1–10. Does Andrew think taking risks is a good or bad thing?

EXAM TIP

Before you listen, think about what kind of words are missing (a noun, verb etc.) or whether a number is needed. Then focus on these words while you are listening.

---

4 ▶ 2.11 Now listen and complete the sentences. Write between one and three words in each space.

Speaking

5 Discuss the questions in pairs.

1 Do you think it's better to be a risk-taker or risk-averse?

2 Which is the riskiest behaviour (A–D), and why?

A not wearing a helmet when cycling or skiing

B driving above the speed limit

C walking home alone late at night

D eating food that's past its sell-by date

Adjectives and verbs with prepositions

1 Choose the adjective which does NOT fit in the sentence.

1 She's very *committed/involved/dedicated/devoted* to teaching young people about safety.
2 She was very *concerned/worried/timid/anxious* about taking part in the race.
3 He felt *sure/convinced/determined/confident* of his ability to win.
4 He's *thrilled/excited/enthusiastic/keen* about joining the skydiving team.

2 Use four of the adjectives to write sentences that are true for you. Then discuss your sentences with a partner.

3 Complete the sentences with the prepositions in the box.

about	from	in	on	to	with

1 He complained .... the inaccurate map of the area.
2 She always insists .... the best diving equipment.
3 My father admitted .... feeling nervous.
4 He was involved .... a skiing accident.
5 He was prevented .... competing because of an injury.
6 She has to deal .... many dangerous situations.
7 You have to rely .... your partner when you're climbing.
8 He's determined .... enter the race.
9 My boss congratulated me .... my achievement.
10 He's very keen .... sky-diving.

Phrasal verbs with *off*

4 Replace the words in italics with one of the phrasal verbs below.

back off	call sth off	cut off	go off
put sth off	see sb off	tell sb off	wear off

1 They *delayed* the start of the climb because of the storm.
2 Even though he was terrified of the dog he didn't *move away*.
3 The trip was *cancelled* because the weather was too bad.
4 We were *shouted at* by the guide for not following the safety rules.
5 A lot of people came to the port to *say goodbye to us* before we started the yacht race.
6 There was a loud bang and we realised one of the fireworks *had exploded* by accident.
7 When I hit my knee on the rock it hurt really badly but the pain *gradually went away*.
8 The village was *separated from* the outside world by the flood.

Speaking

5 Find out if your partner has

1 ever been cut off by snow or flooding.
2 ever called off something important.
3 ever been told off by a neighbour.
4 put anything off recently.

DANGER AVALANCHES

Hypothetical meaning

wish and *if only*

▶ **GRAMMAR** REFERENCE p.169

1 ▶ **2.12 Listen to a man talking about skateboarding. Why did he give it up?**

A His wife wanted him to.

B He had too many accidents.

C He felt he was too old.

2 Look at the examples and answer the questions.

1 *If only I hadn't given up skating.*
Did he give up skateboarding? Is he sorry he gave up?

2 *If only I could start again.*
Would he like to start skateboarding again? Is this possible?

3 *I wish I was twenty years younger.*
Would he like to be younger? Is this possible?

4 *I wish my wife wouldn't tell me I need a new hobby all the time.*
Does his wife tell him he needs a new hobby? Does he mind?

3 Look at the examples in Activity 2 and match the two parts of the sentences.

1 We use *wish/if only* + past simple

2 We use *wish/if only* + *could*

3 We use *wish/if only* + *would*

4 We use *wish/if only* + past perfect

when we would like something to…

A have been different in the past.

B be different about other people in the present/future.

C change in the present/future about ourselves.

D be different about ourselves now.

LANGUAGE TIP

• Use *If only* when your feelings of regret are strong.

• *I wish/If only* can be followed by *was/were* in spoken English, but *were* is used in formal written English, e.g. **I wish I were** able to help you.

---

4 Complete the sentences to make true wishes about yourself. Then say which of your partner's wishes are also true for you.

1 I wish I could ....

2 I wish I didn't have ....

3 I wish my parents would ....

4 I wish I'd never ....

other expressions with hypothetical meaning

5 Choose the correct alternative so that the second sentence means the same as the first.

1 Suppose we didn't go to work tomorrow…
We *have decided not to go to/are thinking about not going* to work tomorrow.

2 I met an old friend last night and it was as though we'd only seen each other the day before.
It felt like I *had/hadn't seen* my friend Alison very recently.

3 I'd rather you didn't go climbing this weekend.
I don't want you to/You're not allowed to go climbing this weekend.

4 It's time we stopped for a rest.
Let's have/We don't have time for a rest now.

6 Complete the sentences with the correct form of the verb in brackets.

1 Suppose we .... (*go*) there next week instead of tomorrow?

2 I felt as if someone .... (*gave*) me a million dollars!

3 I'd rather you .... (*not take*) so many risks.

4 It's time you .... (*realise*) how dangerous rugby can be.

7 Work in pairs.

Student A: Turn to page 159 and follow the instructions.

Student B: Turn to page 158 and follow the instructions.

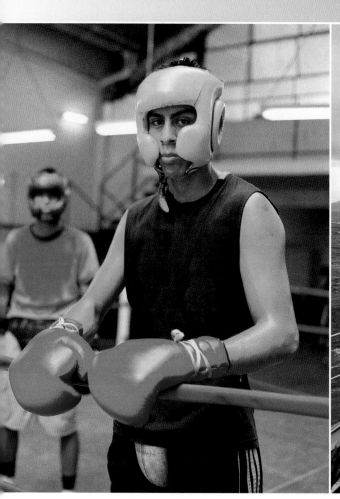

Long turn (Part 2)

responding to your partner's photographs

▶ **EXAM** FOCUS p.206

1　Look at the photographs. Which of the sports would you least like to do?

2　▶ 2.13　Listen to a student called Layla doing the task below and answer the questions.

> These photographs show people taking risks in different situations. I'd like you to compare the two photographs and say which person you think is taking the most risks.

1　Does she cover both parts of the task adequately?

2　Do you agree with her opinion? Why/Why not?

3　Listen again. What words and phrases does Layla use to

1　talk about the similarities and differences between the photos?

2　give her own opinion?

3　describe the people?

4　▶ 2.14　After your partner has finished speaking, the examiner will ask you a question. Listen and say whether you agree with Leo.

EXAM TIP

When you answer the follow-up question, you only have to speak for about twenty seconds. Try not to repeat what your partner has said.

5　Student A, look at the photos on page 153 and do the exam task in Activity 2.

Student B, which of these jobs would you prefer to do?

6　Work in pairs.

Student B, look at the photos on page 155 and do the exam task in Activity 2.

Student A, would you enjoy doing dangerous sports like these?

Semi-formal letter (Part 1)
requesting information

▶ **WRITING** REFERENCE p.182

Kilimanjaro climb

Climb the highest mountain in Africa!

\worried about fitness – training necessary?

7 day trip £555.00——dates available?

For a brochure
Phone: 01892 565677
Write to: Adventure Tours, George Street, Wells,
Kent KT23 NBT
Email: adventuretours@wells.net

WHAT'S INCLUDED?
• Two nights in a hotel
• Four nights' accommodation
  in mountain huts or camping
• Return bus to Nairobi   \meals
• National park fees   included?
• Services of guide and porter
                \equipment needed?
WHAT'S NOT INCLUDED?
• Travel insurance
• Flights

1 **Would you be interested in this trip? Why/Why not?**

2 **Read the exam task and underline the key words.**

> You would like to climb Mount Kilimanjaro this year. Read the advertisement above and the notes you have made. Then write a letter to the company requesting a brochure and more information.
> Write **120–150** words in an appropriate style.

3 **Match the two parts of the requests.**

1 I would be grateful
2 Could you tell me
3 I'd like to know
4 Would it be possible

A whether we will need to bring our own tents
B for you to let me know the name of the hotel
C if it's necessary to pay a deposit
D if you could send me some more details

LANGUAGE TIP

Use indirect questions to make polite requests. They're different to normal question forms. You don't need the auxiliary *do/does/did*, and the word order doesn't change.

4 **Decide if each of the requests in Activity 3 needs a full stop or a question mark.**

▶ **GRAMMAR** REFERENCE p.170

5 **These are the questions you have to ask. Make them more polite.**

1 Is any training necessary?
2 What dates are available?
3 Are all meals included?
4 Do I need to bring any special equipment?
5 Can you send me a brochure?

6 **Now write your letter. The introductory sentence has been written for you.**

> Dear Sir/ Madam,
> I am interested in the trips you organise to Mount Kilimanjaro and I would be grateful if you could give me a few more details.

EXAM TIP

It's a good idea to learn fixed phrases for letter writing e.g. *I would be grateful if you could..., I look forward to hearing from you.*

7 **Check your work for spelling and punctuation mistakes. Then compare your letter with the model answer on page 183.**

1 Complete the second sentence so that it has a similar meaning to the first sentence, using no more than five words, including the word given.

1 Ella is sorry she didn't learn to snowboard when she was younger.
   WISHES
   Ella .... how to snowboard when she was younger.

2 I would prefer you to wear a helmet when you ride your bike.
   RATHER
   I .... a helmet when you ride your bike.

3 I think you should go home now.
   TIME
   I think .... home.

4 It felt like my legs were made of wool.
   THOUGH
   My legs .... were made of wool.

5 I took the bus because the train is so expensive.
   BEEN
   If the .... so expensive, I wouldn't have taken the bus.

6 I didn't get up in time and now I'm late for work.
   WOULD
   I .... late for work if I'd got up in time.

2 Read the text (right) and complete the gaps with the correct preposition.

3 Complete the sentences with the correct form of the word in capitals.

1 Taking her children on such a dangerous trip was very ....   **RESPONSIBILITY**

2 Being caught in the storm at sea was a .... experience.   **TERRIFY**

3 Meeting my hero was very ....   **MEMORY**

4 People were very .... of his decision to climb the mountain in such bad weather.   **CRITIC**

5 The expedition was a great ....   **SUCCEED**

6 It takes determination and .... of character to sail around the world alone.   **STRONG**

Jessica Watson arrives back in Sydney

Returning **(1)** .... her 200-day solo trip around the world, sixteen-year-old Jessica Watson said 'I'm just a girl who believed **(2)** .... her dream. You don't have to be someone special to succeed **(3)** .... achieving something big,' she said. She was congratulated **(4)** .... her success by the Australian Premier.

Critics questioned whether she was experienced enough to take **(5)** .... the treacherous journey and whether her parents should have called it **(6)** .... , but she said: 'The one thing I won't accept is when someone calls this reckless. We spent years preparing **(7)** .... this trip.'

The first few months of the trip went well, although the lack **(8)** .... human contact inevitably had an impact **(9)** .... her state of mind at times. Jessica admitted **(10)** .... being 'pretty moody and a little homesick' and in April wrote on her blog: ' I think I am ready to come home now.'

But harder times were to come. In the final stages of her trip Jessica had to deal **(11)** .... waves as large as a four-storey building and towering 'like liquid mountains'. She had to strap herself into her bunk and put on a crash helmet to prevent herself **(12)** .... being injured in the wild seas.

Crime scene

12

Speaking and vocabulary

1 **Discuss these questions in pairs.**

1 What would be the hardest thing about being in prison?

2 What would it be like to work as a prison officer?

2 **What is the purpose of a prison? Put these reasons in order of importance, then compare with a partner.**

☐ to protect the public

☐ to punish criminals

☐ to discourage other people from committing crimes

☐ to rehabilitate criminals into society

3 **Choose what you think is the most suitable punishment (A–D) for people 1–4.**

1 someone caught shoplifting for the first time

2 an armed robber caught stealing from a jewellery shop

3 a member of a terrorist organisation

4 someone caught driving dangerously

A paying a fine

B doing community service (e.g. street cleaning)

C serving a prison sentence

D having an overnight curfew and wearing an electronic tag

Sentence completion (Part 2)

▶ **EXAM** FOCUS p.204

4 **You will hear a journalist talking about places which used to be prisons, where paying guests can now stay. How would you feel about staying in a former prison?**

5 ▶ **2.15** **Listen and complete the sentences.**

6 **Work in pairs and discuss the question.**

Which of the former prisons would you prefer to stay in?

> **EXAM TIP**
>
> Words that are spelt out for you to write down must be spelt correctly, but you won't lose marks if you make a minor spelling mistake on other words.

CHECK-IN

Prison hotels

The growth in ' _____ ' 1 has encouraged former prisons to become hotels.

Most of the guests at Karosta prison are on _____ 2 trips.

Each guest's _____ 3 is inserted in a prison document.

Only _____ 4 is available to drink at dinner.

When they are in their cells, guests must remain _____ 5 , unless given permission to do otherwise.

The speaker says the advertisement's description of the _____ 6 at the prison is accurate.

For a three-day trip to Latvia which includes a one night stay at Karosta, go to www. _____ 7 tours.com

The speaker does not recommend the _____ 8 in cell rooms at the Alcatraz Hotel.

In the Alcatraz Hotel, the _____ 9 are very different from those in a real prison.

One night in a single cell room at the Alcatraz prison hotel costs _____ 10 euros.

Vocabulary

crime

7 Use the words in the box to complete the sentences.

arrest	suspect	witness	fine	sentence

1 The police made the _____ only a few hours after the crime was committed.

2 A _____ has to give evidence in court about what he saw.

3 The police began to _____ the woman's husband of committing the crime.

4 Everyone thought the judge had given a very harsh _____ .

5 The police asked each _____ who they were with on the night of the crime.

6 I'd hate to _____ an accident.

7 I had to pay a large _____ for speeding on the motorway.

8 The police were able to _____ the burglar at the scene of the crime.

9 In some cases it's better to _____ people than send them to prison.

10 At the end of a trial the judge has to _____ the defendant, if the jury decides he or she is guilty.

8 Look at Activity 7 and answer the questions.

1 Are the noun and verb forms the same?

2 Is there any difference in pronunciation between the verb and noun?

3 Do any of the words have other meanings?

9 Use the vocabulary in Activity 7 to describe recent crime stories in the news.

collocations with *catch, follow, reach*

10 Write the correct form of one of the verbs in the box below in each gap 1–6.

catch	follow	reach

1 Sometimes it's hard for a jury to _____ *an agreement* or *a verdict*.

2 Local crime rates dropped again last year; this _____ *a trend* that has continued for three years.

3 The criminals were _____ *in the act of* breaking into the car and arrested at the scene of the crime.

4 I had to stop running to _____ *my breath*, and the criminals got away.

5 The police haven't succeeded in _____ *their target* for crime convictions this year.

6 The police are _____ *a lead* which they think will help solve the crime.

Modal verbs

obligation, prohibition and necessity

▶ **GRAMMAR** REFERENCE p.170

1 **Read the statements and decide who said each one: a) a police officer, b) a prison officer or c) a prisoner.**

1 We *have to* inspect all mail sent to prisoners.

2 We *mustn't* talk to journalists about cases we are investigating.

3 We *don't have to* work or go to classes if we don't want to.

4 We *are not allowed to* have more than three visitors at a time.

5 I *must* try and stay positive until I am freed.

6 I *needn't have* spent so long preparing for the trial because in the end the defendant pleaded guilty.

2 **Which of the statements in Activity 1 refer to**

A an obligation the speaker feels is necessary?

B an obligation someone else says is necessary?

C things that aren't permitted?

D a lack of necessity/obligation?

E something that was done but wasn't necessary?

LANGUAGE TIP

Must is only used in the present. To talk about obligation in the past or future, use *have to*.

We **had to wear** a school uniform until we were sixteen; I **will have to save more** if I want to buy a car.

3 **Choose the correct modal verb.**

1 If you are arrested you *don't have to/are not allowed to* answer all the police's questions.

2 Witnesses *mustn't/don't have to* tell lies in court.

3 We *must/had to* stay in our prison cells for up to twenty-three hours per day. It was awful.

4 We *must/have to* carry our identity cards at all times.

4 **Complete the second sentence so that it has a similar meaning to the first sentence, using the word given. You must use between two and five words.**

1 It was good to see you but it wasn't necessary for you to visit me in prison.
   NEED
   You .... visited me in prison but it was good to see you.

2 You mustn't open the door to strangers.
   ALLOWED
   You .... the door to strangers.

3 It is prohibited for members of the jury to talk to the press.
   MUST
   Members of the jury .... to the press.

4 It isn't necessary for suspects to answer the police's questions.
   HAVE
   Suspects .... answer the police's questions.

5 He is responsible for collecting evidence at the scene of a crime.
   HAS
   He .... evidence at the scene of a crime.

6 Was it necessary for him to get advice from a lawyer?
   NEED
   Did .... advice from a lawyer?

Speaking

5 **Discuss what members of the jury/crime scene investigators/prison officers**

1 have to do.

2 mustn't do/aren't allowed to do.

3 are allowed to do.

4 needn't do/don't have to do.

Vocabulary and speaking

cybercrime

1 Work in pairs and discuss the questions.

1 In what ways do you think the internet can be a dangerous place?

2 How seriously do you take cybercrime?

3 What can people do to protect themselves against cybercrime?

2 What do activities 1–5 involve? Match them with A–E.

1 identity fraud

2 cyber bullying

3 identity theft

4 hacking

5 libel

A publishing something that is harmful to someone's reputation

B illegally gaining access to a computer or network.

C pretending to be someone else

D deliberately hurting or embarrassing someone by email, text or on social networking sites

E stealing personal details for criminal purposes

3 Which of activities 1–5 do you think is a) the most serious? b) the most common?

4 What do you think of people who

1 download music/films illegally?

2 post a picture of someone without their consent on Facebook?

3 give false information online?

5 What could the possible consequences of doing these things be? Think about

1 the individuals.

2 society.

3 the industries involved.

Discussion (Part 4)

▶ **EXAM** FOCUS p.207

6 Join with another pair. Look at the examiner's questions and, in pairs, take turns to answer them. Listen carefully to the other pair and note down whether they

A only gave very short answers/spoke too much.

B tried to include each other in the discussion.

C used a variety of phrases for agreeing/disagreeing.

1 Which is more important to you, your phone or your computer?

2 Do you think people rely too much on computers?

3 How would you feel if you couldn't access the internet for a month?

4 Do you think the internet is the best way to shop?

EXAM TIP

You can expand your ideas by giving specific examples (e.g. examples of people you know who rely too much on computers).

---

7 Discuss your feedback in groups.

Speaking

1 Discuss the following questions.

1 Why do you think crime fiction is one of the best-selling genres in many countries?

2 Which crime novels, films or TV programmes are popular in your country?

Multiple choice (Part 1)

▶ **EXAM** FOCUS p.200

2 You are going to read an extract from a crime novel. For questions 1–8, choose the answer (A, B, C or D) which you think fits best according to the text.

EXAM TIP

Make sure you read all the options carefully before making your decision.

1 The writer mentions Martin's unwillingness to kill flies to show that he

A has a lot of patience.

B wishes he was braver.

C avoids being aggressive.

D is fond of small creatures.

2 The people in the queue didn't try to stop the violence because they

A were afraid of getting involved in it.

B realised it was none of their business.

C wanted to know what would happen next.

D didn't want to lose their place in the queue.

3 What was Martin's initial reaction to the situation?

A He was in a state of disbelief.

B He felt disinterested in what was going on.

C He felt he had a responsibility to do something.

D He thought about what his father would have done.

4 Martin threw his bag at the Honda driver

A to protect himself from being hit by the bat.

B because the Honda driver was damaging the victim's car.

C because he had decided it was the only sensible solution.

D to distract the Honda driver from killing the Peugeot driver.

5 *ducked* in line 39 means

A found it exciting.

B tried his best to catch it.

C moved to avoid being hit.

D could never see anything.

6 What do we learn about Martin in Paragraph 5?

A He was hoping to become a crime writer.

B He disliked people making jokes about him.

C He preferred the company of women to men.

D He felt he made a negative impression on people.

KATE ATKINSON

Martin had never done anything like that in his life before. He didn't even kill flies in the house, instead he patiently <u>stalked</u> them, trapping them with a glass and plate before letting them free. The meek shall inherit the earth. He was fifty and had never knowingly committed an act of violence against another living creature, although sometimes he thought that might be more to do with cowardice than pacifism.

He had stood in the queue, waiting for someone else to <u>intervene</u> in the scene unfolding before them, but the crowd were in audience mode, like promenaders at a particularly brutal piece of theatre, and they had no intention of spoiling the entertainment. Even Martin had wondered at first if it was another show – a faux impromptu piece intended either to shock or to reveal our immunity to being shocked because we lived in a global media community where we had become passive voyeurs of violence (and so on). That was the line of thought running through the detached, intellectual part of his brain. His primitive brain, on the other hand, was thinking, Oh, this is horrible, really horrible, please make the bad man go away. He wasn't surprised to hear his father's voice in his head (*Pull yourself together, Martin*). His father had been dead for many years but Martin often still heard the bellow and yell of his parade-ground tones.

When the Honda driver finished breaking the window of the silver Peugeot and walked towards the driver <u>brandishing</u> his weapon and preparing himself for a final victory blow, Martin realised that the man on the ground was probably going to die, was probably going to be *killed* by the crazed man with the bat right there in front of them unless someone did something and, instinctively, without thinking about it at all – because if he'd thought about it he might not have done it – he slipped his bag off his shoulder and swung it, hammer-throw fashion, at the head of the insane Honda driver.

· 124 ·

7 *that* in line 56 refers to

   A using magic.

   B closing his eyes.

   C trying to hide from people.

   D making himself anonymous.

8 Martin was astonished that

   A his bag had missed the Honda driver.

   B the Honda driver had decided to leave.

   C the Honda driver was unable to find him.

   D the crowd were supporting the Honda driver.

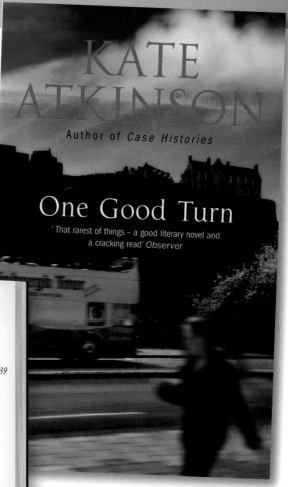

ONE GOOD TURN

He missed the man's head, which didn't surprise him – he'd never been able to aim or catch, he was the kind of person who ducked when a ball was thrown in his direction – but his laptop was in the bag and the hard weighty edge of it caught the Honda driver on the shoulder and sent him <u>spinning</u>.   *line 39*

The nearest Martin had been to a real crime scene previously had been on a Society of Authors' trip around St Leonard's police station. Apart from Martin, the group consisted entirely of women. 'You're our token man,' one of them said to him, and he sensed a certain disappointment in the polite laughter of the others, as if the least he could have done as their token man was to be a little less like a woman.

Martin expected the Honda driver to pick himself up off the ground and search the crowd to find the culprit who had thrown a missile at him. Martin tried to make himself an anonymous figure in the queue, tried to pretend he didn't exist. He closed his eyes. He had done that at school when he was <u>bullied</u>, <u>clinging</u> to an ancient, desperate magic – they wouldn't hit him if he couldn't see them. He imagined the Honda driver walking towards him, the baseball bat raised high, the arc of annihilation waiting to happen.   *line 56*

To his amazement, when he opened his eyes, the Honda driver was climbing back into his car. As he drove away a few people in the crowd gave him a slow hand-clap. Martin wasn't sure if they were expressing disapproval of the Honda driver's behaviour or disappointment at his failure to <u>follow through</u>. Whichever, they were a hard crowd to please.

Martin knelt on the ground and said, 'Are you OK?' to the Peugeot driver, but then he was politely but firmly set aside by the two policewomen who arrived and took control of everything.

· 125 ·

Speaking

3 **Discuss these questions.**

1 Do you think that Martin was right to get involved? What would you have done?

2 What examples of road rage have you experienced or witnessed?

Vocabulary

verbs

4 **Match meanings 1–8 to the verbs underlined in the text.**

1 do what is necessary to complete something

2 turn around quickly

3 follow something quietly in order to catch it

4 hold something or someone tightly

5 become involved in a difficult situation

6 hurt or frighten someone who is less powerful than you

7 wave something (e.g. a weapon) in a threatening way

8 move someone or something away

5 **Work in pairs. Choose three verbs from Activity 4 and use them to make two true sentences and one false sentence about your life. Take turns to read your sentences out. Can your partner guess which one is false?**

have/get something done

▶ **GRAMMAR** REFERENCE p.169

1 **Read the dialogue. Which of the phrases in italics refer to**

1 something over which people had no control?

2 something which happened as a result of an arrangement?

> **Zara:** I heard there was a break-in at your office the other night. Did they take anything?
>
> **Dan:** Luckily, not much. We *had some computers stolen* but that was about it.
>
> **Zara:** What did the police do about it?
>
> **Dan:** The usual. They *got the rooms fingerprinted*, but I don't expect they'll catch anyone.

2 **Complete the rule to show how causative *have/get* is formed.**

have or .... + object + ... of the verb

3 **Read the dialogues 1–6 and complete the responses using the correct forms of the words in brackets.**

1 **A** This room looks different?
   B Yes, we .... (*have/just/paint*)

2 **A** This tooth has been aching for ages now.
   B Why don't you go to the dentist's and ....? (*get/look at*)

3 **A** My hair is so long it takes ages to wash and dry.
   B Why don't you ....? (*have/cut*)

4 **A** I think I must be getting a bit short-sighted!
   B Go to the optician's and .... (*get/test*)

5 **A** Did you build that shed yourself?
   B No, I .... last year. (*get/a friend/make it*)

6 **A** What a beautiful family photograph.
   B Yes, we .... by a professional. (*have/take*)

4 **Look at the list (below) of some things victims have to do after a crime has been committed.**

1 Put a tick (✓) next to the things people often do themselves.

2 Put a cross (✗) next to the things people would probably have done for them/get somebody to do for them.

3 Add anything else you can think of to the list.

4 Discuss your lists in groups. Have you ever had to do any of these things?

- ☐ report the crime to the police
- ☐ change their locks
- ☐ repair broken windows
- ☐ buy a guard dog
- ☐ stop their credit cards
- ☐ clean the house
- ☐ find their insurance policy
- ☐ install an alarm

LANGUAGE TIP

- *Get* is more informal than *have* and is not usually used to describe unpleasant experiences (e.g. *I* **had** *my identity stolen* NOT *I got my identity stolen*).

- We can also use *get somebody to do something/make somebody do something* when we make or persuade somebody to do something.
  I **got** *my dad* **to change** *the tyre for me.*
  I **made** *my brother* **help** *me.*

Vocabulary

phrasal verbs with *go*

1 Replace the words in italics with the correct form of one of the phrasal verbs with *go*. There may be more than one possible answer for each question.

go off	go over	go on	go ahead
go down			

1 The policeman had no idea what was *happening*.
2 They decided to *continue* with the original investigation.
3 Jack has *lost interest in* the idea of becoming a detective.
4 The computer network has *stopped working*.
5 The dog started shaking when the fireworks *exploded*.
6 I didn't keep the milk in the fridge and it *became sour*.
7 The lights *stopped working* for no apparent reason.
8 I finished early so I *revised* what I'd written.

2 Work in pairs and ask each other these questions.

1 Have you ever gone off someone or something?
2 Have you ever gone ahead with something against someone's wishes?
3 Do you always go over your work before you hand it in?
4 Do you usually know what is going on in the world?

Open cloze (Part 2)

▶ **EXAM** FOCUS p.202

3 Read the text quickly. In what way has tourism been affected by crime novels?

4 Read the text again and think of the word which best fits each gap. Use only one word in each gap. There is an example at the beginning.

5 Have you ever been on, or would you consider going on a tour of a place where a book, film or TV show was set? Why/Why not?

In the footsteps of the fictional detective

Detective novels have been widely popular **(0)** *since* Sherlock Holmes and Maigret first caught the public's imagination, but nowadays this particular genre of novel seems to **(1)** _____ selling more than ever before. Dan Brown's *The Da Vinci Code*, **(2)** _____ example, has sold millions of copies all **(3)** _____ the world since its publication. In fact, it is **(4)** _____ popular that walking tours have been set **(5)** _____ so that people **(6)** _____ visit the places mentioned in the novel. The novel has also been made into a very successful film.

One of the **(7)** _____ popular fictional detectives these days is Wallander, the main character in a series of novels written **(8)** _____ the author Henning Mankell. Divorced and unlucky in love, Wallander survives by eating too much junk food and working far too hard. He is kept very busy tracking **(9)** _____ criminals and killers. For millions of people worldwide, **(10)** _____ small Swedish town of Ystad is now synonymous with murder and the man who solves them.

And, **(11)** _____ the fact that it is well over a hundred years since the first Sherlock Holmes story was published, tourists still flock to visit Baker Street in London, the place associated with that famous detective. It appears that crime, **(12)** _____ it is true or fictional, is still a tourist attraction!

Story (Part 2)

▶ **WRITING** REFERENCE p.184

1 **Read the exam task carefully.**

1 Who is your target audience? What style should the story be in?

2 What kind of story do you think it will be? romantic/ funny? crime/adventure?

3 Think about the characters: who is Stefan, and what is his relationship to the writer?

> You are going to enter a short story competition which was advertised in an English language magazine for students. The story must end with these words.
>
> *I saw Stefan off at the airport and decided that, after all the scary experiences we had been through together that summer, it would be safer never to have contact with him again.*
>
> Write your **story**. Write your answer in **120–180** words in an appropriate style.

2 **Work in pairs and think about what might have happened.**

3 **Discuss how you are going to organise your story. Think about**

1 how many paragraphs you'll have and what will be in each one.

2 starting with a strong opening sentence to attract the reader's attention.

3 a title for the story.

EXAM TIP

Include a range of language in your story, including

- linking words to make your story flow well. (e.g. *as well as, if, although…*)
- time expressions to make the sequence clear (e.g. *at first, then, in the end…*)
- descriptive, interesting adjectives, verbs, adverbs (e.g. *terrified, crept, incredibly…*)

---

4 **Work in pairs. Match the adverbs in italics in sentences A–E to their uses (1–5).**

1 showing your attitude

2 giving extra emphasis

3 saying how sure you are

4 giving details about *when*

5 giving details about *how*

A I was told to report to the police station *straight away.*

B I didn't like my lawyer *at all.*

C *To my surprise*, the police let him off with a warning.

D I had *definitely* seen him somewhere before.

E I spoke to the accused very *calmly.*

▶ **GRAMMAR** REFERENCE p.162

5 **For each sentence, decide whether the adverb is in the correct place. If it is, tick the sentence, If not, correct it, There may be more than one possibility.**

1 Probably he is going to plead not guilty.

2 Did you yesterday phone the police?

3 I didn't remember, personally, anything.

4 Quickly, we explained what had happened.

5 The novel was incredibly interesting.

6 **Write your story. When you have finished the first draft, check your work, including your spelling and punctuation. Make sure you have organised your story into paragraphs, and used suggestions from the Exam tip box.**

1 **Choose the correct option A, B, C or D to complete sentences 1–6.**

1 The police .... an arrest and took the suspect to the station.
   A made   **B** did   **C** had   **D** got

2 Because it was his first offence, the judge let him .... with a warning.
   A up   **B** off   **C** down   **D** in

3 The police are .... a lead which they hope will help solve the crime.
   A reaching   **B** catching   **C** following   **D** inspecting

4 The jury took over a week to .... a 'guilty' verdict.
   A do   **B** make   **C** arrive   **D** reach

5 The defendant went .... a long trial before he was sentenced.
   A off   **B** over   **C** through   **D** by

6 As the burglar was breaking into the shop, the alarm .... off.
   A went   **B** came   **C** sounded   **D** let

2 **Complete the second sentence so that it has a similar meaning to the first sentence, using the word given. You must use between two and five words.**

1 We went to the lesson, but it wasn't necessary because it was cancelled. **NEED**
   We .... to the lesson because it was cancelled.

2 The policeman didn't give us permission to go into the courtroom. **ALLOWED**
   We .... go into the courtroom.

3 During the lesson, raise your hand if you want to speak. **UNLESS**
   During the lesson, ... you raise your hand.

4 Why don't you talk Harry into checking your brakes for you? **GET**
   Why don't you .... your brakes for you?

5 I"ve asked the newsagent's to deliver me a newspaper every day. **DELIVERED**
   I've told the newsagent's that I want to .... every day.

6 I'm going to ask a friend of mine to make my wedding dress. **HAVE**
   I'm going to .... by a friend of mine.

3 **Complete the text, using the correct form of the word in capitals.**

What happens when you report a crime?

A woman went into the police station to report a **(1)** .... , and was able to give a full description of the man who took her purse. Since there was also a witness, it wasn't very long before the police were able to arrest a **(2)** .... At the station, a request was made for a **(3)** .... to be present while the interviews were taking place. This was done, and in the meantime, the police discovered that the man had several other **(4)** .... to be taken into account.

THIEF

SUSPICIOUS

LAW

CONVICT

In court, the jury took a long time to reach an **(5)** .... but evidence found at the crime scene meant he was eventually found **(6)** .... of the crime and had to be sentenced.

AGREE

GUILT

Surprisingly, despite his previous **(7)** .... record, the judge chose not to give the man a prison sentence, deciding instead to make him do six months' community **(8)** ....

CRIME

SERVE

Who are you again?

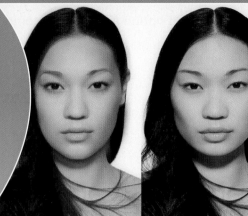
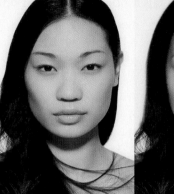

Multiple matching (Part 3)

▶ **EXAM** FOCUS p.201

1 **Look at the small photos and put the faces in the order that they most resemble the big photo (below left). Then answer the questions below.**

1 Did you find this task easy or difficult? Did other people do better/worse than you?

2 How did you do the task? Did you have to study the features carefully?

EXAM TIP

Leave any questions you are not sure about and go back to them later. Always answer them as you will not lose marks for a wrong answer.

2 **Read the title and introduction. You are going to read an article about people who suffer from 'face blindness.' For questions 2–15, choose from the people (A–D). The people may be chosen more than once.**

Which person

says that <u>location</u> is her biggest clue to recognising people?	1	C
is in difficulty when everyone dresses the same?	2	
has problems if people change their appearance?	3	
once failed to recognise a friend until he spoke?	4	
fears that her disability might affect her work?	5	
says she has mistaken a stranger for her boyfriend?	6	
suspects that people must think she is unfriendly?	7	
can sometimes find watching certain things on TV confusing?	8	
has had problems identifying herself?	9	
identifies people she works with by their style of dressing?	10	
pretends to be distracted in case she ignores people she knows?	11	
says it can be misleading to rely too much on context?	12	
thinks that face blindness may have affected her childhood?	13	
prefers to avoid large social gatherings?	14	
believes the condition can be passed down the generations?	15	

IDENTITY CRISIS

We can all forget a face but some people – around one in fifty – can't recognise their colleagues, friends, even their parents. It is a condition known as 'face blindness.'

A Emily's worst experience was arriving at a restaurant to meet the man she'd been going out with for a month. 'Seeing him sitting alone at the bar, I gave him a kiss on the cheek and we talked for a few minutes. Then an embarrassing thought struck me. 'We've never met before, have we?' I asked. 'I don't think so,' he replied, 'but you seemed pretty sure.' This incident, along with many similar experiences, led me to realise that I am face-blind. I'm OK if I can rely on facial clues other than features, such as glasses or an unusual hairstyle, but it means I can be completely thrown if someone has their hair coloured, grows a beard or gets contact lenses. People aren't always found where they 'belong', either. I once assumed a tall man who greeted me warmly at work was just a new colleague. I later realised that he was actually a friend's flatmate who had just started working there, but who I'd met many times before at her flat!'

B Andrea works in a design studio. 'It's a really good profession for me as people tend to express themselves through clothes and jewellery and it's easier to remember who usually wears a huge watch or very bright tops or whatever rather than faces. So you can imagine how tricky it is at meetings when clients are all in suits and white shirts, looking identical. And when I'm the only one in the office and I have to open the door, I might say 'Hello, how can I help you?' when I have done business with them ten times before. In fact, I worry that I'm going to lose my clients because of this. I am also expected to meet clients outside work. I obviously try to get out of going to big parties because it's a nightmare with my condition. If I have to go, I always memorise what people are wearing when I'm first introduced to them.'

C Laura tells us about an experience she had recently. 'I was coming out of the cinema and a woman smiled at me. I assumed I must know her, but I usually depend on venue and this one didn't help me to work out whether she was a colleague, a parent at my son's school, or a friend. So what I did was smile faintly. Not too much, in case I was wrong. I then hoped desperately that if she spoke, a few moments' conversation would place her. Sure enough it did, I realised she is someone who sits in an office quite near to me. Embarrassing, but an everyday occurrence for people like me; and I probably come across as rather a cold person for never speaking first. If people have features that stand out from the crowd, such as gappy teeth or a birthmark, I'm not too bad. But I'm hopeless if you have regular features like my colleague. Most actors do too, which is why I find it so hard to follow the plot of a film, especially if there are a lot of characters. My daughter is just the same. So is my mother, which leads me to believe the disorder must run in families.'

D Chloe admits that when she's out, she now puts earplugs in and pretends she's listening to music, or consciously looks deep in thought as if she had a lot on her mind. 'I came up with this plan because I've so often offended people by not recognising them. I once thought I was being followed by a man. I walked faster, ignoring him and it was only when his American accent triggered my memory that I realised it was a man I've known really well since university. Even worse, though, I've caught sight of myself in a shop window and not realised it was my own reflection! When I look back there were hints even when I was very young of my disorder. I tended to have just one close friend at school. I now put this down to missed opportunities because I was a perfectly friendly child. I probably just didn't recognise people again.'

SUNDAY SUPPLEMENT

Speaking

3 **Discuss these questions.**

1 Which of the strategies mentioned in the article do you think would be the most effective in helping with face-blindness?

2 What advantages and disadvantages would there be of being a 'super-recogniser' – someone who can recognise people again many years after they've seen them just for a moment?

Vocabulary

phrasal verbs with *come*

4 **Match the phrasal verbs with *come* in sentences 1–8 with the definitions A–H.**

1 I *came across* a pile of old letters while I was tidying up my office.

2 I probably *come across* as unfriendly to some people.

3 I *came up* with this plan because I've so often offended people.

4 I'm sure Paolo will *come round* to the idea sooner or later.

5 I think Jess has *come down* with flu.

6 If I *came into* money, I'd give some to medical research.

7 My exam results are *coming out* next week.

8 She's got her twentieth birthday *coming up* soon.

A find by chance

B happen

C give the impression/appear

D think of

E inherit

F get/catch something

G agree to something you're not sure about

H be made public

5 **Work in pairs. Ask each other questions using the phrasal verbs in Activity 4.**

Examples:
Do you think you come across as a different kind of person to who you really are?
Have you ever come down with an unusual illness or condition?

Modal verbs

ability

1 Read the forum extracts. Which person is
a) a 'super recogniser'? b) face-blind?

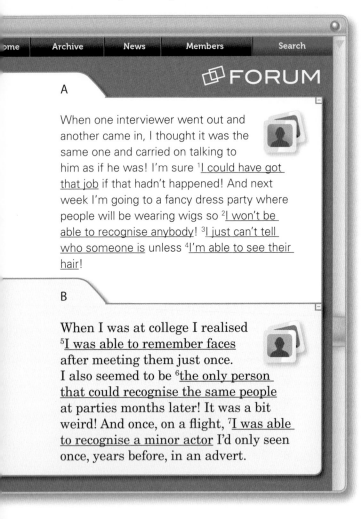

A

When one interviewer went out and another came in, I thought it was the same one and carried on talking to him as if he was! I'm sure ¹I could have got that job if that hadn't happened! And next week I'm going to a fancy dress party where people will be wearing wigs so ²I won't be able to recognise anybody! ³I just can't tell who someone is unless ⁴I'm able to see their hair!

B

When I was at college I realised ⁵I was able to remember faces after meeting them just once. I also seemed to be ⁶the only person that could recognise the same people at parties months later! It was a bit weird! And once, on a flight, ⁷I was able to recognise a minor actor I'd only seen once, years before, in an advert.

2 Which of the underlined phrases (1–7) are examples of the following?

A general ability in the past ..5.. ....
B ability on a particular occasion in the past ....
C ability in the present ....
D ability in the future ....
E things which were possible but did not happen ....

▶ **GRAMMAR** REFERENCE p.170

LANGUAGE TIP

- We can also use *know how to* to talk about ability. *I don't **know how to** drive.*
- *Succeed in* and *manage to* give the idea of overcoming difficulty. *I finally **succeeded in** contacting Josh. He finally **managed** to find his way home.*

3 Choose the correct verb form to complete the sentences. Both may be possible.

1 After we'd tried everything, we *could/were able to* get the computer to work at last.
2 When we lived on the coast we *could/were able to* swim every day in the summer.
3 She must *can/be able to* leave earlier than that!
4 If you'd got here earlier we *could catch/could have caught* the fast train together.
5 *I've been unable to/can't* recognise faces since I had the accident last winter.
6 I hope *can/to be able to* finish this today.

4 Complete the second sentence with between two and five words including the word given so that it has a similar meaning to the first sentence.

1 I couldn't finish the competition because I wasn't feeling well.
WAS
I .... the competition because I wasn't feeling well.
2 When I was younger, I was the best football player in my year.
PLAY
When I was younger, I .... anyone else in my year.
3 As it's such a long way, I don't think I'll be able to run all of it.
SUCCEED
As it's such a long way, I don't think I'll .... all of it.
4 I didn't take the job, even though I was offered it.
COULD
I .... the job I was offered, but I didn't.
5 I knew how to cook before I went to university.
ABLE
I .... before I went to university,

5 Complete the sentences with an expression of ability so they are true for you. Use the ideas in the box to help you.

| ride a horse/motorbike | speak a language fluently |
| play a musical instrument | run a marathon   cook |

1 I used to…
2 Once, I…
3 One day, I hope…
4 I've never…
5 It would be nice…
6 I should…

Speaking

1 Look at the photos of people keeping a record of their memories, and discuss the questions.

1 What kind of things do people often want to keep memories of?
2 Which of these two methods do you think is best? Why?
3 What other ways are there to record your memories?

Vocabulary

useful phrases for Part 2

2 Match expressions 1–6 to the reasons for using them (A–F).

1 Both of these photos…
2 What I meant was…
3 Did you say we had to…?
4 It's a kind of…
5 It might be a good way of…
6 One shows… while the other shows…

A making sure you understand
B correcting yourself/making something clearer
C talking about how things are similar
D talking about differences
E speculating
F saying something in a different way if you don't know the word

3 Work in pairs and think of as many other useful expressions as you can for each category.

Long turn (Part 2)

▶ **EXAM** FOCUS p.206

4 Work in pairs.

Student A: Compare the two pictures in Activity 1, and say why people might choose to record their memories like this. You should speak for about a minute.

Student B: Do you prefer to write down your memories or keep photographs?

5 Now turn to the photos on page 156.

6 Discuss how well you feel you did the activity.

1 Were you able to speak for a minute without pausing too much?
2 Did you use 'fillers' (e.g. *er…*, *well…*, *right…*) when you paused, rather than leave long silences?
3 Did you compare the photos rather than just describe them?
4 Did you give your personal opinion?

7 Tell your partner two things they did well, and two things they could improve.

EXAM TIP

You will know when your minute is up because the examiner will say *thank you.*

Expressions with *mind*

1 Choose the correct meaning, A or B, for the expressions with *mind.*

1 I just couldn't think what the answer was. *My mind had gone completely blank.*

   A I'd forgotten all the numbers.

   B I wasn't sure of the correct number.

2 I had no idea where I was. I thought I was *losing my mind.*

   A getting lost

   B going mad

3 OK, thanks for your suggestion. *I'll bear that in mind.*

   A I've changed my mind.

   B I'm going to remember that.

4 *I'm in two minds about* whether to go to the party.

   A I haven't decided yet.

   B I'm really looking forward to it.

5 *It had crossed my mind* that she would forget to come.

   A I was convinced.

   B It occurred to me.

6 I'm really sorry I didn't phone you back last night. *It slipped my mind.*

   A I forgot.

   B I was really busy.

7 I must *put his mind at rest* and tell him I've found his credit card.

   A make him lose his memory

   B stop him worrying

8 To *take her mind off* breaking up with her boyfriend, we threw a party.

   A make her forget

   B persuade her not to do it

Speaking

2 Use the expressions with *mind* to talk about something

1 you're not sure about.

2 you forgot recently.

3 you're worried about.

4 you think about often.

Verbs with similar meanings

3 Choose the correct verb.

1 I always *store/record/preserve/maintain* my favourite photos in a special box.

2 The photos helped her to *preserve/recall/reflect/maintain* the events of that day.

3 We *recalled/remembered/reflected/reminded* on what had gone wrong and how we could improve.

4 He *recalled/recorded/reminded/remembered* her of her grandfather.

4 Complete the sentences with the correct form of the verbs. Sometimes more than one word is possible.

believe	consider	judge	think

1 I don't .... in doing exercises to improve your memory.

2 I am in no position to .... whether they are doing the right thing.

3 I am .... writing a family history.

4 He is .... of becoming a journalist.

5 It is .... that memory declines as people get older.

6 I .... myself lucky that I have such a good memory.

7 You need to .... for yourself whether or not the job is a good opportunity.

8 They are .... about starting a family.

5 Which answers in Activity 4 depend on you knowing

1 whether the verb can be used with a particular preposition?

2 a fixed phrase?

LANGUAGE TIP

• *think of/about* can mean *consider,*
 e.g. I'm **thinking of/about** doing a journalism course.

• *think of* is used to ask about someone's opinion,
 e.g. What did you **think of** the film?

• *think about* is used to talk about the action of thinking,
 e.g. I'm **thinking about** how to solve the problem.

Multiple-choice cloze (Part 1)

▶ **EXAM** FOCUS p.202

1 **Read the text quickly (don't worry about the gaps yet). What problem does the writer describe?**

A not having enough storage space for all his text messages

B making difficult choices about what to keep

C keeping too much unnecessary information

135

The lost art of forgetting

Of the (**0**) _A approximately_ 1,500 text messages I have stored on my phone, around three quarters of them are very (**1**) .... Of the remaining quarter, most are significant in some way, but also not really worth (**2**) .... forever. And then there are maybe a (**3**) .... of text messages that I really do want to save for future reference. Yesterday as I was trying to (**4**) .... my mobile phone files, I could have searched for those few precious messages, saved them and deleted the rest. But I didn't. Instead I saved the whole lot. That was much easier, took about five seconds and only used a fraction of the storage space (**5**) .... But this really wasn't a good idea. In (**6**) .... , I have effectively 'deleted' the few (**7**) .... messages I wanted to keep, because I will never have time to search for the ones that I might, someday, like to re-read. And although I (**8**) .... myself quite an organised person, the chances are I won't be able to (**9**) .... I've even got them.

I see this as part of a (**10**) .... problem. In the digital age it's too easy to hang onto every little social exchange and every photo. We are no longer in a position to (**11**) .... whether something is valuable or worthless. We need to keep (**12**) .... ourselves that we can't remember everything.

EXAM TIP

When you have finished, read the whole text to make sure it makes sense and there are no gaps. If necessary, make a guess.

2 **For questions 1–12, decide which answer (A, B, C or D) best fits each gap. There is an example at the beginning (0).**

0 **A** approximately	**B** generally	**C** normally	**D** probably
1 **A** uninteresting	**B** right	**C** useless	**D** meaningless
2 **A** preserving	**B** maintaining	**C** recording	**D** remembering
3 **A** quantity	**B** total	**C** handful	**D** list
4 **A** sort out	**B** make up	**C** work out	**D** take up
5 **A** open	**B** available	**C** empty	**D** vacant
6 **A** time	**B** reality	**C** certainty	**D** agreement
7 **A** definite	**B** suitable	**C** relevant	**D** sure
8 **A** believe	**B** think	**C** consider	**D** judge
9 **A** remind	**B** memorise	**C** reflect	**D** recall
10 **A** grander	**B** wider	**C** clearer	**D** looser
11 **A** believe	**B** consider	**C** judge	**D** think
12 **A** recalling	**B** reminding	**C** reflecting	**D** memorising

3 **Check your answers and make sure you understand why the incorrect options are incorrect.**

4 **Discuss in pairs: What do you do with old text messages?**

Multiple choice (Part 1)

▶ **EXAM** FOCUS p.204

1 ▶ **2.16 You will hear people talking in different situations. For each question, choose the best answer, A, B or C.**

> **EXAM TIP**
>
> Underline the key words in the question and make sure the option you choose answers this question.

1 You overhear a conversation between two friends. What did the woman find difficult when she was learning Chinese?

    A the writing

    B the grammar

    C the pronunciation

2 You hear a woman describing her work colleagues. What does she say about her colleagues?

    A They are unsociable.

    B They only talk about work.

    C They gossip about each other too much.

3 You hear a man telling a friend about travelling alone. What disadvantage does he mention?

    A There is no support when things go wrong.

    B There is no opportunity to share memories afterwards.

    C There is no one to discuss problems with at meal times.

4 You hear a student talking about his future plans. What is the student thinking of doing as soon as he finishes university?

    A getting a job in a zoo

    B becoming a journalist

    C working as a conservation volunteer

5 You overhear a woman talking on the phone. Who is she talking to?

    A her son

    B her boss

    C her friend

6 You hear two friends talking at a party. Why doesn't the woman enjoy parties?

    A She finds them tiring.

    B It's difficult to meet new people.

    C She can't hear what people are saying.

7 You hear a woman describing a problem. How does she feel about the problem?

    A sorry

    B angry

    C confused

8 You hear a man and a woman talking about an old photo. Why do they like the photo?

    A They think they look young.

    B It reminds them of a happy event.

    C They prefer the fashion at that time.

Speaking

2 **How do you feel about the following things?**

1 learning a language

2 going to parties

3 travelling alone

4 remembering phone and pin numbers

5 looking at old photos

Vocabulary

expressions with *time*

3 **Match sentences 1–4 with the responses A–D.**

1 I can't believe it's the end of July already.

2 Granddad had a computer before anyone else in his office, didn't he?

3 My dad has finally bought a new car.

4 My boss is always telling us to stop chatting.

A I know. Doesn't time fly?!

B He's right. Time is money!

C That's right. He was ahead of his time.

D At last! That's not before time!

4 **How far do you agree that**

1 time is money?

2 time flies?

Reflexive pronouns

▶ **GRAMMAR** REFERENCE p.173

1 **What's the difference in meaning between the following sentences?**

1 **A** Florence reminded herself that there was nothing to worry about.
   B Florence reminded her that there was nothing to worry about.
   C Florence herself reminded her that there was nothing to worry about.

2 **A** Suzy and Sam blamed themselves for losing the photographs.
   B Suzy and Sam blamed each other for losing the photographs.

3 **A** I went there myself.
   B I went there by myself.

LANGUAGE TIP

- Use reflexive pronouns with transitive verbs (verbs that take a direct object) when the subject and object are the same person. *I keep reminding **myself** (NOT me) of the number.*
- Intransitive verbs (verbs which do not take a direct object) e.g. *remember, relax, feel* etc. do not need a reflexive pronoun.

---

2 **Complete the sentences with a pronoun (e.g. *me*), a reflexive pronoun (e.g. *myself)* or (-) when no pronoun is needed.**

1 At the party a man I didn't know recognised me from work and came and introduced .... to me.

2 We enjoyed .... a lot at the party.

3 My boyfriend is very forgetful so I always remind .... to take his keys and wallet when he goes out.

4 My parents think because I forget things a lot, I don't know how to look after ....

5 My husband can't relax .... at parties because he's worried he'll forget someone's name.

6 Stop pulling my hair. You're hurting ....!

7 She blames .... for the flood because she forgot to turn off the taps.

8 My brother was so good at the piano that our parents always compared .... to Mozart!

3 **Decide where the reflexive pronoun can go in these sentences to give emphasis.**

1 The president of the bank apologised for losing my money.

2 I never have a problem remembering numbers.

3 Even Einstein occasionally made mistakes with numbers.

4 I think you should tell him.

4 **Work in pairs. Think of at least three pieces of advice to give people who have difficulty remembering names, numbers, English vocabulary or dates. Use the verbs in the box to help you.**

give	remind	send	tell	test	write

Example: Keep reminding yourself of the number.

5 **Share your advice with the class. Did you have anything on your list that nobody else thought of?**

Speaking

1 **Discuss the questions with a partner.**

1 Do you always apologise in these situations?

    A being late
    B forgetting a friend's birthday
    C forgetting your homework
    D losing your temper
    E breaking something
    F having an argument

2 When you know you've done something wrong, is it better to deny it or take responsibility?

Informal email of apology (Part 2)

▶ **WRITING** REFERENCE p.185

2 **Choose the correct word.**

Apologising

1 I'm afraid I *offer/owe* you an apology.

2 I *can/can't* apologise enough for *forgetting/forget* your birthday.

3 I'm *terribly/absolutely* sorry for…

4 I *would/must* apologise for…

5 Please could you also *give/make* my apologies to (name of person).

Explaining and giving excuses

6 It happened *by/with* accident.

7 I didn't *aim/mean* to upset you.

8 I did it *by/for* mistake.

9 It wasn't my *fault/problem*.

Claiming responsibility

10 I'm afraid it was all my *fault/responsibility*.

11 I must *have/take* the blame.

Asking for forgiveness

12 I hope you will *accept/take* my apology.

13 I hope you can *forgive/forget* my stupidity.

Offering to make things better

14 To make it *over/up* to you, how about I buy you another?

3 **Which phrases in Activity 2 are semi-formal and which are informal?**

4 **Work in pairs. Read the exam task and discuss the kind of information you should include, and in which paragraph.**

> You received an invitation to a friend's party but you lost it, forgot to reply and missed the party. Write an email apologising to your friend and explaining your behaviour. Suggest how you could make it up to your friend.
> Do not write any postal addresses. You should write **120–180** words.

5 **Write your email. Then check your work for spelling, grammar and punctuation mistakes, and make sure you have written between 120 and 180 words.**

1 Complete the text with one of the words in the box. You will need to use some words more than once.

ability	able	could	couldn't
know	managed	unable	

Learning to live again

Six years ago, Claire Robertson woke from a coma, surrounded by her husband and children. She had no idea who they were.

One day I woke up in hospital surrounded by my husband and four children. I (**1**) .... recognise any of them. I had lost my memory. The first person I was (**2**) .... to recognise was my youngest son. This was after I had been in hospital for over five weeks. He spoke to me from behind a curtain and it was his voice that I was (**3**) .... to recognise.

I had to believe that my husband was who he said he was but I was (**4**) .... to remember anything about him or our previous life together. I was convinced that I (**5**) .... never have been married to him or lived in our house. I didn't (**6**) .... how to find my way around the house and I'd lost the (**7**) .... to cook. Things started to get better when I began to write things down. And slowly I've (**8**) .... to piece together some memories. But much of the time I am still a stranger in my own world. I'm (**9**) .... to watch family videos, which remind me of the twenty years I've lost, without crying. Still, I'm very grateful for the love of my family. I (**10**) .... have got this far without them.

2 Choose the correct word, A, B or C.

1 She comes .... as being very shy.

   A across   **B** up   **C** round

2 We came .... the idea after a lot of consideration.

   A out   **B** up with   **C** across

3 I'd never come .... him before but he seemed to know who I was.

   A out   **B** across   **C** up

4 We've got a revision test coming .... soon.

   A down   **B** up   **C** over

5 My parents eventually came .... to the idea of having a party at home for my eighteenth.

   A out   **B** up   **C** round

6 She's always coming .... with coughs and colds.

   A up   **B** down   **C** across

7 His secret will come .... one of these days.

   A out   **B** round   **C** up

8 The film comes .... on Friday. We'll need to book tickets.

   A across   **B** up with   **C** out

3 Complete the second sentence so that it has a similar meaning to the first sentence, using no more than five words, including the word given.

1 'We did it on our own', they said proudly.
   THEMSELVES
   They said they ...., which made them proud.

2 'The accident was all my fault', she cried.
   BLAMED
   She .... accident.

3 'I always put a note in my diary about my friends' birthdays', she said.
   REMINDS
   She always .... her friends' birthdays by putting a note in her diary.

4 'I am very sorry I'm late', he said.
   APOLOGISED
   He .... late.

5 'I might become a doctor. I haven't decided yet', she said.
   THINKING
   She said that she .... a doctor.

6 'I believe I am a very lucky person', he said.
   CONSIDERS
   He .... a very lucky person.

Say what you mean

Speaking

1 **Work in pairs and discuss the questions.**

1 How much variation is there in people's speech in different parts of your country?

2 Are there any accents you find particularly attractive?

3 How easy is it to change your accent? Why might some people want to do this?

2 **When people make these gestures, what are they trying to communicate?**

1 shrugging their shoulders

2 raising their eyebrows

3 shaking their head

4 crossing their fingers

5 rolling their eyes

3 **What gestures do you frequently use when speaking? Do you think gestures mean the same in all languages? Why do some cultures use gestures more?**

Multiple matching (Part 3)

▶ **EXAM** FOCUS p.205

4 ▶ **2.17** **You will hear five different speakers talking about communicating with people. For speakers 1–5, choose from the list (A–F) what each person says. Use the letters only once. There is one extra letter which you do not need to use.**

A It's a mistake to think that all women are good communicators.

B Some people give the wrong impression by the way they speak.

C Some accents are considered more attractive than others.

D Most people change the way they speak in different situations.

E The gestures people use give away important information about them.

F The way people speak is an important part of their identity.

Speaker 1 ☐
Speaker 2 ☐
Speaker 3 ☐
Speaker 4 ☐
Speaker 5 ☐

5 **Work in pairs and discuss how true you think these statements are.**

1 Women are better listeners than men.

2 Men are better at public speaking.

3 Women are better at expressing their emotions than men.

4 Men don't really talk about personal issues with their friends.

say, speak, talk and *tell*

6 **Complete the sentences with the correct form of the verbs.**

say   speak   talk   tell

1 I don't .... a word of Chinese but I want to learn.

2 Everyone .... I have a big mouth and I shouldn't talk so much.

3 Don't .... me you haven't sent the invitations yet!

4 Why don't you just .... there's been a misunderstanding? I'm sure she'll forgive you.

5 That was a very silly thing to .... to her.

6 We're not very good at .... about our feelings.

7 **Which of the words go with *tell* or *talk*? Copy and complete the table below.**

the difference   a joke   lies   rubbish
(someone) a secret   sense   a story
the truth   to yourself

tell	talk

8 **Choose the correct verb to complete the expressions. Then match the examples with the meanings A–F.**

1 It goes without *speaking/saying* that it's easier to learn a language when you're young.

2 Actions *speak/say* louder than words.

3 Just *say/speak* the word if you need anything.

4 He hasn't got much to *say/speak* for himself.

5 Generally *speaking/saying*, I think women are better communicators than men.

6 I have more respect for a politician who *says/speaks* their mind.

A says what they are thinking

B on the whole

C don't hesitate to ask

D everyone knows this

E says very little

F what you do is more important than what you say.

Ways of speaking

9 **Complete the sentences with the correct form of the verbs in the box.**

mumble   mutter   whisper   yell

1 My teacher .... at me in front of the whole class because I'd forgotten my homework again.

2 You can only .... in the library.

3 My dad .... to himself when he doesn't agree with politicians on the TV.

4 Some people in my class always .... the answers and I can't understand what they're saying.

10 **Work with a partner. Think of some situations when**

1 actions speak louder than words.

2 it's best to speak your mind.

3 it's acceptable to yell at someone.

4 it's rude to whisper.

it is, *there is*

▶ **GRAMMAR** REFERENCE p.170

1 **Choose the correct pronoun. Both answers may be possible.**

1 *It/There* will be very hot so you don't have to wear a jacket and tie.
2 *It/There* always used to be arguments about who paid the bill when we ate out.
3 *It/There* seems to be a lack of communication.
4 *It/There* once used to be unacceptable to eat in the street.
5 *It/There* might be a good idea to find out what the customs are before you visit a country.
6 *It/There* is a long time until dinner so have a snack now.

2 **Complete these sentences with *it* or *there* and a form of *be* if necessary.**

1 .... not unusual to have dinner at 10.30p.m.
2 .... common for men to greet each other with a kiss on the cheek.
3 .... might sometimes be applause when a guest arrives.
4 .... no need to tip the waiters in restaurants.

3 **In which countries are the customs in Activity 2 true? There may be more than one answer.**

Argentina   China   Japan   Saudi Arabia

4 **Use sentences with *it* and *there* to describe customs in your country.**

Use of English (Part 4)

▶ **EXAM** FOCUS p.203

EXAM TIP

Don't add any words that are unnecessary or change the meaning of the sentence. The 'key word' must not be changed and must be included in your 2–5 words.

5 **For questions 1–8, complete the second sentence so that it has a similar meaning to the first sentence, using the word given. Do not change the word given. You must use between two and five words, including the word given.**

1 Someone said the town has a good Chinese restaurant. **THERE**
I believe .... Chinese restaurant in town.

2 I had a wonderful time and I really enjoyed seeing everyone again. **GREAT**
I had a wonderful time and .... everyone again.

3 The weather forecast has predicted more snow. **GOING**
According to the weather forecast, ... more snow.

4 She said she was really pleased you could all come. **WONDERFUL**
She said .... you could all come.

5 The park used to have a playground for children. **BE**
In the park .... a playground for children.

6 Most people think that nurses need to be paid more. **NECESSARY**
Most people think that .... nurses more.

7 He said I didn't need to make an appointment. **NO**
He said .... for me to make an appointment..

8 I would suggest taking your coat. **MIGHT**
I think that .... a good idea to take your coat.

Interview (Part 1)

▶ **EXAM** FOCUS p.206

1 Tick the things you should do in Part 1 of the Speaking test.

1 ask the examiner questions ☐
2 speak to both examiners ☐
3 answer personal questions ☐
4 give opinions about things ☐
5 talk to your partner ☐
6 answer the same questions as your partner ☐

2 Check your answers by looking at the Exam focus.

3 Choose a topic and write three questions about it to ask other students. Use the ideas in the box to help you.

family	free time	future plans	holidays
home town	likes and dislikes		work/studies

4 Work in groups. Practise asking and answering each other's questions.

Long turn (Part 2)

▶ **EXAM** FOCUS p.206

5 Look at the photos and the exam task. Which of the following will you need to do?

1 compare ☐
2 speculate ☐
3 describe in detail ☐
4 give a personal reaction ☐
5 discuss advantages and disadvantages ☐
6 give examples ☐
7 use paraphrases ☐
8 agree and disagree ☐

6 Work in pairs.

Student A: Do the task on this page.

Student B: Turn to page 156. Take turns to do your task. Try to speak for a minute each.

> Student A: Here are your photographs. They show people trying to communicate a message. I'd like you to compare the photos and say which of these ways of communicating messages is most effective.

EXAM TIP

The examiner will tell you the task but it is also written on the paper with the pictures, so you can remind yourself of it.

Speaking and vocabulary

1 How do dogs communicate with each other and with humans? Use some of this vocabulary.

bark   growl   lick   sniff
mark their territory   raise the hair on their backs
wag their tail

"What? You want something? It has something to do with your food dish? Darn, I wish dogs could talk!"

Gapped text (Part 2)

▶ **EXAM** FOCUS p.201

2 You are going to read an extract from a book about how dogs communicate. Seven sentences have been removed from the article. Choose from sentences A–H the one which fits each gap (1–7). There is one extra sentence which you do not need to use.

EXAM TIP

When you have finished, read through the text to check that it makes sense and that you haven't used a sentence more than once.

3 Compare your answers. Which words or expressions in the text helped you to decide?

Inside a dog's world

Alexandra Horowitz, a psychologist who studies dog behaviour, describes dogs as 'anthropologists among us,' and in her engaging book *Inside of a Dog*, she studies them with the same intensity and affection that they devote to us.

Even in the middle of a busy modern city, we're surrounded by all kinds of animals that share our space and our food, but only one of them bothers to study us.

To rats, crows and cockroaches, we're mostly an irritation and sometimes a threat. Dogs are different. [____ **1**] They also try to control us, persuading us to provide them with food and shelter. People are used as tools to solve the puzzles of closed doors and empty water dishes.

Most interestingly, dogs confirm our prejudices about other people. [____ **2**] But in fact, when their dog greets a stranger with a wagging tail or a growl, he is copying his owner's unconscious signals, which he has gradually worked out through smells and body language.

If we want to understand the life of any animal, we need to think about it from their perspective. We need to know what it can sense and how it responds to this. And, whereas humans see the world, a dog smells it. [____ **3**] Instead they bravely stride up to an unknown object and take a nice deep sniff. When a dog turns its head towards you, it is to let his nose 'look' at you. The eyes just come along for the ride.

Sniffing objects gets smells to the brain via receptor cells in the nose. Humans have around six million of these. Six million seems an enormous amount but some dogs have more than 300 million, which explains their remarkable sense of smell. They put this to great use socially, especially by lifting a leg at every lamp post to convey a message. [____ **4**] Instead, the purpose is for them to leave information about themselves; how often they walk by that spot, their recent victories and how interested they are in mating. In this way, the pile of scents becomes a kind of noticeboard.

Having assumed that the 'kisses' they receive when they return home are a sign of their pet's affection, dog owners might be disappointed to hear of research into wild dog packs, which reports that these puppies also lick their mother's faces on return from hunting, in the hope of getting some food. However, the good news for dog owners is that this behaviour now seems to act as a greeting, to welcome another dog home and find out where they've been and what they've done. So it is not an exaggeration to say that a dog licking you is a way to express happiness that you have returned.

5

All mammals tend to produce the same kinds of sounds to express certain meanings and dogs take advantage of this when they communicate with humans. They are able to vary the length, range, pitch and frequency of their barks in different situations. **6** It has been suggested that dogs learned to develop a wider vocal range as they became domesticated.

7 Look a dog in the eyes, and you get a definite feeling that he's looking back. When information, reassurance or guidance is needed, they seem to inspect our faces. In fact, we are known by our dogs probably far better than we know them. They are amazingly skilful at spying on our every move, knowing about our comings and goings and whether we are anxious or sad. They are students of our behaviour and what makes them especially good is that they never tire of watching out for changes in our expressions, and moods.

A All dog owners think that their pet is a good judge of character.
B Because of this, forgetting what we think we know about dogs is the best way to begin to understand them.
C But what about a dog's ability to see and understand?
D Especially since this behaviour is often accompanied by wagging tails and general excitement.
E However, contrary to popular belief, the main point of this kind of communication is not to mark their territory.
F As a result, most people can tell whether a dog is happy, lonely or aggressive just by listening.
G Unlike wolves, they inspect our actions, interpret our emotions and, over time, learn how to please us.
H Dogs don't touch new things or stare at them as we do.

Speaking

4 **Discuss these questions in groups.**

1 In what ways have any pets you have had communicated with you?
2 In what ways do animals have a good or bad effect on our lives? Use the topics below to help you think.

entertainment   environment   food
health   sport   transport

Vocabulary

idioms: animals

5 **Read sentences 1–8. Then try to work out the meaning of the idioms in sentences A–H and match the two sentences.**

1 Why don't we have the meeting during lunch?
2 I've never seen Anna so nervous.
3 Tom's party was meant to be a secret.
4 My boss is actually quite nice when you get to know her.
5 Nobody even knew Kate was going out with anyone.
6 My kids never care when I tell them off.
7 When she went to university there were lots of other people just as clever as her.
8 The team were really thirsty after playing tennis in that heat.

A Her *bark is worse than her bite*.
B However, Lucy *let the cat out of the bag* by letting him see the invitation.
C So she really *put the cat among the pigeons* by announcing she was getting married.
D This was a shock, because she was *a big fish in a little pond* at school.
E She's *having kittens* about what to do next.
F That way we could *kill two birds with one stone*.
G It's like *water off a duck's back*.
H At the end, they *made a beeline* for the café.

6 **Work in pairs. Make sentences about your own lives, using some of the idioms in Activity 5.**

Subject/verb agreement

▶ **GRAMMAR** REFERENCE p.175

1 Look at examples 1–7 from the article on page 144–5 and choose the correct option.

1 Only one of these animals *bother/bothers* to study us.

2 People *is/are* used as tools to solve the puzzles of closed doors and empty water dishes.

3 All dog owners *think/thinks* that their dog is a good judge of character.

4 Sniffing objects *get/gets* smells to the dog via receptor cells in the nose.

5 Six million *seem/seems* an enormous amount.

6 The good news *is/are* that this behaviour now seems to act as a greeting.

7 When information, reassurance or guidance *is/are* needed, dogs seem to inspect our faces.

2 Match the examples in Activity 1 with the following rules.

A singular verb is used after

A nouns which end in *s* but are not plural.

B expressions of quantity, measurement, time and distance.

C words/expressions such as *everyone, anything, hardly anyone, only one of, more than one.*

D abstract/uncountable nouns.

E an *-ing* clause as the subject.

A plural verb is used after

F nouns which are plural but don't end in *s*.

G words/expressions such as *both of, all, plenty of, the majority of.*

3 Choose the correct alternative in each of these sentences. Both may be possible.

1 The police *has/have* charged him with animal cruelty.

2 We gave her advice on looking after her dog, but she didn't take *it/them*.

3 1,000 dollars *is/are* a lot of money to pay for a puppy.

4 Both my sisters *understand/understands* what a commitment having a pony can be.

5 Everyone *has/have* fallen in love with my new kitten.

6 Neither of them *know/knows* how to train a dog properly.

7 Our family *has/have* always had a variety of different pets.

8 There *is/are* a couple of dog bowls over there.

4 Read this information about animals and decide which form of the verb goes in each gap.

Did you know?

- Despite the saying 'as blind as a bat', the majority of bats **(1)** .... (*be*) able to see perfectly well.

- The name 'mouse' comes from the Sanskrit for 'little thief'. People **(2)** .... (*have*) provided food for them ever since farming began. However, although everyone **(3)** .... (*seem*) to believe that mice like cheese, most **(4)** .... (*prefer*) chocolate.

- Rabbits are the world's third most popular pet. All modern rabbits **(5)** .... (*have*) been bred from the European wild rabbit.

- 85 percent of cats' time **(6)** .... (*be*) spent doing nothing.

- Medical advice **(7)** .... (*have*) suggested that owning a pet is good for your health.

- Current news **(8)** .... (*be*) claiming that dogs can be successful at detecting cancer.

5 Complete these sentences so that they are true for you.

1 Some of my friends…

2 The news these days…

3 People who live in towns…

4 The majority of football fans…

5 The staff at the school I go/went to…

6 Most of my family…

Open cloze (Part 2)

▶ **EXAM** FOCUS p.202

1 **Read the article and answer the questions in pairs.**

1 What is unusual about Kanzi and Rico?

2 In what ways do scientists disagree about why animals can't speak?

3 Which group of animals are scientists particularly interested in studying, and why?

2 **For questions 1–12, read the text and think of the word which best fits each gap. There is an example at the beginning.**

The animal world's communication kings

In an attempt to understand how human language came about, scientists are studying animals that, like us, use sound to communicate.

The majority of mammals **(0)** _are_ able to understand some language, even though they can't 'talk back'. Kanzi, a bonobo ape, understands about 3,000 words. Even for our closest relatives, 3,000 words **(1)** .... a very impressive number to know. In fact, **(2)** .... is more than any other mammal, with the exception of humans. But even apes **(3)** .... Kanzi can only produce a very small number of sounds, **(4)** .... they can 'talk back' using hand gestures. And Rico, the famous dog **(5)** .... is believed to be able to recognise the names **(6)** .... over 200 toys, can only bark and growl, rather **(7)** .... actually being able to 'speak'.

So why is it that most mammals can understand but not speak? There is a small **(8)** .... of scientists who believe that it is due to physical factors such as tongue control. However, others **(9)** .... suggested that the key could be genetic, as with some humans.

Despite this inability to speak, **(10)** .... are some animals – around six species in all – that can hear a sound, copy it and then reproduce it in order to interact socially. Dolphins can copy whistles, whales can learn and copy songs and parrots are famous for copying sounds. Interestingly, the animals that can do this are dissimilar both to humans and to **(11)** .... other. As a result, scientists are eager to study **(12)** .... brain pathways in order to find out what gives this group of animals their unique 'vocal learning ability.' They hope that this will shed some light on our unique talent.

3 **Check your answers. Which answers related to subject/verb agreement?**

4 **Discuss these questions.**

1 Which method of animal communication do you think is the most interesting?

2 Which animals would you most like to be able to communicate with?

Speaking

1 **Have you ever owned a pet? What are the good and bad things about it?**

2 **What pet do you think would be a good choice for someone who**

1 wants to get healthy?
2 hasn't got much money?
3 hasn't got much time?
4 is lonely?
5 lives in a small flat with no garden?
6 has children?

©Glenn and Gary McCoy/Distributed by Universal Uclick via CartoonStock.com

3 **Tick (✓) the three ways of giving advice which you would be more likely to use in a formal situation.**

1 You could…
2 In my view, you ought to…
3 If I were you, I'd…
4 Why don't you…?
5 Wouldn't it be better to…?
6 I'd strongly advise you to…
7 You should…
8 The best solution would be to…

▶ **GRAMMAR** REFERENCE p.171

4 **Work in pairs.**

Student A: you want to get a pet. Choose one of the situations in Activity 2 and ask your partner for advice.

Student B: give advice.

Letter of advice (Part 2)

▶ **WRITING** REFERENCE p.185

5 **Read the exam task. What advice would you give to the friend?**

> A friend of yours has written to you asking for advice. She lives alone and wants a pet for company, but she is out at work all day and hasn't got a garden.
>
> Write your **letter** in **120–180** words.

6 **Work in pairs and plan your letter.**

1 How many paragraphs will you write?
2 What information will you include in each paragraph?
3 Who is the target reader? Will your language be informal or semi-formal?
4 How will you begin and end the letter?

7 **Now use your plan to write the letter.**

EXAM TIP

You should end a letter to a friend with an informal phrase such as *Love, All the best* or *See you soon.*

8 **Check your first draft. Think about the following things. Have you**

1 answered the question and included all necessary information?
2 checked the number of words you have written?
3 organised your writing into paragraphs?
4 written your letter in the appropriate style for the target reader?
5 used a range of vocabulary and different grammatical structures?
6 made any grammatical, spelling or punctuation mistakes?
7 written clearly?

1 Choose the correct word.

1 *It/There* is unlikely to be time for questions after the presentation.

2 A high percentage of people *is/are* unable to remember their own mobile phone number.

3 *It/There* is some evidence that owning a pet is good for your health.

4 Both cats and dogs *is/are* unable to recognise human faces.

5 Only one of my brothers *has/have* a problem with remembering people's names.

6 Neither my brother nor my sister *like/likes* cats.

7 The police *has/have* found my grandmother's missing dog.

8 Information on ways to improve your memory *is/are* available on the website.

9 I think *it/there* can be a huge problem if you don't understand someone else's culture.

10 *It/There* may be a problem with our computer.

2 Choose the correct option to complete these sentences.

1 My students take no notice when I shout at them. It's like water off a duck's ....
   A head   **B** back   **C** feathers

2 Cycling to work means I get exercise too, so I'm killing two .... with one stone.
   A birds   **B** ducks   **C** rats

3 In her school sports club, Jo was a big fish in a little..........
   A river   **B** lake   **C** pond

4 Dan put the cat among the .... when he resigned.
   A blackbirds   **B** owls   **C** pigeons

5 Actions .... louder than words.
   A speak   **B** say   **C** talk

6 He's very quiet and never seems to have much to .... for himself.
   A speak   **B** say   **C** talk

7 I wish you would speak more clearly and not .... like that.
   A whisper   **B** mumble   **C** mutter

8 He really does .... rubbish sometimes.
   A say   **B** speak   **C** talk

3 Choose the correct preposition to complete the sentences. Sometimes more than one answer is possible.

off ahead through in over down into on of

1 We went .... the plan for his escape many times.

2 The climb was called .... because of bad weather.

3 The prison officers had to give .... to the prisoners' demands.

4 The effect of the medicine soon began to wear .... and my headache returned.

5 He insisted .... carrying all my equipment because I was so tired.

6 I've never been involved .... a serious accident.

7 She seems confident .... her ability to pass the test.

8 They had been .... a lot of difficult times so they deserved their success.

9 We were asked to hand .... our documents to the police for them to check.

10 The instructor told us .... for not using the equipment safely, like he taught us.

11 The search for the missing boy turned .... a murder hunt.

12 Against everyone's advice the team went .... with the bike race.

13 The computer network has gone .... so I can't send any emails this afternoon.

14 The police succeeded .... catching the thief very quickly and efficiently.

15 He was suspected .... the crime even though there were no witnesses.

4 There is a mistake in each of the following sentences. Underline the mistakes and correct them. There may be more than one possibility.

1 If Sarah had listened to her parents she will never have become a world champion.

2 If my father doesn't speak Russian, he wouldn't have got the job in Moscow.

3 If I had saved more money I would been able to go on holiday next month.

4 If I were younger I work much harder.

5 If only that car doesn't cost so much, I would buy it.

6 I wish my brother helped me more with my homework.

7 Suppose we will not go to the party this evening.

8 I'd rather you come home before midnight.

9 You aren't allowed using Facebook in the college library.

10 It was a waste of time doing all that research. We needn't to do it.

11 They have just have their car stolen.

12 We're getting a friend looked after our house while we're away.

13 After trying several times we could finally get tickets for the show.

14 I need to remind me of my passwords.

15 You shouldn't blame myself for losing your wallet – it wasn't my fault.

PROGRESS TEST 3

Multiple-choice cloze (Part 1)

5 For questions 1–12, read the text below and decide which answer (A, B, C or D) best fits each gap. There is an example at the beginning.

Watch your (body) language

Most research now shows that as much as 70–80% of human communication may be non-verbal. This kind of communication has been **(0)** _widely_ studied since ancient times in an **(1)** .... to understand people's characters, and experts have endlessly **(2)** .... the significance of the way we move and position our bodies. **(3)** .... many feel that the study of body language can be over-simplistic, there is some evidence to show that some postures and movements indicate **(4)** .... emotional states clearly.

The **(5)** .... people shake hands, for example, can be a good indicator of the power balance between them. Pulling the person towards you or grabbing hold of someone's elbow can show you want to **(6)** .... control.

Personal space is another interesting area. The vast **(7)** .... of westerners feel uncomfortable if a friend stands closer than 45cm, although this will **(8)** .... from country to country.

(9) .... eye contact makes you appear more confident, whilst glancing away at key points in the conversation or rolling your eyes can make you seem dishonest or bored. **(10)** .... of these should be **(11)** .... during an interview!

And finally, it is likely that, if someone is **(12)** .... to you, they will copy the way you stand or move. If you're trying to make somebody relax, it can also help to 'mirror' their movements in this way.

Open cloze (Part 2)

6 For questions 13–24, read the text below and think of the word that best fits each gap. Use only one word in each gap. There is an example at the beginning.

Life without limits

Tim Shieff shouts from a rooftop nine metres **(0)** _above_ us. 'You should see the view from here! It's awesome!' Just a **(13)** .... seconds earlier Tim was down among the shoppers, on the streets of his hometown. He suddenly began climbing up a series of walls **(14)** .... he reached a rooftop world, **(15)** .... is invisible to **(16)** .... rest of the city's residents. Then, with a leap, he was over a 3.6m gap to the next building, landing on a flat roof and pausing for a one-armed handstand.

This is nothing extraordinary for Shieff. The 22-year-old is a world champion of freerunning, which he defines **(17)** .... 'the way you create a path without following the normal options presented to you.'

Shieff **(18)** .... to be a breakdancer, and now combines dance moves with those from gymnastics and acrobatics to create **(19)** .... own very individual style of movement. It was after he **(20)** .... seen the TV programme *Jump London* that he became inspired to discover rooftops **(21)** .... other young freerunners who he met online. He has now found **(22)** .... at the forefront of a young sport which is attracting more and more international attention, especially since freerunning started **(23)** .... used in music videos, films and advertisements.

Shieff agrees that it is a risky sport, but adds that it is a calculated risk, based **(24)** .... years of practice, and he is always in control.

0	**A** highly	**B** deeply	**C** widely	**D** strongly
1	**A** act	**B** action	**C** attempt	**D** approach
2	**A** talked	**B** argued	**C** disagreed	**D** discussed
3	**A** But	**B** Although	**C** However	**D** Nevertheless
4	**A** actual	**B** typical	**C** particular	**D** singular
5	**A** way	**B** style	**C** custom	**D** manner
6	**A** be	**B** take	**C** bring	**D** stay
7	**A** number	**B** quantity	**C** majority	**D** amount
8	**A** vary	**B** alter	**C** compare	**D** contrast
9	**A** Being	**B** Doing	**C** Giving	**D** Making
10	**A** Both	**B** Some	**C** Neither	**D** All
11	**A** missed	**B** avoided	**C** removed	**D** prevented
12	**A** attracted	**B** appealed	**C** approved	**D** fascinated

Word formation (Part 3)

7 For questions 25–34, read the text below. Use the word given in capitals at the end of some of the lines to form a word that fits the gap in the same line. There is an example at the beginning.

Creating a palace for your memories

Memory champions use 'memory palaces' that (0) ..*rely*.. on the human brain's natural (25) .... with spatial and visual memory. They think up images to represent everything they want to remember – the most effective images are often the (26) ....

These images are then (27) .... inside the rooms of the 'palace', an imaginary (28) .... in the brain that can be anything from a childhood home to the city library. For example, if you're trying to remember groceries you need to buy at the store on the way home, (29) .... your memory palace with the butter on the doors and the soap on the stairs. Many people find it hard to believe at first that this method is (30) .... but it does actually work.

The 'mind sport' of Memory was (31) .... in 1991. Today there are competitors from thirty countries (32) .... in the sport, with the aim of becoming the next World Memory Champion. None of the top memory champions would (33) .... claim to be born with a great memory. All of them have learnt special (34) .... to develop their skills, and practise to a high level to get them to the top of the sport.

RELIABLE
ABLE

STRANGER
STORAGE

BUILD

IMAGINATION

HELP

CREATIVE

PARTICIPATION

NECESSARY

TECHNICAL

Key word transformations (Part 4)

8 For questions 35–42, complete the second sentence so that it has a similar meaning to the first sentence, using the word given. Do not change the word given. You must use between two and five words, including the word given. Here is an example.

Example:
I'd strongly advise you not to get a dog just yet.

IF

I wouldn't get a dog just yet ....*if I were*...... *you.*

35 Maybe it's possible to get someone to train it.
COULD
Maybe .... to train it.

36 Apparently, the health benefits of owning a pet are huge.
THERE
Apparently, ... to owning a pet.

37 You mustn't cycle without wearing a helmet.
ALLOWED
You .... cycle without wearing a helmet.

38 Someone had already called the police so it wasn't necessary for you to call them.
NEED
Someone had already called the police so you .... them.

39 My parents would prefer me not to travel alone.
RATHER
My parents .... travel alone.

40 My grandfather would love to do extreme sports but he's too old.
WISHES
My grandfather .... do extreme sports but he's too old.

41 'Don't forget to text me when you arrive,' Jake's mother said.
REMINDED
Jake's mother .... when he arrived.

42 I couldn't finish the race.
MANAGE
I .... finish the race.

Visuals for Speaking Tests

Unit 3, Speaking focus, Activity 7
Student A

Your photos show people preparing or receiving gifts. Compare the photos and say what makes people happy about giving or receiving gifts.

> **What makes people happy about giving or receiving gifts?**

Unit 5, Speaking focus, Activity 5
Task 1

Student A: Look at the photos, which show people shopping for food. Compare the photos and say what the advantages and disadvantages are of shopping in these different ways.

Student B: Do you prefer to go shopping in the town or shop online?

> **What are the advantages and disadvantages of shopping in these different ways?**

Unit 11, Speaking focus, Activity 5

> **Which person is taking the most risks?**

Unit 7, Speaking focus, Activity 5
Task 1

Student A: Look at the photos, which show unusual places to live. Compare the photos and say why you think people might choose to live in these places .

Student B: Which of these places would you prefer to live in?

> **Why do you think people might choose to live in places like this?**

Unit 3, Speaking focus, Activity 7

Student B

Your photos show people who love horses. Compare the photos and say what might make these people feel so strongly about their horses.

> **What might make these people feel so strongly about their horses?**

Unit 5, Speaking focus, Activity 5

Task 2

Student B: Look at the photos, which show people having dinner. Compare the photos and say what the people enjoy about eating in these different ways.

Student A: Do you prefer to eat in front of the TV or sit at the table with other people?

> **What might the people enjoy about eating in these different ways?**

Unit 7, Speaking focus, Activity 5

Task 2

Student A: Look at the photos, which show unusual places to work. Compare the photos and say how difficult you think it would be to work in these places.

Student B: Are you an adventurous person?

> **How difficult do you think it would be to work in these places?**

Unit 11, Speaking focus, Activity 6

> **Which person is taking the most risks?**

Unit 13, Speaking focus, Activity 5

Student B: Compare the two different ways of remembering vocabulary and say what the people might find effective about doing these things.

Student A: How do you remember vocabulary best?

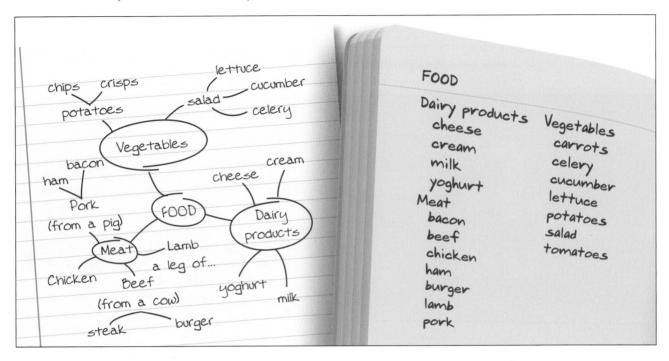

Unit 14, Speaking focus, Activity 6

Student B: Here are your photographs. They show people communicating in different ways. I'd like you to compare the photos and say which form of communication would be the most difficult to learn how to do.

Communication activities

Unit 2, Use of English focus, Activity 3

PERSONALITY QUIZ

How to score:

Very likely = 5 points
Quite likely = 4 points
Neither likely nor unlikely = 3 points
Quite unlikely = 2 points
Very unlikely = 1 point

1 + 4 + 2 + 2 + 1 → 5
5   5   +5
*   15*

Find out

how *sociable* you are (add your scores for questions 1 and 5)
how *organised* you are (add your scores for questions 2 and 6)
how *creative* you are (add your scores for questions 3 and 4)

1 + 1
4 + 5
2 + 2

	7–10 points	5–6 points	1–4 points
Sociability My score =	You are adventurous and sociable. You enjoy going out and meeting new people. You're confident and fun to be with but you get bored easily.	You are a bit of both. Read both descriptions to find out more.	You are independent and shy. You need time to be alone. You take a long time to make new friends. You aren't easily led by other people.
Organisation My score =	You are organised and practical. You like to be in charge. You're very good at getting things done but you find it difficult to relax.	You are a bit of both. Read both descriptions to find out more.	You are relaxed and spontaneous. You don't like to plan ahead. You think there are more important things than being on time and meeting deadlines.
Creativity My score =	You are imaginative and creative. You're always full of ideas. You prefer to look at the big picture rather than focusing on detail.	You are a bit of both. Read both descriptions to find out more.	You are thoughtful and realistic. You pay attention to detail. You're cautious when making decisions. You always see both sides of an argument.

Unit 10, Listening focus, Activity 2

LIFESTYLE

Results: Add up your scores.

	1	2	3	4	5	6	7	8
3 points	A	C	C	A	B	C	C	A
2 points	B	A	B	C	A	A	B	B
1 point	C	B	A	B	C	B	A	C

Circle friendships
Score: 12 or less

You have, or want, a wide circle of friends, and people might say you have a gift for friendship. You seek to know people in many walks of life, with different lifestyles and characters. You like nothing more than being with them all but you may also worry that different friends of yours won't get on. This shows that you have many parts to your character, and different friends appeal to different parts. The risk of your friendship type is that you may not actually get to know any of your friends very well. They are drawn to your extrovert character though that can act as a barrier to intimacy.

Ladder friendships
Score: 13-18

You view life as a journey of change, evolution and progress. You therefore value friends who share your journey, or who are experiencing the same things as you. You like to encourage and help your friends get on in life, and value it when they encourage and help you. You're very self-confident and enjoy meeting new people and make friends easily. But sometimes old friends will feel you've left them behind, though they will admit that you are an inspiring person to be with, someone who both challenges and excites them.

Soulmate friendships
Score 19-24

You value a small number of close friends, perhaps just one, and regard other people in your life as acquaintances. The benefit of soulmate friendship is the chance of knowing someone well, and allowing them to know you. You are loyal and completely trustworthy. You are self-sufficient and don't depend on friendship to maintain your self-esteem. The risk you face is of disappointment with friends, since it's quite hard to meet someone you connect with so strongly. In fact, you may well have had a close friend in the past, and now feel that you don't. You value friendship so much because you know the treasure it offers.

Unit 11, Grammar focus, Activity 7, Student B

Think of what you might say in the following situations. Use *I wish/ if only* and other expressions with hypothetical meaning. Then role-play the situations with your partner.

Situation 1: You are at a theme park with Student A. Student A wants to go on a new roller coaster ride at the theme park. You are afraid of heights and don't want to go on the ride. Try and persuade Student A to choose a different activity.

Situation 2: You are on a walking trip in the mountains with Student A. You are reading the map but you think you are lost. Suggest what action you should take.

Unit 8, Grammar focus, Activity 3

Match the underlined examples to the verb forms in the box.

---

present simple   going to   might   past simple
present continuous   past perfect   will   would

Interviewer: Lauren, how [1]did you hear about this job?

Lauren: Well, I [2]spotted the advert while I was on the internet. [3]I think it's something [4]I'd be good at.

Interviewer: Being an entertainment coordinator [5]will involve looking after very young children. [6]Have you had much experience of doing this?

Lauren: Well, [7]I look after my niece and nephew every month and [8]I'm taking them on a cycling holiday tomorrow.

Interviewer: Well, [9]you might be unlucky, I'm afraid, because [10]I've heard that [11]it's going to rain.

Lauren: Oh [12]I'm sure [13]we'll still have a lot of fun.

Interviewer: Well, [14]you sound very positive, and this is one of the qualities [15]we're looking for. Anyway, enjoy your weekend!

Lauren: Thanks.

Interviewer: Lauren, thanks for coming. [16]We'll write soon, but don't worry if [17]you don't hear anything for a few days.

Find the 'reported' versions of the underlined examples above in the email on page 84.

Unit 11, Grammar focus, Activity 7, Student A

Think of what you might say in the following situations. Use _I wish/if only_ and other expressions with hypothetical meaning. Then role-play the situations with your partner.

Situation 1: You are at a theme park with Student B. You want to go on a new roller coaster ride.

Situation 2: You are lost in the mountains and Student B is reading the map. You know that you are better at reading maps than Student B. You are angry with yourself for getting into this situation.

Unit 4, Listening focus, Activity 1

1B   2A   3C   4A   5C

Unit 8, Listening focus, Activity 3

In my work as a counsellor, I'm already seeing a huge increase in the number of victims of cyber bullying on social network sites and this is a trend that can only get worse. To deal with bullying or other problems that can occur online, social networking counsellors will support people in their cyber relationships using the same counselling skills we use today. The only difference is that, because we'll be online, it'll be easier for people to contact us when they need us – in the evenings, for example. This may mean that we'll have to change our working patterns and work out of office hours.

Unit 5, Grammar focus, Activity 7

Look at the table and choose the correct words in sentences 1–8.

	much	many	a lot of/ lots of	some	a few/ very few	hardly any	a little/a bit of/very little	any	no
In positive sentences		•	•	•	•	•	•		•
In negative sentences	•	•	•					•	
With countable nouns		•	•	•	•	•		•	•
With uncountable nouns	•		•	•		•	•	•	•

1 I don't eat *many/much* fresh fruit.
2 There aren't *a lot of/hardly any* healthy snacks in my local shop.
3 I drink *very few/very little* water.
4 We eat *hardly any/any* meat at home.
5 I drink *a lot of/many* orange juice.
6 I only eat *a little/a few* eggs a week.
7 There isn't *no/any* chocolate in my bag.
8 I always have *some/a few* rice with dinner.

Grammar reference

Contents

1 Adverbs

1.1 Formation of adverbs from adjectives

1 Many adverbs are formed by adding *-ly* to the adjective form of the word, e.g. *clear* → *clearly*.
For adjectives ending in *-y*, drop the *y* and add *-ily*, e.g. *happy* → *happily*.
For adjectives ending in *-le*, drop the *e* and add *-y*, e.g. *gentle* → *gently*.
For adjectives ending in *-ic*, add *-ally*, e.g. *automatic* → *automatically*.

2 Some words ending in *-ly* are adjectives only, not adverbs, e.g. *cowardly, friendly, silly*. If an adverb is needed, a phrase must be used:
*They greeted us **in a friendly way/manner**.*

3 Some words ending in *-ly* can be used both as adjectives and adverbs, e.g. *hourly, daily, nightly*.
*Take the medicine twice **daily** (adv). There is a **daily** (adj) flight to the island.*

4 Some adverbs have the same form as adjectives, e.g. *early, fast, hard, still, straight, better, best, worse, worst.*
*He's got a **fast** (adj) car and he drives it **fast** (adv).*
*She has **straight** (adj) hair. He looked **straight** (adv) at me.*

5 Some adverbs have two forms, one like the adjective and the other form ending in *-ly*, e.g. *clear, close, direct, easy, free, hard, high, late*. There is usually a difference in meaning.
*Stand **clear** of the doors.* (= keep away)
*Try to speak more **clearly**.* (= so we can understand)
*He works very **hard**.* (= he makes a lot of effort)
*He had **hardly** any petrol left.* (= almost none)
*The balloon was **high** up in the sky.* (= a long way up)
*They think very **highly** of you.* (= have a good opinion)
*Children under twelve travel **free**.* (= don't have to pay)
*You can walk **freely** in the hotel grounds.*
(= without restrictions)
*The train arrived **late**.* (= after the time it was expected)
*He's not been very well **lately**.* (= recently)

1.2 Comparison of adverbs

The comparison of adverbs is similar to that of adjectives. See 4.5.

1.3 Adverbs of manner

These adverbs are used to say how the action of the verb is carried out.

1 Common adverbs of manner include *accurately, badly, carefully, patiently, straight* and *well*. They usually come in the middle of the sentence, after the main verb. If the verb has an object, the adverb comes after the object.
He spoke (the words) **clearly**.
She went **straight** *to the house.*

2 Prepositional phrases may also be used adverbially to answer the question *How?*
I ordered the book **over the internet**.
He shouted **in a loud voice**.

1.4 Adverbs of frequency

1 These adverbs are used to talk about how often we do things. We can put them in order from most often to least often like this

always	▲ most often
almost always	
generally/normally/regularly/usually	
frequently/often/sometimes	
occasionally	
almost /never/hardly ever/rarely/seldom	
not ... ever/never	▼ least often

2 In statements and questions, these adverbs come

- after *be* when it is the only verb in the sentence.
  I am **always** *a bit depressed in winter.*
- after the first auxiliary verb when there is more than one verb.
  I have **often** *seen her walking here.*
- before the main verb when there is only one verb.
  We **sometimes** *watch a video on Friday evenings.*
- in questions, after the subject.
  Don't you **usually** *work with Jenny?*

3 In negative sentences, *not* comes before *always, generally, normally, often, regularly* and *usually*.
We **don't often** *see him nowadays.*

4 With imperatives, *always* and *never* come at the beginning of the sentence.
Always *look on the bright side of life.*
Never *refuse an opportunity.*

1.5 Other types of adverbs used to describe frequency

1 These are common adverbs of frequency:

once
twice   } *a day/week/month/year*
five times
several times

every day/week/month/morning/afternoon/evening
every three/couple of/few years
on Monday/Wednesday/weekdays, etc.

2 These adverbs usually come at the end of the sentence, e.g. *I phone my sister* **several times a day**.
He goes jogging **every morning**.
They go abroad **every few years**.
However, they may come at the beginning for emphasis.
Several times a month, *I go to the cinema.*

1.6 Adverbs of attitude

These adverbs do not modify the verb, but express the speaker's opinion or attitude.

1 The following adverbs explain how he/she is feeling: *honestly, personally, seriously,* etc.
Personally, *I think it's wrong to hunt animals.*
Seriously, *this is an important question.*

2 The following adverbs comment on how likely something is: *actually, certainly, clearly, definitely, maybe, obviously, perhaps, possibly, probably, surely,* etc.
Perhaps/Maybe *it will rain tomorrow.*
Surely *he is going to come?*
We'll **probably** *be late.*

3 The following adverbs explain the speaker's reaction to some event: *annoyingly, hopefully, luckily, naturally, surprisingly, understandably,* etc.
Hopefully, *we'll win the match.*
Annoyingly, *I forgot my phone.*

4 Adverbs of attitude usually come at the beginning of the sentence. However, the adverbs *certainly, definitely, possibly* and *probably* usually come in the middle of the sentence, after the verb *be*, before the main verb, or after the first auxiliary verb.
He is **definitely** *not a friend of mine.*
I'll **certainly** *be seeing her tomorrow.*

1.7 Modifiers and intensifiers

USE We can use adverbs to make adjectives, other adverbs and verbs stronger (intensifiers) or weaker (modifiers).

1 We can use these adverbs before gradable adjectives (i.e. adjectives that can be used in the comparative) and adverbs

- *very, extremely, really, particularly, terribly* (emphatic)
- *quite, pretty, fairly, rather* (weaker than *very*)
- *a bit*

I felt **terribly upset** when I heard the news.
He drives **rather fast**.
I thought the story was **a bit silly**.

> **Watch Out!** *quite* has two meanings.
> The picture was **quite** good. (= good but not very good)
> Her cooking was **quite** wonderful. (= very, very good)

2 Adverbs such as *almost, barely, hardly, nearly* and *scarcely* have a negative meaning. They come in the middle of the sentence.
I **almost/nearly** missed the train.
We could **barely** hear the speaker.
She **hardly** knew anyone at the party.

3 Extreme or absolute (non-gradable) adjectives include: *amazing, boiling, disastrous, fantastic, freezing, impossible, marvellous, superb, wonderful*, etc. We can use the following adverbs with extreme adjectives: *absolutely, really, completely*.

The special effects were **absolutely amazing**.
I've just read a **superb** new book about Egypt.
I love swimming in the sea, but it's **absolutely freezing** at this time of year.

4 We can use these adverbs to emphasise both adjectives and verbs: *just, completely, totally* (= in every way).
I **completely/totally** forgot about your birthday.
It's **completely impossible** to finish in time.
You look **just fantastic**.
Let's **just** go.

2 Articles

2.1 The definite article: *the*

We use the definite article *the*

- when the person or thing referred to is unique
  The sun came out and soon we were dry.
  The President is giving a speech tonight.
  the London Marathon, **the Olympic Games**

- to talk about specific things when the context makes it clear what we are referring to
  Your shoes are in **the cupboard**.
  Your dinner's in **the fridge**.

- to talk about previously mentioned things
  A man and a woman walked into the room. **The man** was wearing sunglasses.

- with superlatives
  He's **the bravest person** in the team.

- to talk about a generic class of things
  The bicycle was invented about 200 years ago.
  The tiger is in danger of becoming extinct.

- with oceans, seas, rivers and deserts
  He's sailed across **the Atlantic** and **the Pacific**.
  We went by canoe up **the Orinoco**.
  She said she'd driven across **the Sahara**.

- with plural mountain ranges and island groups
  Are **the Andes** as high as **the Himalayas**?
  The British Isles include **the Isle of Wight** and **the Isle of Man**.

- with continents and countries whose name includes a common noun
  He's from **the Czech Republic**, but he's living in **the United States**.

- with areas
  There is a range of mountains in **the north**.

- with hotels, cinemas, theatres
  They had afternoon tea at **the Ritz**.
  That new Polish film is on at **the Odeon**.

- with newspapers
  The Times, **The Guardian**, **The Independent**

- with national groups
  The English are a mixed race.

2.2 The indefinite article: *a/an*

We use the indefinite article *a/an*

- with (singular) jobs, etc.
  She's **an architect**.
  Is your sister **a football fan**, too?

- with singular countable nouns (mentioned for the first time or when it doesn't matter which one)
  I'd like **a sandwich** and **a glass of orange juice**.
  What you need is **a rest**.

2.2 The indefinite article: *a/an* (continued)

We use the indefinite article *a/an*

- with these numbers: 100, 1,000, 1,000,000
  *There were over **a hundred** people at the wedding.*
  *He made **a million** dollars in one year.*

- in exclamations about singular countable nouns
  *What **an amazing view**!*

2.3 Zero article

1 We use no article (zero article) when talking about

- uncountable, plural and abstract nouns used in their general sense
  *We had awful **weather** on holiday.*
  ***Happiness** isn't the only thing in life.*

- continents and countries
  *They are going to visit **Africa**.*
  *Have you been to **Nepal**?*

- mountains and lakes
  *They are going to climb **Mount Everest**.*
  *Is **Lake Titicaca** in Peru?*

- villages, towns and cities
  ***San Marco** is a pleasant little fishing village.*
  ***Saffron Walden** is a small market town near Cambridge.*
  ***Auckland** is the biggest city in New Zealand.*

- streets, roads, etc.
  *In London, there are some huge shops on **Oxford Street**.*

- magazines
  *Do you read **Time** magazine?*

- illnesses
  *I've got **flu** and Sue's got **indigestion**.*

> **Watch Out!** *I've got **a headache** and I think I'm getting **a cold**.*

2 Also use no article in the following expressions:
to/at/from school/university/college
at home
go home
in/to class
to/in/into/from church
to/in/into/out of prison/hospital/bed
to/at/from work
for/at/to breakfast/lunch/dinner
by car/bus/bicycle/plane/train/tube/boat
on foot
by accident/chance

3 *as/like; as if/as though*

3.1 *like*

1 *like* can be a preposition, meaning *similar to* or *in the same way as*.
  *Do you look **like** your sister?*
  ***Like** John, I hate cooking.*

2 We use the question *What … like?* when we are asking for a description of a person, place or thing.
  *'What's the restaurant **like**?' 'Oh, really good.'*

3 *like* can mean *such as/for example*.
  *Let's buy him something nice **like/such as** a CD.*

4 *feel like* + object/*-ing* is used to talk about something that we want or want to do.
  *I **feel like (eating)** some crisps.*

5 *seem/sound/look like* + object is used to introduce an idea we may not be completely sure about.
  *It **seems like** a good idea.*

6 *like* is not used before an adjective on its own.
  They seem happy. It feels cold.

3.2 *as*

1 *as* can be a preposition, coming before the name of a job or a role, or to describe the purpose of something.
  *She works **as** a sales manager.*
  ***As** your father, I can't allow you to do this.*
  *We use the loft **as** a play room for the kids.*
  *I think of her **as** my best friend.*

2 *as* can be a conjunction, followed by subject + verb.
  *You should do **as** your parents say.*
  *I'll do **as** we agreed earlier.*

> **Watch Out!** In colloquial English *like* is also used as a conjunction in this way, but this is regarded as incorrect by some people, and is not used in formal writing.
> ***Like** I said, he's a really nice guy.* (colloquial)
> *I want you to do **like** I tell you.* (colloquial)

3.3 *as if/as though*

As if/as though are conjunctions followed by subject + verb.

- They are followed by the present or present perfect when referring to something likely.
  *He looks **as if he's crying**.*
  *It looks **as if it's stopped raining**.*

- To show that something is imaginary or unlikely, they can be followed by the past tense.
  *He looked **as if he had seen** a ghost!*
  *He behaves **as if he knew** more than us.*

> **Watch Out!** In colloquial English like is often used instead of *as if/as though*.
> *You look **like** you're worried.* (colloquial)
> *It looks **like** we're going to win.* (colloquial)

4 Comparing

4.1 Types of comparison

There are three types of comparison

1 to a higher degree (comparative form + *than*)
*Mountain climbing is **more dangerous than** windsurfing.*
*The Andes mountains are **higher than** the Alps.*

2 to the same degree (*as … as*)
*Hiring a car would cost **just as much as** getting a taxi.*
*I don't enjoy swimming **as much as** I used to.*

3 to a lower degree (with *less + than* and *the least*)
*I am **less keen** on taking risks **than** I used to be.*
*Antarctica is **the least** densely populated continent.*

4.2 Comparative and superlative adjectives

1 With one-syllable adjectives
Add *-er* and *-est* to form the comparative and superlative of one-syllable adjectives.
*Which is the **highest** mountain in the world?*

For one-syllable adjectives ending in a vowel + a consonant, double the consonant, e.g.
hot → *hot**ter*** → *hot**test***.

For one-syllable adjectives ending in *-e*, add *-r* and *-st*, e.g.
fine → *fin**er*** → *fin**est***.

2 With two-syllable adjectives ending in *-y* and *-ow*
For two-syllable adjectives ending in *-y* after a consonant, drop the *-y* and add *-ier* and *-iest*.
*Childhood is the **happiest** time of your life.*
For two-syllable adjectives ending in *-ow*, add *-er* and *-est*.
*The road became **narrower** as we went along.*
For other two-syllable adjectives see 4.3.

4.3 *more* and *most* + adjective

Use *more* and *most* with

* two-syllable adjectives (except for those listed in 4.2)
  *Walking at high altitudes is **more tiring** than at sea level.*
  *It was the **most boring** magazine I'd ever read.*

* adjectives with three or more syllables
  *This exam was **more difficult** than the last one.*
  *This is the **most interesting** book I've read.*

4.4 Irregular comparative and superlative adjectives

These are the most common irregular forms:
good → *better* → *best*
bad → *worse* → *worst*
little → *less* → *least*
much → *more* → *most*
far → *further/farther* → *furthest/farthest*

*Jim is a **better** player than I am, but John is **the best.***
*It's **the worst** game I've ever seen.*
*It's even **worse** than their last one.*
*You live **further** from the station than I do, but Pedro lives **the furthest** away.*

4.5 Comparing adverbs

1 Most adverbs of manner have two or more syllables. Therefore they form their comparatives and superlatives with *more* and *most*.
*If you speak **more clearly**, everyone will be able to hear you.*
*Sami works **the most quickly**.*

2 Adverbs with the same form as adjectives form their comparatives with *-er* and *-est*.
*I can run **fast**, but Toni can run even **faster**.*
*We were **the earliest** people to get to the party.*
*He'll need to work **harder** if he's going to pass the exam.*
*It'll take much **longer** if we walk – let's get the bus.*
*Who's **the quickest** at mental arithmetic?*
*We'll get there **sooner** if we walk.*

4.6 Irregular comparative adverbs

1 *badly* and *well* use the same comparative and superlative forms as *bad* and *good*.
*I did **worse** in maths than I'd expected, but **better** in English.*
*The weather's getting **better**, but I'm worried it will turn **worse** at the weekend.*

2 Other irregular forms include:
late → *later* → *latest*
much → *more* → *most*
little → *less* → *least*
*Tom arrived **later** than Peter, but Mary arrived **last**.*
*I don't go to the cinema **much**, but I go **more** than I used to.*
*She likes Saif **less** than Dean, but she likes Ali **least** of all.*

4.7 Intensifying and modifying comparisons

modifiers	comparative/superlative	
(by) far	the most/least expensive the cheapest the most time	
much a lot far a bit	more/less expensive cheaper more time	than…
just almost/nearly not quite not nearly	as cheap/expensive as much time	as…

- We can use the following words to intensify and modify comparatives.

  far/much/a lot cheaper/less expensive
  very much bigger/better
  rather harder
  a bit/slightly/a little faster
  no worse than
  not any quicker
  just as good as
  almost/not quite as expensive as
  not nearly as cheap

> **Watch Out!** You cannot use *very on its own* with comparatives.

5 Conditionals

5.1 Alternatives to *if*

- Common conditional linking words are: *if, as/so long as, unless, even if, whether, providing, provided (that), on condition that*.

- When the clause with the conditional linking word is at the beginning of the sentence, there is a comma. When the main clause begins the sentence, there is no comma.
  If you give me your number, I'll phone you tomorrow.
  As long as you take your mobile, I can phone you.
  I won't go **unless you come with me**. (= if you don't come with me)
  We're going on the walk **even if it rains**.
  I'll help you **provided that you don't tell**.

- *in case* is used to describe things we do as precautions against what might happen.
  I'll take the mobile **in case** I need to phone you.

- *otherwise* is used to describe what would happen if we did things differently. It usually begins a new sentence.
  I must leave by 3.30. **Otherwise** I'll get stuck in traffic.

5.2 Zero conditional

FORM *If* + present simple + present simple in the main clause

USE to describe a general truth
> If there **is** life on other planets, we **are not** alone.

Alternatives to *if*
Unless lions **are** frightened or hungry, they**'re not** dangerous.
When people are under stress, they often **perform** better.

5.3 First conditional

FORM *if* etc. + present simple + future in the main clause

USE
- to describe what is possible or likely in the present or future
  I'**ll be** so disappointed **if we lose** the match **on Saturday**.

- You can also use *if*, etc. + present continuous/present perfect + future/imperative in the main clause to talk about possibility/likelihood in the present/future.
  You **won't get** an interview **unless** you'**ve filled** in an application form.
  If you'**re watching** TV, you **will see** him on the news.

5.4 Second conditional

FORM *If* + past simple/continuous + *would/could* etc. + past participle in the main clause

USE
1. To talk about something
   - that is contrary to the present facts, or seen as very unlikely to happen
     If I **was/were** twenty years younger, I**'d emigrate**.
     If I **was/were** Prime Minister, I'**d make** health care free.
   - which is very unlikely to happen in the future
     I **wouldn't apply** for that job **unless I thought** I had a good chance of getting it.
2. To give advice. I'**d write** it out again **if I were you**.

5.5 Third conditional

FORM *If* + past perfect + *would/could/might have* + past participle in the main clause

USE to describe something in the past that could have happened but didn't, or that shouldn't have happened but did.
> I **wouldn't have told** her that **if I'd known** she'd tell everyone else.
> She **could have got** there on time **if** she **hadn't missed** the bus.

5.6 Modal verbs in conditional sentences

Modal verbs *can, could, might*, etc. can be used in all types of conditional sentences.

*I **might send** him an email **if** I **can find** his address.*
*If she **had** someone to look after the children, she **could go out** to work.*

5.7 Mixed conditionals

It is possible to have sentences that mix conditionals in

- an *if* clause referring to the past with a main clause referring to the present or future
  *If I **had invested** in that company ten years ago, I **would be** rich now.*
  *If we **hadn't been given** all that homework, we **could go** swimming.*

- an *if* clause referring to the present or future with a main clause referring to the past
  *If you **don't like** sweet things, you **shouldn't have ordered** that dessert.*
  *If you**'ve got** an exam tomorrow, you **ought to have started** revising by now.*

5.8 Polite expressions

1 *would* can be used after *if* in polite expressions.
  *If you **wouldn't mind** waiting here, I'll find someone to help.*

2 *If + should* is common in formal letters.
  *If you **should** require any further information, please do not hesitate to contact us.*

> **Watch Out!** For even greater formality, *if* can be omitted, and *should* can begin the sentence.
> ***Should** you wish to contact me, I can be reached at the above address.*

6 Countable and uncountable nouns; expressions of quantity

6.1 Uncountable nouns

These have no plural. The following are common nouns that are usually uncountable: *accommodation, advice, behaviour, bread, copper* (and all other metals), *meat, sugar, English,* (and all other languages), *furniture, health, information, knowledge, luggage, maths* (and all other school subjects), *news, progress, research, rice* (and all other grains and cereals), *salt,* (and all other condiments, e.g. *pepper*), *scenery, spaghetti, traffic, transport, travel, trouble, water* (and all other liquids), *weather, work.*

> **Watch Out!** Use *a slice,* and *a piece* with uncountable nouns for food.
> *I'll just have **a small slice** of cake.*
> *Would you like **another piece** of toast?*

6.2 Nouns which can be countable or uncountable

1 Nouns we can think of as a single thing or substance, e.g. *chicken, chocolate, egg, hair, iron, paper, stone*
  *There are only **two chocolates** left in the box.*
  *You've got **chocolate** on your T-shirt.*
  *We'll have to buy **a new iron**.*
  *Green vegetables are rich in **iron**.*
  *Have you read today's **paper**?*
  *I need to go and buy **some paper** for the printer.*
  *There's **a hair** in my soup.*
  *She's got short dark **hair**.*
  *The house is built of **stone**. (= rock)*
  *The necklace is made of semi-precious **stones**. (= gems)*

2 Nouns which are used to refer to particular varieties, e.g. *wine, country*
  *Would you like **some wine**? This is **a** very good **wine**.*
  *I'd like to have a house **in the country**. He's worked in **five different countries**.*

3 Words for some drinks, e.g. *coffee, beer*. The countable noun means *a glass of, a cup of, a bottle of,* etc.
  ***Coffee** is produced in Africa and South America.*
  *Shall we have **a coffee** and a piece of cake?*

4 *time, space, room*
  *There's **no time** to talk – we have to rush!*
  *I didn't have **a** very **good time** at the party.*
  *There's **no space** left. You'll have to get another bag.*
  *Fill in the **spaces** with the correct preposition.*
  *There's **room** for seven people in this car.*
  *This house has seven **rooms**.*

6.3 Expressions of quantity used with countable/uncountable nouns

1 *lots/a lot of* + plural countable and uncountable nouns (informal)
*I've got **lots/a lot of** homework, so I can't go out.*
*I've got **lots/a lot of** brothers and sisters.*

2 *much* + uncountable nouns
*We don't have **much homework**.*
***How much money** do you need?*

3 *many* + plural countable nouns
*How **many** bags have you got?*
*There are **many** interesting places in the world.*

> **Watch Out!** In positive statements *lots/a lot of* is less formal and is more commonly used in spoken English

4 *little, a little, a bit of* + uncountable nouns

  A *a little, a bit of* means *at least some*
    *Just **a little rice**, please – not too much.*
    *I've got a **bit of money**, but not enough to get a taxi.*

  B *little* without *a* means *almost none*. This can be emphasised with *very*.
    *The government has done **very little** to improve the situation.*

5 *few, a few* + plural countable nouns (= some but not many)

  A Before *few* you can use
    • the indefinite article *a*
      *There were quite **a few people** in the room.*
      *There were only **a few people** staying at the hotel.*

    • the last, the first, the next, every
      *Over **the next few weeks**, we have a lot to get ready.*
      *For **the first few minutes**, you may feel a bit nervous.*
      *I phone her **every few days**.*

  B When *few* is used without *a*, it means *almost no*. This can be emphasised with *very*.
    *(Very) **few** people know the secret.*

6 *some* + uncountable nouns and plural nouns (= between *a little* and *a lot*)
*There's **some** useful **information** on that website.*
There are some good scenes in that film.

> **Watch Out!** If *some* is stressed, it often means *not many*.
> *I suppose he's written **some** good books.*

7 *hardly any* + uncountable nouns and plural countable nouns
*There were **hardly any customers** in the shop.*

8 *no, not any* + uncountable nouns and plural countable nouns
*There was **no milk** left./There was**n't any milk** left.*
*There were **no students** on the bus./There weren**'t any students** on the bus.*

7 Emphasis with *what*

This structure is a relative clause introduced by a *wh-* word. We use it to emphasise key information in a sentence. It is more common in spoken English, but is also used in writing.

People do not realise that these accidents can be avoided.
***What people do not realise is** that these accidents can be avoided.*

The authorities are collecting information.
***What the authorities are doing is** collecting information.*

You should learn to say no.
***What you should learn to do is** say no.*

Friends are important to young kids.
***What is important to young kids is** their friends.*

8 Habit in the past

8.1 Past habit: *used to*

FORM Positive statements: *used to* + *infinitive*
Negative statements: *did/didn't* + *use to* + *infinitive*
Questions: *Did you/she/they*, etc. *use to* + *infinitive*

USE We use *used to* to talk about past habits and states that do not occur now or no longer exist.
*We **used to** be driven to school, but now we walk.*
*What did people **use to** do before electricity was invented? Ken **used to** be shy, but he's more confident since he met Cindy.*

> **Watch Out!**
> **1** *used to* is not used to say how often things happened or how long they took.
> **2** Be careful not to confuse *used to* with *be/get used to* + noun/-ing). This means *be/become accustomed to something* because you have been doing it for a while.
> *I'**m used to** making my own meals.*
> *I can't **get used to** the cold winters.*
> *Do you think we'll ever **get used to** eating dinner at 6.00?*

8.2 Past habit: *would*

Would is also used to talk about past habits and repeated actions but NOT about past states.
*When I was little, I **would/used to** play with my brother's toys.*
NOT *We ~~would~~ live in a small village.*

8.3 Past habit: past simple

This can also be used to describe past habits and states.
*When I **was** a child, I **walked** to school every day.*

9 have/get something done

FORM *have* + object + past participle (the most common form)

get + object + past participle (also possible when people are speaking informally)

USE **1** to say that someone else did something for you because you wanted them to.

He **had his hair cut** *specially for the interview.*
He's got such big feet he **has to have** *shoes specially* **made***.*
Where can I **get these papers photocopied***?*
He decided to **get the photograph enlarged***.*

2 We also use *have something done* to say that someone else did something to you even though you didn't want them to.

He **had to have a kidney removed***.*
She said she'd **had her necklace stolen***.*

3 We use *get somebody to do/make somebody do something* when we want to persuade or force somebody to do something for us.

I **got my friend to drive me** *to the shops.*
The police **made the man hand over** *his car keys.*

10 Hypothetical meaning

10.1 *wish*

1 We use *wish* + past simple to express a wish that has not come true in the present or to talk about wishes that might come true in the future.

We use this structure when we want our situation (or the situation of the person who is doing the wishing) to be different.

I wish *Eleanor* **liked** *me.*
Don't you wish *you* **had** *a big car?*
I wish *she* **was/were** *going out with me.*
We all wish *the weather* **wasn't/weren't** *so bad.*

2 We use *wish* + *would/could* to refer to general wishes for the future.

I wish *the sun* **would shine***.*
I wish *I* **could be** *in the basketball team.*

3 *wish* + *would* is used to talk about wishes we have for other people.

I wish *my sister* **would** *stop smoking.*
I wish *he* **wouldn't** *chew gum all the time.*

> **Watch Out!** This form is not often used with *I* or *we*. To talk about wishes we have for ourselves we use *could*.
> **I wish** *I* **could** *have a holiday.*

4 We use *wish* + past perfect to refer to things we are sorry about in the past.

I wish I had been invited *to the party.*
She wishes she hadn't told *him about Carlo.*

10.2 *if only*

If only is used with the same verb forms as *wish*, and is used when your feelings are stronger. It is often used with an exclamation mark (*!*). It is often used with *would/wouldn't* to criticise someone else's behaviour.

If only I could *find the answer!*
If only they would *stop talking!*
If only I had never met *him!*

10.3 *it's time*

It's time is used with the past simple to talk about the present or future. We mean that the action should have been done before. For emphasis, we can also say *It's* **about** *time* and *It's* **high** *time.*

It's (about) time you started *revising for the exam.*
It's (high) time we set off*. The train leaves in half an hour.*

10.4 *would rather*

1 We use *would rather* + past simple to say what we want someone or something else to do in either the present or the future.

I'd rather you didn't tell *anyone about all this.*
Would you rather I asked *someone else?*
I'd rather we didn't discuss *that, if you don't mind.*

2 We use *would rather* + past perfect to say what we wanted to happen in the past.

I'd rather you hadn't told *her that.*
I'd rather you had asked *me first.*

> **Watch Out!** *would rather* + infinitive without *to* is used to talk about our or other people's preferences in the present or future.
> **I'd rather go** *to the concert than to the opera.*
> **They'd rather go** *on foot.*

10.5 *suppose/what if?*

Suppose means *What if…?* It is used with

1 the present simple to describe something that may possibly happen or may have happened.

Suppose *someone* **sees** *her with us.*
Suppose *someone* **hears** *you coming in.*

2 the past simple to talk about something that is just imagination or which is unlikely to happen in the future.

Suppose *Eleanor* **knew** *you loved her. What would you do?*
Suppose *you* **won** *the prize. How would you feel?*

3 the past perfect to talk about something that could have happened in the past but didn't.

Suppose *we* **hadn't told** *her. Would she have found out?*
Suppose *you* **had married** *Carlos. Would you have been happy together?*

11 Indirect questions

1 Indirect forms are often used when you want to be polite. This may be because you don't know someone very well, or when you want to ask someone a request and you feel uncertain about their reaction

2 The first part of the question often begins with a modal such as *would, could, I was wondering*. In the second part of the question the word order is the same as in a statement; auxiliaries such as *do/does/have/be* are not used and the subject and verb are not inverted.

  A Direct question:
    When does the film start?

  B Examples of indirect questions:
    *Could you tell me **when the film starts**?*
    *Do you know **when the film starts**?*
    *Would you mind telling me **when the film starts**?*
    *I was wondering **when the film starts**.*

12 *it is, there is*

1 We use *There is/There are* to begin a sentence describing whether or not something exists. It is often followed by an indefinite noun.
  There is *a little house at the foot of the hill.*
  There are *some trees growing along the side of the road.*
  There's *no point in worrying about it.*

2 We use *It is/was,* etc. to begin a sentence giving information about time, weather and distance.
  It is *a bright, sunny day.*
  It was *half past six in the morning.*
  It's *just over ten kilometres to the nearest town.*

3 We use *It is* as the subject of a sentence to refer forwards to a later clause with *that*, an infinitive or an *-ing* form.
  It is *a pity that no one can help.*
  It's *good to see you again.*
  It's *no use crying over spilt milk.*

13 Modal verbs and expressions with similar meanings

13.1 Possibility

1 We use *can* or *could* for theoretical possibility.
  Can *there be life on Mars?*
  Can *that be Peter over there?*
  *The weather **could be** better tomorrow.* (= it's possible)

2 We use *may, might, could* + infinitive to talk about likelihood in the present or future.
  *He **may be** in a meeting.*
  *She **might/could be** here already.*

3 We use *could/may/might* + *have* + past participle (perfect infinitive) to talk about the possibility that past events happened.
  *His face was familiar. We **may have met** somewhere before.*
  *He's not in the office. He **might have finished** work early.*
  *She **could have been** at the party, but I didn't see her.*

13.2 Certainty (deduction)

1 We use *must* to say that we are sure about something in the present or past.
  *You **must be** pleased with your exam results.* (= present)
  *He **must have touched up** the photograph.* (= past)

2 We use *can't* or *couldn't* in negative sentences. We do not use *mustn't*.
  *That **can't be** Keira Knightley. She's too old.* (= present)
  *They **can't have got lost**. They know the area really well.* (= past)
  *It **couldn't have been** Tom that I saw.* (= past)

13.3 Obligation, prohibition and necessity

1 We use *must/mustn't* and *(not) allowed to* to talk about present and future obligations/prohibitions imposed by the speaker, often on him/herself.
  *Payment **must** be made in cash.*
  *I **must** get some new shoes.*
  *You **must** read that book, it's excellent!* (= recommendation)
  ***Must** I really go now?* (= appeal)
  *You **mustn't** park here.* (= prohibition)
  *You **mustn't** eat so much.* (= strong advice)
  *You **aren't allowed to** wear trainers to school.*

2 We use *have to/have got to* to talk about present and future obligations that are imposed by someone other than the speaker.

> **Watch Out!** *have got to* is more common in British than American English.
> *I **have (got) to take** my holiday in February.*
> *Do we **have to pay** to go in?*

3 We use *had to* to talk about past and reported obligations of all kinds.
  *They told us we **had to** leave our bags in the cloakroom.*
  *We **had to** stand up when the teacher came in.*
  *I knew I **had to** make a decision.*

4 We use *need to* to talk about obligation and necessity.
  *Do we **need to** type our work?*
  *You **need to** book tickets in advance.*

13.4 Lack of obligation or necessity

1 We use *needn't, don't need to, don't have to* to talk about a lack of obligation in the present or future.
  *You **don't need to/needn't meet** me at the station.*
  *We **don't have to wait**. We can go straight in.*

2 We use *needn't* + *have* + past participle to say that somebody did something, but that it was unnecessary.
  *You **needn't have gone** to all that trouble.*

3 We use *didn't need to* + infinitive to say that something wasn't necessary without saying whether the person did it or not.
  *You **didn't need to bring** any extra money.*
  *She **didn't need to cook** dinner for all of us!*

13.5 Ability

1 We use *can/could* to express general ability and typical behaviour of people or things.
*Temperatures **can rise** to over 30°C in the summer.*
*Employers **can be** unwilling to employ people over fifty.*
*My father **could be** very generous. (= past)*

2 We use *can/be able to* for present and future ability.
*I **can** understand French but I **can't** speak it very well.*
***Will** your parents be able to help you?*
*I like **being able to** cook my own meals.*

3 We use *can* for the future where there is a sense of opportunity.
*I **can come** tomorrow if you like.*
*You **can practise** your French when you go to Paris.*

4 We use *could/couldn't* and *was able to* to talk about general past ability.
*I **could swim** before I **could** walk.*
*I **was able to talk** when I was eighteen months.*
*Andrew's father **couldn't get** a job.*

5 We use *was/wasn't able to* to talk about past ability in a specific situation.
*Fortunately, he **was able to** swim to the shore.*

6 We use *could/couldn't* + perfect infinitive to talk about unfulfilled ability in the past.
*I **could have gone** to university, but I decided not to.*
*I **couldn't have been** a ballet dancer. I was too tall.*

7 Other expressions for ability:
*Do you **know how to** type?*
*He **succeeded in becoming** a professional footballer at eighteen.*
*We **managed to** find our way home. (= suggests difficulty)*

13.6 Advice: *should* and *ought to, be supposed to*

1 We use *ought to* and *should* to talk about obligations and duties in the future, present and past, or to give advice.
*You **ought to/should speak** English in class.*
***Shouldn't we tell** someone about the accident?*
***Oughtn't we to have invited** Mandy? (= more formal)*

2 We can use *be supposed to* when saying what someone should or should not do according to rules or regulations.
*You're **not supposed to park** here.*
*I'm **supposed to call** my mum when we leave the party.*

3 *should* + *have* + past participle is often used to criticise your own or other people's behaviour.
*I **should have told** you before.*
*You **shouldn't have promised** that.*

4 Other phrases for advice include
*You **could get** the next flight.*
***If I were you, I'd** phone him.*
*I'd **advise** you **not to park** there.*

13.7 Asking for and giving permission

1 We use *can* and *are allowed to* to ask for and give permission.
***Can I borrow** your calculator for a few minutes?*
*Yes, you **can stay up** and watch the late night film.*
*You **can't wait** here. It's private. (= not allowed to)*
*You **are allowed to** borrow up to eight books.*

2 We use *could* to ask for permission when we are not sure what the answer will be.
A: Could I *open the window?*
B: *Yes, of course you **can**.*

> **Watch Out!** *could* is NOT used for giving permission.

3 We use *may* to ask for or give permission in formal situations.
***May** I take that chair?*
*You **may** use pen or pencil.*

14 Participles (-*ing* and -*ed*)
14.1 Participles in relative clauses

We can use present participle (-*ing*) and past participle (-*ed*) clauses in place of relative pronouns to make writing more economical.

1 A present participle has an active meaning. It can replace relative clauses which have an active verb.
*This is the road **leading** to the school. (= which leads…)*
*There was a huge lamp **hanging** from the ceiling. (= which hung…)*

2 A past participle has a passive meaning. It can replace relative clauses which have a passive verb.
*The cathedral, **built** in the Middle Ages and recently **restored**, is well worth a visit. (= which was built… which has recently been restored)*

14.2 Other uses of participles (see also 22.1)

We also use participles

1 after certain verbs *I enjoy **running**.*

2 after conjunctions *Before **going** out, I locked the door.*

3 after prepositions *She's really good **at swimming**.*

4 as adjectives *That film was **amazing**.*
*I was **shocked** by his behaviour.*

5 as the subject of a sentence
***Eating** too much is bad for you.*

6 to express reason, condition, or result in place of adverbs
***Seeing** Jim in the distance, I called after him.*
(= because I saw Jim…)
***Having refused** the invitation, I then changed my mind.*
(= after I'd refused…)
***Seen** from a distance, the view is amazing.*
(= if/when you see it…)

15 Passives

15.1 Passive form and use

FORM To form the passive, use the appropriate tense of *be* + past participle.

present simple	Most phone calls **are made** on mobile phones.
present continuous	Calls **are being made** every day.
past simple	The first email **was sent** in the 20th Century.
past continuous	I thought I **was being asked** to help.
present perfect	Millions of text messages **have been sent**.
past perfect	Once personal computers **had been invented**, they spread quickly.
future *will*	She**'ll be given** her own room.
future perfect	The arrangements **will have been made** by the end of the week.
going to	The event **is going to be organised** by the manager.
modals	The machine **must have been** left switched on. Messages **may not be delivered** immediately.
-ing	Our dog doesn't like **being left** on his own.
present infinitive	They hope **to be chosen** to take part.
perfect infinitive	I was happy **to have been selected** for the team.

Watch Out!

1 Verbs that do not take an object (e.g. *ache, arrive, sit down*) do not have passive forms. It is not possible to say *I was ached*.

2 For verbs with two objects, one of them a person, the passive sentence usually begins with the person. *Someone gave Mary a present.* → **Mary was given** *a present.* (NOT ~~A present was given to Mary.~~)

3 The verbs *make, hear, see, help* are followed by the infinitive without *to* in active sentences, but the infinitive with *to* in passive sentences. *They* **made** *him go home.* → *He was made* **to go** *home.*

4 *Let* does not have a passive form. We use *be allowed to* in the passive. *They don't* **let** *us talk in class.* → *We* **are not allowed to** *talk in class.*

USE the passive is used

• to talk about actions, events and processes when the action, event or process is seen as more important than the agent. This is often the case in formal or scientific writing.
The equipment **was checked** *carefully.*
Rats **have been trained** *to open boxes.*

• to put new information later in the sentence
Hamlet **was written** *by Shakespeare.*

15.2 *by* + agent

When we are interested in the agent, we use the preposition *by.*
He was saved **by** *his mobile phone.*
The team were guided **by** *a local climber.*

15.3 Passive reporting verbs

We often use reporting verbs such as *believe, claim, report, say, think* in the following impersonal passive structures when we don't know or don't wish to specify the subject.

• *It + be + verb + that*
It is thought that *the criminal is a local man.* (= present)
It was claimed that *the minister had been involved.* (= past)

• Subject + *be* + reporting verb + infinitive
The criminal is thought to be *a local man.* (= present)
The minister was claimed to have been involved. (= past)

16 Relative clauses and pronouns

16.1 Relative pronouns

• The most common relative pronouns are:
who (= subject) and *whom* (= object) to refer to people
which to refer to things
that to refer to either people or things
whose the possessive of *who* and *which*
when used after nouns referring to time
where used after nouns referring to place
why used to refer to reasons

Watch Out! The relative pronoun replaces the subject or the object.
People **who** (~~they~~) *live in glass houses shouldn't throw stones.*
The vase, **which** *I bought* (~~it~~) *years ago, is very valuable.*
What is not a relative pronoun.

16.2 Defining relative clauses

In defining relative clauses

1 the relative clause defines or identifies the person, thing, time, place or reason.
   *Chris is the son of a woman **who works in television***.
   *That's the man **whose son is an actor***.
   *Winter was the time **when people tended to get insufficient fresh food***.
   *I know the place **where the play is set***.
   *I can't imagine **why he would want to leave you***.

2 *that* can be used instead of *who* or *which*.
   *The girl **that (who) lives next door** rides a motorbike.*
   *The sports centre **that (which) is opening soon** will offer great new facilities.*

3 The relative pronoun can be left out if it is the object of the verb in the relative clause.
   *The person **(who/that)** I spoke to yesterday said it was free.*
   *Sue bought the watch **(which/that)** she'd seen.*

4 No commas are used before and after the relative clause.

16.3 Non-defining relative clauses

Relative clauses give extra information which CAN be omitted. Commas are used before and after the relative clause.
The pronoun *that* CANNOT be used instead of *who* or *which*.

*The museum, **where you can see Roman pottery,** is free.*
*The witness, **who refused to be named,** said the police had acted unwisely.*

16.4 Prepositions in relative clauses

Prepositions can come before the relative pronoun or at the end of the relative clause, depending on whether the sentence is formal or informal.

*The person **to whom I spoke** told me the hotel was fully booked. (formal)*
*John, **who I bought my car from,** has gone abroad. (informal)*

17 Reflexive pronouns

Reflexive pronouns (*myself, yourself, him/her/itself, ourselves, yourselves, themselves*) are used

- when the subject and object of a transitive verb are the same
  *He stopped **himself** from saying something.*
  *I hurt **myself** when I fell over.*

- to mean 'without the help of others'
  *I cleaned the car **myself**.*
  *We booked the holiday **ourselves**.*

- with *by* to mean alone/on your own
  *Are you going to town **by yourself**?*

- with *enjoy, behave,* etc. when there is no object
  *Enjoy **yourself**!*
  *Behave **yourselves**!*

- To add emphasis to the subject or object
  *The President **himself** spoke to me.*
  *The actors were good but the film **itself** was boring.*

18 Reported statements and questions/Reporting verbs

18.1 Reported speech

This is when we report something that has been said or written.

1 If the report is after the time the thing was said or written, the verb form generally changes as follows

Direct speech	Reported speech
present simple/continuous *'I like your shoes, Kate,' said Jack.*	past simple/continuous *Jack said (that) he **liked** Kate's shoes.*
past simple/continuous *'I saw them advertised on TV,' said Kate.*	past simple/continuous or past perfect simple/continuous *Kate said (that) **she saw/had seen** them advertised on TV.*
present perfect simple/continuous *'I've bought a hat,' Helen told me.*	past perfect simple/continuous *Helen told me (that) she **had bought** a hat.*
will *'I'll take you there if you want,' she said.*	*would* *She said (that) she **would** take me there if I wanted.*
must (obligation) *'You must buy a ticket,' he said.*	*had to* *He said (that) we **had to** buy a ticket.*
can *'I can speak Spanish,' said Mel.*	*could* *Mel said (that) he **could** speak Spanish.*

2 The verb form does not need to change when

- the situation being reported is unchanged
  *'Bananas **are** good for energy,' said the doctor.*
  *The doctor told us that bananas **are** good for energy.*
  *'The castle **is** 800 years old,' said the guide.*
  *The guide told us that the castle **is** 800 years old.*

- the thing reported contains the modals *would, could, might, ought to* and *should* or *must* for logical deduction '
  *I **ought to** buy a new car,' she said.*
  *She said she **ought to** buy a new car.*
  *'I think he **must** be coming,' she said.*
  *She said she thought he **must** be coming.*

- the thing being reported contains the past perfect
  *'He **had** already **been given** a prize,' she said.*
  *She said he **had** already **been given** a prize.*

3 Other changes that occur in reported speech are shown in the table below:

Direct speech	Reported speech
tomorrow	*the next day, the day after, the following day*
yesterday	*the day before, the previous day*
last week	*the week before*
here	*there*
this morning	*that morning*
today	*that day*
next Friday	*the following Friday*
ago	*before*

18.2 Reported statements

verb (+ *that*) + clause
'He works in television,' she said.
*She **said (that) he worked** in television.*
'I took the money,' she admitted.
*She **admitted (that) she had taken** the money.*

18.3 Reported questions

1 Reported *yes/no* questions
When there is no question word in the direct speech question, we use *if/whether*. Word order is the same as in the statement. The verb tense and other changes are the same as for other types of reported speech.
'Could I borrow your bike?' she asked.
*She asked **if/whether** she could borrow my bike.*

2 Reported *wh-* questions
The *wh-* word is followed by statement word order (subject followed by verb). All tense and other changes are the same as for other types of reported speech.
'Why did you leave that job?' she asked him.
*She asked him **why he had left that job**.*
'Where is the swimming pool?' he asked her.
*He asked her **where the swimming pool was**.*

18.4 Reported imperatives

verb + object + infinitive with *to*
'Please open your suitcase,' said the customs official.
*The customs official **asked me to open** my suitcase.*
'Don't walk on the grass!' said the official.
*The official **told them not to walk** on the grass.*

18.5 Reported recommendations

recommend (that) + clause; *recommend* + *-ing*
'I'd buy the red coat,' my friend said.
*My friend **recommended buying/(that) I buy/bought** the red coat.*

18.6 Reported suggestions

FORM *suggest* + *-ing*
suggest + *that* + past simple
suggest + *that* + *(should)* + infinitive without *to*
'Let's pay half each,' she said.
*She **suggested paying half each**.*
*She **suggested we paid half each**.*
*She **suggested that we should pay half each**.*

> **Watch Out!** We can't say
> *She suggested ~~to pay/suggested us to pay~~ half each.*

18.7 Reporting verbs

1 verb + infinitive
agree, decide, offer, promise, refuse, threaten
*We **agreed to go** to the meeting.*

2 verb + object + infinitive
advise, beg, encourage, invite, persuade, remind, tell, warn
*She **asked me** to tell the truth.*

3 verb (+ *that*) + clause
accept, admit, claim, explain, recommend, say, suggest
*She **says (that) we should be repaid the money**.*

4 verb + object (+ *that*) + clause
promise, remind, tell, warn
*He **told us (that) he would be on time**.*

5 verb + *-ing*
admit, deny, recommend, suggest
*He **admitted taking** the money.*

6 verb + preposition + *-ing*
apologise for, insist on
*She **apologised for being** late.*

7 verb + object + preposition + *-ing*
accuse (of), blame (for), congratulate (on), discourage (from)
*She **discouraged me from going** in for the competition.*

8 verb + *wh-* word + infinitive
describe, explain, know, wonder
*She **explained what to do**.*

9 verb + object + *wh-* word + infinitive
ask, remind, tell
*They **told us who to see**.*

19 so/such/too/enough/very

19.1 so and such

FORM • *so* + adjective/adverb/determiner (+ noun) (+ *that* clause)
*The journey was **so dangerous that** they gave up after 200 miles.*
*He has travelled **so widely that** he's forgotten what home is like.*
*I had **so little information that** I couldn't make a sensible suggestion.*
*It was **so hot**!* (= emphatic)

• *such* + (adjective) + noun (+ *that* clause)
*The taxi took **such a long time** to come **that I decided to walk instead**.*
*He had **such fun** at the party **that he didn't want to leave**.*
*We had **such a** good time!* (= emphatic)

USE *so* and *such* are used to introduce a clause of result, or for emphasis.

19.2 too

FORM *too* + adjective/adverb/determiner (+ noun) (+ *to* infinitive)

USE *too* has a negative meaning – the speaker is not happy about the situation.
*It was **too hot** to sleep.*
*You**'re speaking too quickly** – I can't understand you I'm afraid.*
*That's **too much (money)**. I can't afford it.*

19.3 enough

FORM • adjective/adverb + *enough* (+ *to* infinitive)
*He's **rich enough to buy up** the whole town.*
*You're not doing that work **carefully enough**.*

• *enough* + noun (+ *to* infinitive/+ *for* + noun)
*Have you got **enough money to get a taxi**?*

USE *enough* has a positive meaning – the speaker regards the situation as possible.

19.4 very

FORM *very* + adjective/adverb/determiner (+ noun)

USE *very* is used for emphasis in either a positive or negative statement. It is sometimes used when we wish to avoid using a negative word.
*It's **very difficult**, but I think I can do it.*
*He's working **very hard** – he's bound to pass.*
***Very few people** agree with her.*

20 Subject/verb agreement

Verbs and their subjects usually 'agree'.
*Plants die if **they aren't** watered.*
*My **car is** very old.*

However, sometimes it's not clear whether the verb should be singular or plural.

1 A singular verb is used:
• with uncountable nouns which end in *s*, e.g. *maths, physics, genetics, aerobics, athletics, news.*
***Maths is** a very difficult subject.*
*The **news is** bad, I'm afraid.*

• with expressions of quantity, time, distance, measurement.
***Twelve dollars is** too much to pay for a sandwich.*
***Ten kilometres is** a long distance to run.*
***Is three hours** long enough for you?*
***Two metres is** too high.*

• after words/expressions such as *everyone, anything, hardly anyone, more than, one of, neither of,* etc.
***Everyone was** waiting for the train to arrive.*
***One of them is** obviously wrong.*

• with abstract nouns
***Happiness is** very difficult to measure.*

• when an *-ing* clause is the subject of a verb
***Fishing is** a very popular activity.*

2 A plural verb is used with nouns that are plural but don't end in *s* (e.g. *people, police*)
***Some people dislike** shopping.*

• after words/expressions such as *plenty of, a couple of, both of.*
*I invited **both of them** back to play football.*

• after nouns which are always plural, e.g. *clothes, glasses, jeans, trousers, pliers, scissors.*
*These **trousers don't fit** me.*

• To refer to a single item, use *a pair of.*
*I need **a** new **pair of glasses**.*

3 Some collective nouns, (e.g. *staff, the team, the army, the public, the media, the United States*) can take a singular verb if we see them as a single unit or a plural form if we are referring to members of the group.
***My family is** very close. (family = a single body)
***My family are** all living quite near to each other.*
(*family* = a collection of individuals)

21 Verb forms

21.1 Present simple

We use the present simple

1 for routine or regular repeated actions (often with adverbs of frequency like *always, usually, often, sometimes, never, every Saturday morning, twice every week*).
*We **go** running **every evening**.*
*She **doesn't do** any work **at weekends**.*
*I **never get** home before eight o'clock in the evening.*

2 for present habits.
*I **generally park** outside the library.*

3 when we are talking about permanent situations.
*She **comes from** South America.*
*They **live** in London.*

4 with scientific facts.
*Water **freezes** at 0°C.*

5 with stative verbs (verbs which are not normally used in continuous forms) e.g. *be, have, depend, know, think, understand, disagree, like, want, hear, love, see, smell, taste.*
*They **don't have** a car.*
***Does** she **understand**?*
*I'm sorry, but I **disagree** completely.*
*That perfume **smells** too strong.*

6 when we are talking about the future as expressed in timetables, regulations and programmes.
*The plane **leaves** at 8.45 a.m.*
*When **do** the holidays **begin**?*

7 in time clauses with a future meaning, e.g. *after, as soon as, if, until, when.*
*I'll see her **when/as soon as** she's free.*
*Give this to Susie **if** you **see** her.*
*Tom can't apply for the job **until** he **gets** the right qualifications.*

21.2 Present continuous

We use the present continuous when we use dynamic (action) verbs to talk about

1 actions happening now.
*I think **he's watching** TV.*

2 changing/developing situations.
*My broken leg **is getting** better.*

3 temporary situations.
*I **am staying** in this hotel for two weeks.*

4 annoying or surprising habits with *always*.
*She's **always losing** her keys.*
*He's **always buying** her flowers.*

5 plans and arrangements in the future.
***Are** you **going out** this evening?*

21.3 Present perfect simple

We use the present perfect simple

1 to talk about states, single or repeated actions over a long period of time up to the present (often with *ever/never, often/always*).
*I**'ve always wanted** to be an actor.*
***Have** you **ever been** to Australia?*
*I**'ve only used** my mobile phone **once** since I bought it.*
*She**'s read** that book **at least ten times**.*
*That's the first time I**'ve ever eaten** octopus.*
*It's the worst concert I**'ve ever been** to.*

2 to talk about recent single actions with a present result (often with *just, already, yet*).
I've already seen that film and I don't want to see it again.
***Have** you **finished** your essay **yet**?*
*Our friends **have** just arrived.*

> **Watch Out!** In American English, it is acceptable to use the past simple in sentences like these.
> *I didn't have breakfast yet.*
> *I already saw that film.*

3 to talk about an unfinished period of time up to the present (often with *for/since, this week/month/year*).
*Tomoko **has lived** in England **for five years**.*
*I**'ve been** in love with Stella **since 2002**.*
*I**'ve loved** travelling **all my life**.*
*I**'ve disliked** bananas **since I was a child**.*
*We **haven't had** a holiday **this year**.*

21.4 Present perfect continuous

We use the present perfect continuous

1 to talk about a recent activity when the effects of that activity can still be seen.
A: *Why are you out of breath?*
B: *I**'ve been running**.*

2 to emphasise how long an action has been going on for, or that it has been repeated many times.
*I**'ve been replying** to emails all morning.*
*I**'ve been cleaning** the house all day.*

3 to suggest that an activity is temporary.
*I**'ve been living** here for five years but I'm going to move soon.*

4 to suggest that an action is not complete.
*I**'ve been reading** 'Ulysses', but I haven't finished it yet.*

> **Watch Out!** We don't use verbs that refer to a state (e.g. *be, know, love*) in the continuous form.

21.5 Narrative forms: past simple

We use the past simple

1 to talk about a finished event that happened at a specific time in the past.
*I **saw** Paul **last night**.*
*I **went** to Brazil five years **ago**.*

2 to describe a sequence of finished events in chronological order.
*I **took** out my key, **opened** the door and **walked** in.*

3 to talk about habits in the past.
***Did** your parents **read** to you when you were younger?*

4 to talk about states in the past.
*When I **was** a child, I didn't enjoy watching TV at all.*
*The house **belonged** to my father from 1990 to 2000.*

5 in reported speech.
*She **said** she **didn't want** to join us.*

21.6 Narrative forms: past continuous

We use the past continuous

1 to describe an action in progress in the past, often to set the scene for a particular event.
*I **was sitting** in the garden, reading a book.*

2 to talk about temporary situations in the past.
*Rodolfo **was living** in South America at the time.*

3 to talk about an event that was in progress in the past and was interrupted.
*I **was going** out of the house when I heard a noise.*

4 to talk about multiple actions in progress at the same time in the past.
*While I **was painting**, you **were watching** TV.*

5 to talk about anticipated events that did not happen.
*We **were going** to Rome for a holiday, but then I broke my leg.*

21.7 Narrative forms: past perfect

We use the past perfect

1 to refer to a time earlier than another past time, when this is needed to make the order of events clear.
*The bird's wings **had been clipped** so it couldn't fly.*
*By the time the fire engine arrived, the house **had** completely **burned down**.*

> **Watch Out!** Be careful not to overuse the past perfect. It is not necessary with *before/after*, which make the sequence of events clear.
> Once we have established the time sequence, we can revert to the past simple.

2 in reported speech.
*They said they **had met** before.*

21.8 Future forms

FORMS *shall/will* + infinitive without *to*
going to + infinitive without *to*
Present continuous (see 21.2)
Present simple (see 21.1)
Future continuous (*will* + *be* + *-ing* form)
Future perfect (*will* + *have* + past participle)

1 We use *will* + infinitive without *to*
- for predicting something based on our belief or our knowledge of characteristic behaviour
*This medicine **will make** you feel sleepy.*
*You**'ll feel** better when you've had a good night's rest.*

> **Watch Out!** We cannot use the present continuous in this case.

- for promises, threats, offers and requests
*If you tell anyone, I**'ll kill** you!*
*I promise I**'ll pay** the money back.*
*I**'ll meet** you at the station if you want.*
***Shall I meet** you at the station?*
***Will you do** the washing-up for me?*

> **Watch Out!** We cannot use *going to* in this case.

2 We use *going to* or the present continuous to talk about things that have already been decided.
*She's decided she's **going to lose** ten kilos.*
*Where are you **going to have** the wedding reception?*

> **Watch Out!** We cannot use *will/shall* + infinitive in this case.

3 We use *going to* to talk about things that are certain to happen because there is present evidence.
*I've got no sense of direction – I know I**'m going to get** lost.*
*Look out – you**'re going to fall**!*

> **Watch Out!** We cannot use *will/shall* + infinitive or the present continuous in this case.

4 We use *will/shall* + infinitive without *to* to talk about future actions decided at the time of speaking.
*I think I**'ll give up** smoking.*
*I**'ll wear** my black dress.*

5 We use the future continuous (*will/shall* + *be* + *-ing*) to say that an action will be in progress at a definite time in the future.
*I**'ll be living** a normal life by this time next year.*

6 We use the future perfect (*will/shall* + *have* + past participle) to describe something that will be completed before a definite time in the future.
*By the end of June I**'ll have been** at this school for a year.*

22 Verb patterns: -ing/ infinitive

2.2.1. Common verbs followed by -ing

admit, appreciate, consider, delay, deny, detest, dislike, enjoy, escape, feel like, finish, give up, imagine, involve, mention, mind, miss, postpone, practise, prefer, put off, recommend, resent, risk, suggest

I **don't recommend going** to that restaurant.

22.2 The infinitive

The infinitive is used
- after some main verbs (see 22.3 and 22.4)
- after some adjectives
  I was **happy to see** her.
  They were **wrong to refuse**.
- after some nouns
  She never regretted her **decision to be** a teacher.
  It's **time to leave**.
- to express purpose
  I **went** to London **to see** my aunt.

22.3 Common verbs followed by infinitive

afford, agree, appear, arrange, ask, attempt, begin, choose, consent, decide, expect, fail, forget, happen, hate, help, hesitate, hope, intend, learn, like, love, manage, mean, offer, prefer, prepare, pretend, promise, refuse, remember, seem, start, swear, try, want, wish

I can't **afford to eat** in that restaurant.

22.4 Common verbs followed by object + infinitive

advise, allow, ask, cause, encourage, expect, forbid, force, get, help, instruct, intend, invite, leave, like, mean, need, order, persuade, prefer, remind, request, teach, tell, tempt, want, warn

He **asked me to help** him.

22.5 The infinitive without to

The infinitive without *to* is used
- after some main verbs (see 22.6)
- after modal verbs
  You **must leave** now.
- after *would rather/had better*
  You**'d better come** in now.

22.6 Common verbs followed by object + infinitive without to

let, make, hear, help, see
He **made me repeat** the exercise.
Her parents **won't let her stay** out late.
I **heard her play** in Milan.

> **Watch Out!** In passive sentences *make, hear* and *help* are followed by an infinitive with *to*.
> He was **made to report** to the police.

Let cannot be used in the passive form. Instead, *allowed* must be used.
My parents **let** me **stay out** late.
I **am allowed to stay out** late by my parents.

22.7 Verbs/expressions followed by -ing or infinitive with a difference in meaning

1 *can't bear/stand, hate, like, love, prefer* When these verbs are used with the infinitive, they refer to more specific situations. When they are used with *-ing*, they refer to more general situations.

> **Watch Out!** The difference in meaning is very slight.

I **prefer to work** on a computer than to write by hand.
I **can't bear listening** to her complaining all the time.

2 *remember, forget, regret, stop, try*
- *remember/forget* + *-ing* refers to an action that happened before the moment of remembering/forgetting
- *remember/forget* + infinitive refers to an action after the moment of remembering/forgetting
  I **remember seeing** you somewhere before. (= that I have seen you)
  Did you **remember to lock** the door?
  She had completely **forgotten telling** him about her cat.
  I **forgot to give** Sally the book.
- *regret* + *-ing* means be sorry about an action that happened in the past
- *regret* + infinitive means be sorry about a present action
  I **regret going** to the party last night.
  I **regret to have to tell** you that your car has been stolen. (= formal)
- *stop* + *-ing* means stop something you do, e.g. a habit
- *stop* + infinitive with *to* means stop what you are doing in order to do something else
  I **stopped drinking** coffee: it kept me awake at night.
  We **stopped to have** a coffee on the way home.
- *try* + *-ing* means do an experiment (= doing the action may not be successful)
- *try* + infinitive means make an effort (= the action may be difficult or impossible to do)
  Try studying in the morning – it might suit you better.
  Try to study at regular times.

Writing reference (Paper 2)

Contents

Checklist of key points for writing

Checklist

Answering the question

Have you

- answered all parts of the question?
- included all the necessary information?
- written the required number of words?
- organised your ideas appropriately, using paragraphs where necessary?
- written clearly so that it is easy to read?

Accuracy

Are there any mistakes in grammar, vocabulary, spelling or punctuation?

Range

Have you used

- a variety of grammatical structures?
- a range of interesting vocabulary?
- a range of linking words?

Style

- Is your language appropriate for the type of writing? (Remember to think about *who* you are writing for.)
- Is your answer interesting for the reader, and would it have a positive effect?

1 Useful linking words and phrases

1.1 Time sequencers

Examples include *before, after, after a while, eventually, later, then, finally, as soon as, at first, at last, when, while*

I immediately phoned the police. **While** *I was waiting for them to arrive, I watched the house.*

At first*, no one got out of the car, but* **after a while** *the driver's door opened.*

And **then** *I* **finally** *found what I was looking for.*

1.2 Listing points

Examples include *first, firstly, first of all, to begin with, secondly, thirdly, finally*

Our holiday was spoiled, **firstly** *because the hotel was uncomfortable and* **secondly** *because the weather was bad.*

1.3 Adding information/emphasising points

Examples include *as well as (that), in addition (to), moreover, furthermore, not only … (but also…), what's more, on top of that, to make matters worse, in fact, as a matter of fact*

The hotel was miles from the beach. **On top of that***, the view from our bedroom window was terrible.*

Not only *was the hotel miles from the beach,* **but** *the view from our bedroom window was terrible too!*

In fact*, everyone is different when it comes to personal taste.*

1.4 Giving examples

Examples include *for example, for instance, such as*

I like pop groups **such as** *Take That.*

My town has a lot of things for young people to do. **For example***, there are three cinemas.*

1.5 Reasons, causes and results

Examples include *as a result, because, because of (this), so, therefore*

I have visited Britain several times and, **as a result***, my English is quite good.*

By the end of the day, you haven't managed to find anything that you like. **So***, you go home frustrated.*

1.6 Contrast

but

But links two contrasting ideas. It is not normally used at the beginning of the sentence.

Many people argue that TV is bad for you, **but** *I disagree with this.*

however

However can come at the beginning or end of a sentence. It must be separated off by commas.

The advert claimed that there were huge discounts for students. **However***, the discount was only five percent.*

I love travelling. I don't enjoy long flights, **however***.*

although, even though, though

These expressions introduce a subordinate clause of contrast. If the subordinate clause comes first, it is separated from the main clause by a comma.

Although *he practised every day, he didn't manage to improve.*

I walked home **even though** *it took me two hours.*

NOTE *though* can be used after a comma at the end of a separate sentence that expresses something surprising.

We lived in the middle of a city. We still had a large garden, **though***.*

whereas, while

- *Whereas* and *while* are used to compare two things and show how they are different.

  She likes football **whereas** *I prefer tennis.*

  My sister is very like my father, **while** *I take after my mother.*

- *While* is also used in the same way as *although*.

  While *computers are important, we shouldn't let them rule our lives.*

in spite of (the fact that), despite (the fact that)

These expressions must be followed by a noun or *-ing* form. *Despite* is slightly more formal than *in spite of*.

In spite of *the fact that they are expensive, many people want to buy designer clothes.*

Despite *all the research that has been done, we still haven't found a cure for cancer.*

in fact, the fact of the matter is

This is used when you are saying what the 'real' truth of a situation is.

According to the brochure, the service is free for students. **In fact,** *students are charged at the same rate as everyone else.*

On (the) one hand … On the other hand …

These expressions are used to introduce opposite points in a discussion.

(On the one hand,) *if I take the job in Milan, I'll be able to go to the opera.* **On the other hand,** *if I take the job in Barcelona, I'll be able to go to the beach.*

otherwise

This is used to say what will happen if something else does not happen first.

You have to choose your holiday carefully. **Otherwise***, you could be disappointed.*

2 Model answers, with hints and useful phrases

2.1 Semi-formal letter/email
(Part 1)

For work on semi-formal letters and emails, see pages 24 and 118.)

TASK

You recently had a short holiday in a large city which you booked through a company called Citibreaks. You were very disappointed with the holiday. Read CitiBreaks' advertisement for the holiday you booked and the notes you have made. Then write a letter to CitiBreaks, explaining what the problems were and telling them what you want them to do.

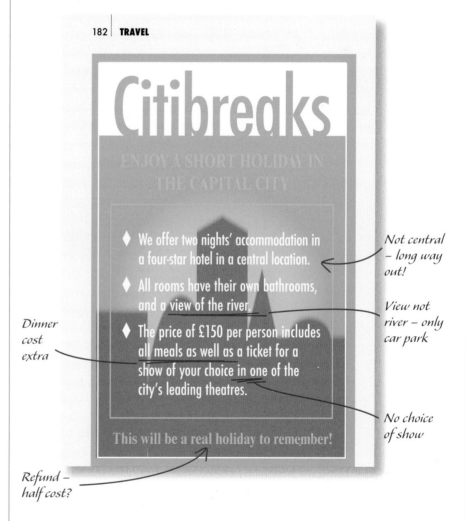

Write a **letter** of between **120** and **150** words. You must use grammatically correct sentences with accurate spelling and punctuation in a style appropriate for the situation.

Model answer

DO begin by saying why you are writing. DON'T begin by saying who you are.

DO list your complaints clearly, using linking words to connect your actual complaint with the details.

When you are writing a letter or an email to someone you don't know, use a semi-formal style. If you don't know their name, a **letter** starts with *Dear Sir/Madam* and ends *Yours faithfully*. If you know their name, a **letter** usually starts with *Dear Mrs/Mr/Miss/Ms* + surname, and ends *Yours sincerely*.

If you're writing an email, you can use *Best wishes'*.

You don't need to put an address for a **letter** in either Part 1 or Part 2.

DO make a clear connection between your answer and the task input. DON'T repeat the exact words in the task input.

If you expect a reply to your **letter**, DO finish with this sentence on a separate line.

In a **letter**, sign and print your full name.

Dear Sir,

I am writing to complain about a short holiday I had recently organised by your company. There were several problems with the holiday.

First, your advertisement promised a hotel in a central location, whereas in fact the hotel was a long way from the centre. You said all rooms had a river view, but my window overlooked a noisy car park. I had to pay extra for dinner, although you stated that it was included. To make matters worse, I couldn't choose which show to go to. I had hoped to go to a new musical, but I had to go to one I had already seen.

I had been looking forward to my holiday very much, but it was completely ruined. I therefore feel that you should refund half the cost of the holiday in compensation for my disappointment.

I look forward to hearing from you soon.

Yours faithfully,

Ursine Schmidt

Ursine Schmidt

(149 words)

Useful language

Complaining

- *I am writing to you about* several problems related to my city break in June.
- *I have been waiting for* two weeks for a reply to my letter.
- *To make matters worse,* we were informed that there was no record of our cheque being cashed.
- *I would be grateful if you could* refund my deposit as soon as possible.

Requesting information

- *I am writing in response to* your advertisement in The Daily Standard on July 20th.
- *I would be grateful if you could* send me further details about the position.
- *I am writing to enquire whether* you could let me have further details about the holiday.
- *I would like to know more about* the arrangements for the evening meal.

Giving information/Responding to requests for information

- *With reference to your letter of …* I enclose details of my qualifications.
- *You asked me to tell you about* my travel plans and I enclose further details.

2.2 Story

For work on stories, see pages 44 and 128.

TASK

Your teacher has asked you to write a story for the school's English language magazine. The story must begin with the following words:

I wanted to do my best, but more than that I wanted the team to win.

Write your **story**. (You should write **120–180** words.)

Useful language

- **We had been** talking about John just before he phoned.
- **It wasn't until** I read the letter **that** I realised how dangerous the situation was.
- **While** I was waiting for my friends, I saw someone go into the house opposite.
- **As soon as** my friends arrived, we went to have a look.
- **I was just about to** open the door, **when** I heard a noise coming from downstairs.
- **By the time** I got back to the house, there was no one to be seen.
- **After waiting** for a few minutes, I decided to climb in through the window.
- **A few seconds later,** the lights went out.
- **Eventually/After a while,** my friends arrived.
- **At last** I knew what I had to do.

Model answer

DO use phrases to show when things happened in your **story** (e.g. *It was the last football game of the season. When the second half started …*).

DON'T make mistakes with narrative tenses.

DO use direct speech because it makes the story more interesting to read.

DO try to create some suspense.

DO try to have a dramatic end to your **story**.

DON'T write about a topic if you don't know some specific vocabulary related to it (e.g. *score, goalkeeper, goal, pitch*).
DO use interesting vocabulary (e.g. *raced, roared*).

DO add extra detail to add to the atmosphere of the **story**.

I wanted to do my best, but more than that I wanted the team to win. It was the last football game of the season, and if we won, we would be the champions. As we ran onto the pitch, I couldn't help feeling nervous. The crowd was cheering, but the opposition looked strong. It wasn't going to be easy.

The game started. I got the ball and raced towards the goal. 'Go on!' roared the crowd, but I kicked it straight into the hands of the goalkeeper. 'Never mind,' yelled my team-mate Joe. 'Good try!' We played hard, but at half-time the score was 0–0.

When the second half started, it was raining heavily. Our chance of winning the championship was slipping away. We struggled to get the ball through the defence, but time after time they stopped us. Now there were only two minutes left. Suddenly I had the ball. I passed it to Joe, who headed it straight into the goal, just as the referee blew his whistle. The crowd went crazy. We were the champions!

(179 words)

2.3 Letter/email to a friend

For work on informal letters and emails, see pages 14, 106, 138 and 148.

TASK

You have received a letter from your pen friend inviting you for a visit in July. Write a letter to your pen friend, accepting the invitation, suggesting something you would like to do and asking what you should bring with you.

Write your **letter**. Do not write any postal addresses. (You should write between **120** and **180** words.)

Useful language

Beginning the letter or email

- *Many thanks for your letter* – *it was really nice to hear from you again.*
- *I thought I'd better write* and give you some more details about …
- *It's been such a long time since we wrote to each other.*
- *How are you and your family?*
- *How are things with you?*
- *How was* your holiday?

Introducing the topic

- *I know you're keen to hear all about* my holiday.
- *You remember I told you in my last letter* that I was going to …

Ending the letter or email

- *Once again,* thanks very much for all your help.
- *Give my love/regards to* your family.
- *Please write soon.*
- *I look forward to* meeting up again soon.

Model answer

DO invent a name. Don't write *Dear Pen friend*.

DO mention a **letter or email** you have received from the person you are writing to, or refer to a shared experience.

DO think of some specific details to include in each paragraph – this will make your **letter or email** more interesting.

DO say what you've been doing recently.

DO mention the next time that you will see the person you are writing to.

DO use an appropriate phrase to end your **letter or email**, e.g. *Love, All the best, Best wishes*. DON'T finish your **letter or email** with *Yours sincerely/ faithfully*.

Dear Carla,

   Thanks for your letter – it was great to hear from you. I'm sorry I haven't written for ages, but I've been really busy preparing for my exams. It's really good news that you've passed your driving test. Congratulations!

   Thank you so much for your invitation to stay with you for a week in July – I'd love to come. I know that you have a wonderful beach near your house, and I'd really enjoy spending some time there. I expect that the weather will be hot, so I hope we can go swimming.

   You said that I don't need to bring much with me. What sort of clothes should I pack? Casual or formal? Would you like me to bring anything for you? I would like to bring something special for you and your family from my country.

   I'd better stop now and get on with my studying. I hope you're enjoying driving your car, and I'm looking forward to seeing you in July!

   Thanks again for the invitation.

   All the best,

   Irene

(169 words)

2.4 Report

For work on reports, see page 66.

TASK

The school where you study English has decided to spend some money on **either** buying more computers **or** improving the library. You have been asked to write a report for the school director describing the benefits to the school of both these things, and saying which one you think should be chosen and why.

Write your **report**. (You should write **120–180** words.)

Useful language

Introduction
- *The aim of this report is to …*
- *This report is intended to …*

Reporting results
- *Most people seem to feel that …*
- *Several people said/told me/suggested/thought that …*

Presenting a list
- *They gave/suggested the following reasons:*
- *They made the following points:*
  - *1 …*
  - *2 …*

Making recommendations
- *I would therefore recommend that we expand the library/ installing a new coffee machine.*
- *It would seem that banning mobile phones is the best idea.*

Model answer

Use of money for school improvements

Introduction
The aim of this report is to compare the advantages of additional computers and of improving the library, and to suggest which of these would be best. I interviewed a number of students to find out their views.

Buying more computers
Some of the students thought that this was a good idea, saying computers were useful for:

- practising writing
- using the internet
- playing games.

However, other students said that they preferred to use their own computers at home.

Improving the library
Most of the students preferred this suggestion, giving the following reasons:

1 Many students do not have a quiet place to study at home. The library would be a good place for private study, but at present there are not enough tables and chairs there.
2 They feel that up-to-date dictionaries and reference books are needed.
3 They want to be able to read modern books written for young people.

Recommendations
Both ideas have benefits, but it was felt by the majority of students that improving the library would be more useful. I would therefore recommend this.

DON'T begin and end your **report** with *Dear Sir/ Madam*, like a letter.

DO use headings because this makes it easier for the reader to find the main information.

DO include two or three points under each heading. DO use numbering or bullet points to highlight main points.

DO use formal language in your **report**.

DO say how you collected the information.

DO use a range of specific vocabulary or set phrases e.g. *Some thought this was a good idea …/other students said they preferred …*, but DON'T use lots of adjectives and dramatic language as you do in a story. A **report** gives factual information.

DON'T include irrelevant details or description.

DO express opinions impersonally. DON'T express recommendations or opinions until the conclusion.

(179 words)

2.5 Article

For work on articles, see pages 34 and 76.

TASK

You see this advertisement in a local English language newspaper.

Hey! magazine is looking for articles about celebrations around the world.

Write us an article about a celebration that is important in your country, explaining why the celebration is important and describing what people do. If your article is chosen for the magazine, you will win a weekend in a city of your choice.

Write your **article**. (You should write **120–180** words.)

Useful language

Involving the reader
- *Are you thinking of* getting married in the near future?
- *I'm sure you'll agree* it was a great idea.

Developing your points
- *Let's start with* why it is so important to take plenty of exercise.
- *Another advantage* of using a computer is that …
- *On top of that,* …

Giving your own opinion
- *I think that/In my opinion* traditional celebrations are very important.
- *It seems to me that* people are much more aware of the importance of a good diet nowadays.

Model answer

DO think of an interesting title. DON'T start and finish your **article** in the same way as a letter.

DO try to involve your reader directly, e.g. by using a question.

DO use informal language to involve the reader.

DON'T forget to express your opinion.

DO finish your **article** by summarising your main point and giving your opinion or expressing your feelings.

Olinda's carnival – something for everyone

When most people think of Carnival, they think of Rio de Janeiro. But Rio isn't the only city in Brazil that knows how to have parties. I live in Olinda, a lovely city in the north-east of Brazil. What can we say about the carnival at Olinda? Just that it's the best in the world!

Carnival has its origins in ancient Egyptian and Roman festivals. It was introduced to Brazil by the Portuguese, and was influenced by African rhythms and Indian costumes. Now it's a big national celebration.

Once Carnival starts, the whole town goes crazy! Everyone's singing and dancing. Parades of people wearing costumes typical of our north-eastern folklore dance through the streets. I love the giant street dolls, both the traditional ones such as 'the man of midnight' and the new ones that appear each year.

The best thing about our carnival is that no one has to pay and there are no big stars. Everyone takes part, rich and poor, old and young, residents and tourists. If you come, I promise you'll never forget it!

(179 words)

2.6 Letter of application

For work on writing applications, see page 86.

TASK

You see this advertisement in a local English language newspaper.

> **We are looking for students of English to spend two mornings a week helping in the local tourist office.**
>
> *Good pay and conditions for the right applicants.*
>
> Write to us, giving information about your level of English, and explaining why you would be suitable for the job.

Write your **application**. Do not write any postal addresses. (You should write between **120** and **180** words.)

Useful language

- *I have always been interested in* using English in my work.
- *One of the main reasons I am applying for this job is that* I want to work in England.
- *I have a lot of experience of* dealing with the public.
- *I am available to start work* at any time/from the end of the month.
- *Thank you for considering my application.*
- *I would be grateful if you would* send me further details of the job.
- *I can be contacted* on 0849 58 48 43 *at any time.*
- *I look forward to hearing from you soon.*

Model answer

Dear Sir/Madam,

I am writing to apply for one of the positions helping in the local tourist office which were advertised in 'Kent Weekly' on August 23rd.

I am 19 years old and come from Switzerland. German is my mother tongue and I have been learning English and French for five years at a comprehensive school. At the moment I'm a student at English International, studying for the FCE.

I have always been interested in working with people. As I have already spent three months in England, I know the local tourist attractions quite well. I would also say that I have a good knowledge of history and old places, because I have read a lot about the subject recently. In the near future, I would like to continue studying English, and so the job in your tourist office would be a great opportunity for me to improve my speaking.

I am available for interview at any time. I can be contacted on 0795 51 32 41 after 6p.m. every evening.

Thank you for considering my application. I look forward to hearing from you.

Yours faithfully,

Gabriella Daniels

Gabriella Daniels

(183 words)

DO say which job you are applying for and where and when you saw it advertised. You can invent a newspaper and date if you need to.

DO organise your application so that you mention each of the areas in the advertisement.

DO say when and how you can be contacted.

DON'T make mistakes with time expressions and tenses.

DON'T forget to mention why you think you are suitable.

DO begin and end your letter as you would other formal letters.

2.7 Essay

For work on essays, see page 96.

For work on essays, see page 96.

TASK

You have been doing a class project on technology. Your teacher has asked you to write an essay giving your opinion on the following statement:

People in the modern world depend too much on computers.

Write your **essay**. (You should write **120–180** words.)

Useful language

- *Some people claim that* your teenage years are the best years of your life.
- *It is often said that* TV is a bad influence on young people.
- *However, in my view/opinion,* …
- *Firstly, it is clear that* money cannot buy happiness.
- *While it is true that* computer games are stimulating, they may not be good for you in the long term.
- *From my point of view,* job satisfaction is more important than a large salary.
- *Finally, it is important to remember that* …
- *On balance then, I feel that* …
- *To sum up/In conclusion, it seems to me that* …

Model answer

DO state the topic in your first sentence, but use your own words.

DON'T start by saying *I agree with this* – your **essay** should present your own argument.

DO include supporting detail for the points in each paragraph.

DO use linking expressions to introduce points in an **essay**.

DON'T forget to express your opinion in the conclusion.

In today's world, nearly every aspect of life is affected by computer technology. Computers are used for business, public services, education and entertainment.

Some people are concerned by this development. They fear that vital skills are being lost as computer technology replaces traditional ways of working in a wide variety of areas, from art and design to banking and commerce. They point out the chaos that can occur when computer systems fail, leading to the breakdown of essential services such as transport, law and order.

However, people could not continue to enjoy their present standard of living without computer technology. There are now far more people in the world than there were a generation ago. The fact that there is enough food for them, that they can travel safely from one place to another, and that they can be provided with medical care, is largely due to computer technology.

In my opinion, therefore, we have to accept our dependence on computers, but at the same time we should work to find ways of making this dependence less dangerous.

(178 words)

2.8 Review

For work on reviews, see page 54.

TASK

You recently saw this announcement in an English language magazine called **Film Scene**.

Have you ever thought of writing a review?

We need a young person's perspective on films today. Write us a review of the last film you saw. Include information on the story, characters and any special features of the film, and say whether you would recommend the film to other people. The best review will be published in next month's edition of the magazine.

Write your **review**. (You should write between **120** and **180** words.)

Useful language

Introduction
- *The film I would like to review is* …
- *The last film I saw / book I read was* …

Summarising the story
- *It's set in* …
- *The story is based on* a book …
- *It's about* …
- *There are many memorable characters including* …
- *The main theme of the* film is …
- *What the* film *is saying is* …

Recommending the film
- *I would recommend* this film **to** anyone.
- *Although I enjoyed it, I would not recommend it for* …
- *It's one of the best* shows *I've ever seen.*
- *Although I am not normally keen on* musicals, *I'm glad that I decided to go.*
- *The* film **lifts you out of your everyday life**.

Model answer

DO say what the film is about, but not in too much detail.

DO try to use a range of interesting vocabulary, to bring the film to life for the reader.

> The last film I saw was not new; in fact it was *The Lord of the Rings*.
>
> It is based on the well-known book, and tells the story of a creature called a hobbit who takes a dangerous magic ring back to the place where it was made in order to destroy it. There are many memorable characters apart from the hobbit and his friends, including a wizard called Gandalf and a suspicious creature called Gollum.
>
> This is a film about friendship and loyalty. However, it is the special effects that make it truly magical. There are vivid battle scenes with fantastic animals and birds, and sets that are so imaginative that you want to believe they are real. But as well as this, the actual locations are beautiful, too.
>
> I would recommend this film to anyone, even those who do not usually enjoy fantasy films. What I would say to them is – go and try it! Like me, you might find that the film lifts you out of your everyday life into a world you will not want to leave.

DO remember to mention important or memorable characters, but don't spend too much time just describing them.

DO remember to link ideas clearly, and to link paragraphs together.

DO remember to give your opinion clearly, as this is the purpose of a **review**, but not until the end.

(180 words)

2.9 Set book

About the exam: In Question 5, you answer one of two questions based on your reading of one of the set books. You may be asked to write an essay, an article, a report or a letter.

You do not have to answer Question 5. If you do, make sure that you know the book well enough to be able to answer the question properly. Here is a suggested **procedure** for writing about the set text.

1 Read the book all the way through, to get a general idea of the story and the characters – and to enjoy it!

2 Read the book again, this time more carefully. Make notes under the following headings.

Plot Include the main events and the order they come in the story.

Characters Include information about what they are like and how important they are in the story.

Relationships Include information about who likes/dislikes who, and the things that affect their relationships.

Places Include quick descriptions of the most important places.

Your own reactions Write down your feelings about the book, with some reasons for your opinion.

3 Make a list of the kind of questions you might be asked to write about, and discuss them with other students. Here are some ideas:

- What makes the book interesting/ exciting? Describe an exciting or memorable moment in the book.
- Choose the most interesting character in the book. Describe him/her. Is this your favourite character?
- Is the title a good one for the book? Why/Why not?
- Does the book have a good ending? Explain why/why not.
- Do you think the book would make a good film? Explain your reasons.
- Would you recommend the book to a friend? Say why/why not.

TASK

(a) An international student magazine is running a series of articles on interesting characters in fiction, and has asked readers to send in their suggestions. Write an **article** on the character you found most interesting in the book you have read, saying who the character is and why you think they are so interesting.

(b) Your friend is going on holiday and wants to take a book to read on the journey. Write a **letter** to your friend, recommending the book you have read and giving reasons why you think they will enjoy it.

Model answer (article)

A lady with no name

It seems strange to experience a story through the eyes of a nameless person - but this is the case in 'Rebecca', by Daphne du Maurier. Rebecca is the name of the first wife of Maxim de Winter. She dies before the story begins, and the novel is narrated by Maxim's second wife, whose name we never learn, but who is to me the most interesting character in the book. As we read, we learn of her feelings for Maxim, and of what she discovers about his past life and the wife she has replaced.

So why do I think the narrator is such an interesting character? Although she is nameless, she has a strong personality. She is emotional and her problems and feelings are vividly described, so that you feel sorry for her. She has not had an easy life, and you want her to be happy, in spite of the strange things that happen after her marriage.

All in all, her lack of an identity makes her all the more memorable - and perhaps that is why I find her so fascinating.

DO focus on what you have been asked to do. DON'T just tell the story of the book.

DO make links between paragraphs clear.

DO describe a characteristic and then say why you like it so much.

(182 words)

Useful language

- **The book is really exciting because** it starts with a murder.
- **The best moment is when** the murderer is revealed.
- **The book tells the story of** a family who have been separated.
- **The first thing that happens is** Sarah leaves home.
- **The main character,** Marian, is a teenager who …
- **The most interesting character is** Joe, the young man who lives …
- **The title is really good, because** it is mysterious and it makes you want to find out what it really means.
- **The story takes place in** the South of France.
- **Events revolve around** a robbery.
- **The ending is very exciting because** it is completely unexpected.
- **It would make** a really good film, **because** it is such an exciting story.
- **The best thing about the book is that** the characters are so interesting.
- **I would recommend this book because** it is easy to read.

3 Sample answers

The following scripts were written by students. Read the Paper 2 general marking guidelines on page 199, and use them to help you evaluate each answer and decide on its strong and weak points. Then read the comments given and the suggested band score, and compare your ideas.

3.1 Semi-formal letter
(Part I)

TASK

You recently entered a competition for learners of English, and have just received a letter from the organisers of the competition. You have made some notes on the letter.

Congratulations! You have won first prize in our competition – a two-week trip to Vancouver or San Francisco.

Your prize includes
* FREE return flight to the city of your choice — *Direct flight?*
* FREE two-week course at the Vancouver or San Francisco School of International English — *Hours? Morning/ afternoon?*
* Two weeks' FREE accommodation with a family — *Distance from school? Meals?*

We need to know your choice of city, your preferred dates, and if you would like us to make any special arrangements for you. — *Stay an extra week?*

We look forward to hearing from you. Once we have the information we will send you your tickets and further details.

Yours sincerely

Jacky Thompson
Jacky Thompson
Competition Manager

Write a **letter in 120–150** words in an appropriate style. Do not write any postal addresses.

Sample answer

Dear Mrs Thompson,

Thank you very much for the letter. I am very pleased that I've won the prize. I would like to go to San Francisco because I have never been to the USA before. However, there are several questions I would like to ask.

First of all, I would like to know whether the return flight is a direct flight or not. I would like to book a direct flight because it is much more comfortable.

Secondly, I would like to know how long we are being teached every day and if there are classes in the morning or the afternoon. Is there a difference between Vancouver and San Francisco concerning this point?

You wrote about a free accommodation with a family. Are the meals included and/or do I have the opportunity to cook by myself? Please let me also know the distance from the school.

Finally, I would like to ask you if it is possible to stay at school for an extra week. If it is possible please let me know the price I have to pay.

I like to thank you in advance for your assistance and I look forward to hearing from you soon.

Yours sincerely,

Lennart Moser

Comments

This is rather long, but there is no irrelevant information and the student answers all parts of the question. He makes a couple of grammatical mistakes (e.g. *we are being teached; a free accommodation*), but these don't cause problems in understanding the meaning. He uses quite a wide range of structures, although he tends to repeat *I would like to know.* Vocabulary is appropriate and ideas are organised in clear paragraphs. The style is sometimes too formal (e.g. *concerning this point*) but the letter would have a very positive effect on the reader.

Band 5

3.2 Story

> **TASK**
>
> Your teacher has asked you to write a short story for the school's English language magazine. Your story must begin with the following words:
>
> *It was not easy, but Carol knew she had to do it.*
>
> Write your **story**.

Sample answers

A

It was not easy, but Carol knew she had to do it. In front of her there was this big river, with water that was running very fast, and this rubber dinghy. Behind her she could hear the guide explaining that the water is only about 8°C warm. Furthermore, he told to Carol's group that there are some dangerous places, where they have to take special care. After that, the guide smiled and cried: 'Let's go!' For one moment, Carol was thinking of an escape. But this river-rafting tour was her birthday present from her friends, and they were all there. She was the last one who got into the boat, and sat down at the back of it. She tried to smile and join the others pleasure, however, she wasn't very successful. She closed her eyes and the boat set off. After a while, Carol began to enjoy the trip. In fact, it was great fun, and at the end, when they arrived, Carol decided to book a next trip two weeks later.

B

It was not easy, but Carol knew she had to do it. She was in Trieste, Italy. She came there to visit her friend. His name is Stefano who she met in their language school in England. Actually she didn't know about Italy until she met him. So she couldn't speak Italian, was not good at Italian geography.

As the first mistake, she thought that Trieste was close to his house, but it was his fault. He lived in Trento, near Verona. She should have used a different airport. Trieste airport was quite small. She wasn't able to find a person who can speak English.

As the biggest mistake, she couldn't call him!! She usually contacted with him by emails, so she didn't know how to call.

She tried to communicated with Italian people with body language many times. She didn't give up. If she gave up, she couldn't meet him. One hour past ... and she learned how to call him!! Eventually she was able to talk with him.

Three hours later Stefano come to her at the airport. She shouted for joy "Stefano!! I missed you!!"

Comments

A This answers the question and gives some detail, and there is a clear beginning, middle and end. There is some good accurate use of language (*Behind her she could hear the guide explaining; After a while, Carol began to enjoy the trip*) but there are several mistakes with reported speech (e.g. *he told ~~to~~ Carol's group that there <u>are</u> some dangerous places*) and other mistakes (e.g. *~~an~~ escape; a <u>next</u> trip*). There is some use of direct speech to add interest and there is quite a good range of vocabulary, but the student has not divided the story into paragraphs. It has a positive effect on the reader.

Band 4

B This is a lively story. There are quite a lot of grammar mistakes (e.g. *who she met* instead of *and she had met him, she tried to communicated with*). However, the student also uses a range of structures accurately (e.g. *She should have used; She didn't give up.*) There are some mistakes in vocabulary so that the meaning is not always clear (e.g. *it was his fault* instead of *He'd made a mistake; she learned how* instead of *she found out how*). Linking of ideas and sentences is not always clear. However, there is good use of direct speech and a strong ending which has a positive effect on the reader.

Band 4 (low)

3.3 Letter to a friend

> **TASK**
>
> You have received a letter from a pen friend who is planning to visit you in July. Write a letter to your pen friend, describing the activities you have planned for his/her visit. Give them advice on what to bring and ask about any special requests.
>
> Write your **letter**. Do not write any postal addresses.

Sample answers

A

Dear Carria,

Nice to hear from you. I'm so surprised that you are on your way to come here this summer. I have to say that you've made a good decision.

First of all, I would like to recommend you some places where you shouldn't miss such as Sentosa island. You can have different activities there. For example, if you would like having sunbathing. I think 'Sun World' is the best choice to relax. Don't forget to bring swimwear! I don't think Bird Park is a good place to visit. It's quite boring I have to be honest to say that. However if you are really interesting in visiting there I could show you around.

Secondly, it's the best time come here if you enjoy the shopping. We have big on sale in July. Therefore, I can arrange the shopping table for you. I will be very please to show you how interesting on big sale in here!

I don't think you need to bring any special stuff. That's because you can buy them here. Don't forget to prepare some more empty suitcase for your shopping.

If you have any question just ask me. I'll do my best to solve them.

I'm looking forward to hearing from you again!

Best wishes,

Carel

B

Dear Diego,

Hi! How are you? Thank you for your letter! I'm very happy about your plan!

OK! If you let me know your arrival time, I will come to you, at Narita airport. I've thought about our plan in Japan. I know you really like football! So, how about visiting stadiums of the World Cup? You can visit a locker room in Yokohama International Stadium where the final was held, and you can see autographs of Brazilian national team members.

In July, Japan is very hot, but sometimes there is a heavy rain so you have to bring an umbrella. And there are lots of mosquitoes, you must bring a medical cream to protect yourself against them.

Do you have any special requests? If you have any, please let me know. I'll try to do it!

I'm looking forward to your reply and to meeting you in July!

Lots of love,

Yuka

Comments

A This is a full answer to the question, with a fairly good range of grammar, but there are quite a few grammatical problems (e.g. *recommend you some places where you* instead of *recommend some places to you which; interesting in* instead of *interested in*). Vocabulary problems sometimes make the meaning unclear (e.g. *I can arrange the shopping table for you*). Paragraphs and connecting words are well used and the style is generally suitable for a letter from a friend. It has a satisfactory effect on the reader.

Band 3

B All parts of the question are dealt with, in an informal style. There are some grammatical mistakes (e.g. *there is a heavy rain*) and problems in pronoun use (e.g. *I'll try to do it!*) but the student uses tenses accurately and shows a good range of vocabulary, and the paragraphs are clear and well constructed. The letter has a positive effect on the reader.

Band 4

3.4 Essay

TASK

You have had a class discussion on what people do in their free time. Your teacher has now asked you to write an essay, giving your opinions on the following statement:

Shopping has little value as a leisure activity.

Write your **essay**.

Sample answers

A

Does shopping have little value as a leisure activity? I think most people are really keen on shopping but is it really useful?

For example, if we ask students what they're going to do in a big city, the answers are almost always 'shopping', and they don't think about going to museums and sight-seeing. Most tourists go shopping sometime instead of to see the famous places and so they don't learn about places they visit.

However, people who enjoy shopping like every stage about shopping, from window shopping, trying clothes on, thinking if they should buy or not, to buying. The final stage is to be satisfied with seeing what they have bought in their house or wearing it in front of their mirror like a fashion show.

This activity is proved to be a complete leisure activity. Indeed, I read an article in a newspaper called 'Shopping is a way to relax'. We should all use this nice relaxation and not feel guilty. Don't you think so?

B

I believe that shopping can be one of the important things people do, like eating and sleeping, and for some shopping is their chance to do their favourite things like walking and meeting friends.

On the one hand, I think that is true that shopping has no value in some lifestyles. People think of shopping only as a chance to do whatever they want, and then it is an escape from doing things they should do. I mean people go shopping instead of do work.

However, others think of it as a chance to meet some friends who you only see from time to time. In addition, it is useful time to discuss every day problems - for example, if you have got some problems, in that shopping time you might listen to others problems and think that yours are nothing compared to theirs. It can make a break from every day work pressure and so it is valuable for some who have a hard job and lifestyle.

In conclusion, it's true that buying things has little value, but people are different, which means that shopping will be priceless for some.

Comments

These answers are both **Band 4**, for different reasons.

A This has clear organisation, with paragraphs giving points for and against the statement. However, the first sentence just repeats the task. There are some good expressions (e.g. *if we ask … the answers are almost always 'shopping'*) but also some grammatical mistakes (e.g. *go shopping sometime instead of to see*). There is quite a good range of topic-related vocabulary, but the style is too informal in places (e.g. *Don't you think so?*). It has a positive effect on the reader.

B This answers the question clearly and uses a wide range of vocabulary and some good expressions (e.g. *think that yours are nothing compared to theirs*). However, there are grammatical mistakes (e.g. *instead of do work*). The style is appropriate. The conclusion clearly returns to the question and gives a nice summary of the writer's opinion. It has a positive effect on the reader.

3.5 Report

TASK

The owner of the school where you study English has decided to make some changes to the school classrooms. He has asked for ideas from students about what should be done to make the classrooms better places to study in. Write a report making suggestions for how the classrooms could be improved.

Write your **report**.

Sample answer

Introduction

This report is to suggest what we need to make the classrooms better in our school. I asked students for their ideas.

Background situation

What it's need to be inside a good school classrooms is that they all have all the equipment students might need starting from the essential things like chair, blackboards, finishing with accessories like televisions.

Suggestions

I certainly believe that two things need to start our plan to improve the school classrooms, they are money and good management. My idea of improving the classrooms is to start with what we have and see what needs to be repared and what has to be thrown away and replaced with a new equipment and some computers that the students might need also having a massive liberrary is one of the more important things that students request. Heating and air conditioning are necessary to make the atmosphere in the classrooms cosy.

Personal opinion

In conclusion, the chance of having a good classrooms looks easy from a distance, in fact it isn't, and that we must try to find the balance between having a very good school and not spending too much.

Comments

This report makes some relevant points, but the style is more suitable for a composition than a report. It would be much better in bullet points.

It is not easy to identify the main suggestions because of problems with sentence linking and punctuation. *My idea of … is to start with what we have* is good. The problem is the sentence is too long and needs splitting up, e.g. *My idea of improving the classrooms is to start with what we have. Then we can see … .* There are some problems with passive forms (e.g. *what it's need instead of what is needed*) but also some good expressions (e.g. *to start with what we have; we must try to find the balance between*). The student has a good range of vocabulary although this is not always appropriately used (e.g. *massive, cosy*) and there are some spelling mistakes (e.g. *repared, liberrary*). It has a satisfactory effect on the reader.

Band 3

3.6 Article

Sample answer

I'd love to have a lot of money although I think money is not a perfect solution. Of course not! However, if I had enough money, I could do a plenty of things which I want to do.

Above all, I want to study in other countries, because. It is a good chance to develop my abilities. In this case, I don't need to worry about the fee of education in my life. I can only concentrate on studying as long as I do my best.

Secondly, I would like to prepare a lovely house for my parents. Although they didn't say to me at all, I think the work of electric services is so hard to continue at their ages within 10 years. Therefore, I hope that I could make them relax and enjoy their life.

On the other hand, I can help the other people who are suffering from lack of food, illness and so on. When I saw a TV programme which announced those people's stories, I thought if I were them I would get really depressed.

Sometimes, money can be used in a bad way, but if I am a rich person, I will spend them on not only for me, but I also give an opportunity to others.

Comments

This answer gives relevant information and answers the question. There is quite a good range of structures and vocabulary but these are not always used very accurately (e.g. *If I am a rich person, I will spend them on not only for me* instead of *If I were rich, I wouldn't just spend the money on myself*). It is also difficult to understand exactly what she wants to say about her parents in the line *Although they didn't say to me at all, I think* ....

The paragraphs are well planned but there are mistakes with linking words (e.g. *On the other hand* instead of *As well as that* or similar) and with punctuation. There is a mixture of informal language (e.g. *Of course not!*) and formal language (e.g. *Therefore*). It has a satisfactory effect on the reader.

Band 3

3.7 Review

TASK

Reviews needed!

We need a young person's perspective on films today. Write us a review of your favourite film. Include information on the story, characters and any special features of the film and say why you would recommend the film to other people. The best review will be published in next month's edition of the magazine.

Write your **review**.

Sample answers

A

I want to tell you about a movie really discussed in Italy, 'L'Ultimo Bacio' (The Last Kiss) directed by Gabriele Muccino in 2001.

It is set in an Italian city in the same time in which actors play, in fact, the director's purpose is take a plausible picture of people's life. The movie tell us about the crisis of two different generations worried by the difficulty of grow up and take their responsibility.

On the one hand, there are thirty years old people who think wedding like an important change of life but sad and serious, therefore they are very frightened of doing it, preferring an affair with someone else to solving their couple's problems.

On the other hand, fifty years old people are frightened of growing old.

I think the story is really topical and show a widespread situation, the actors' performance is really good, the dialogues are fast and accurate. Although is a great film I must admit that it is a bit too shouted, but this is Muccino's style.

A good story, great actors and good dialogues and editing, 'L'Ultimo Bacio' is really interesting, not boring at all.

B

My favourite film is called 'If only'. It's the best romantic film I have ever seen.

It's set in London and about a hard-working businessman and a lovely violinist woman. The man is too busy to take care his love. He thinks work is more important than his girlfriend. On the concert of her graduation he meets a taxi driver and talks with him about their love. He realises something but it's too late because his girlfriend dies by car accident. He regrets everything, but surprisingly there is a great chance of living with her again. Finally he can appreciate her, but sadly he has to die instead of his girlfriend.

I have seen it 5 times. Until I saw it 3-4 times it was just love story with strange situation, but last time, I can feel character's feelings. So it was a really romantic film. The plot and the song of the actress was fantastic. The story could be a bit artificial and far-fetched. But if you focus on character's feelings you can be given a good precept. Don't calculate your love, just appreciate her!

If you fall in love or like romance you'll love this film.

Comments

A This review is a bit long, has some style problems and is not always easy to follow. *On the one hand / On the other hand* does not link well to *two different generations*. There is a good range of vocabulary (*plausible picture, taking responsibility, widespread situation*) but some words are misused, e.g. *too shouted*. There are basic grammatical mistakes, e.g. *-ing* form after prepositions (*difficulty of grow up*). The review only has a satisfactory effect on the reader

Band 3

B This is a bit long, but is organised and easy to follow. The style and paragraphing are both generally appropriate, and the writer has given her opinion. There is some interesting vocabulary although some words are misused, e.g. *precept*. The sentences are simple, but there is a range of structures including present perfect and modals. Mistakes do not usually impede communication. The review generally has a satisfactory effect on the reader.

Band 3

4 General marking guidelines

Both Parts of the Writing paper carry equal marks. When marking, examiners use the general assessment guidelines below for both Parts, as well as a task-specific mark scheme for each question on the paper.

Band 5

- Answers the question completely and makes some original points
- Uses a wide range of grammatical structures at this level with almost no mistakes
- Uses a wide range of vocabulary appropriately
- Uses clear paragraphs with well-organised ideas
- Uses a variety of appropriate connecting words
- Uses the correct style for this type of writing throughout

Band 4

- Answers the question giving enough detail to be effective
- Uses a good range of grammatical structures at this level with few basic mistakes
- Uses a wide range of vocabulary, mostly appropriately
- Uses paragraphs with logically organised ideas
- Uses suitable connecting words appropriately
- Uses the right style for this type of writing most of the time
- Has a positive effect on the reader

Band 3

- Answers the question
- Uses a satisfactory range of grammatical structures at this level, with some errors
- Uses a satisfactory range of vocabulary, with some errors in appropriacy
- Organises ideas into paragraphs, though not always clearly
- Uses some simple connecting words
- Mostly uses the right style for this type of writing, though there may be some lapses
- Has a satisfactory effect on the reader

Band 2

- Does not answer the question fully, and/or is not always relevant to the question
- Uses a limited range of grammatical structures, with errors which interfere with communication
- Uses a limited range of vocabulary, with errors that cause difficulty in understanding
- Does not organise ideas into paragraphs
- Uses very few connecting words, or does not use them correctly
- Uses a style that is not appropriate for this type of writing
- Has an unsatisfactory effect on the reader and does not communicate clearly

Band 1

- Omits some parts of the question and/or is irrelevant
- Uses a narrow range of grammatical structures, with many basic errors
- Uses a narrow range of vocabulary, with errors that prevent understanding
- Does not organise ideas at all
- Does not use connecting words
- Does not demonstrate any understanding of the style and format needed for this type of writing
- Has a very negative effect on the reader

Exam focus

Contents

Paper 1: Reading (1 hour)

Part 1 (Multiple choice)

What is being tested?

Part 1 focuses on your ability to understand a text in detail. Questions will focus on different things such as the main idea of a text, specific details in a text, the writer's opinion, attitude or purpose, your ability to understand the meaning of words or phrases from the context, and to follow features of text organisation such as examples, comparisons and references.

What do you have to do?

- Read the text and answer eight questions. Each question has four possible answers (A, B, C or D) and the questions follow the order of the text.
- Choose the correct option for each question, based on the information in the text.
- Mark the correct letter A, B, C or D for each answer on your answer sheet.

Strategy

1 Read the instructions, title and sub-heading of the text.
2 Skim the text to get a general idea of what it is about.
3 Read each question and highlight the key words (don't worry about the four options yet).
4 For each question, highlight the part of the text that the question relates to.
5 Read the text again carefully. When you find a part of the text you have highlighted, look at the question and the four options and decide on the answer. The meaning will be the same but the language will be different.
6 Check all the options again carefully, crossing out ones that are obviously wrong.
7 Make your decision. If you are not sure, choose the option that seems most likely.
8 When you have completed all the questions, transfer your answers to the answer sheet.

Part 2 (Gapped text)

What is being tested?

In Part 2, you will be tested on your understanding of how a text is structured.

What do you have to do?

- Read through the text, from which seven sentences have been removed.
- Read the eight sentences (there is an extra one which doesn't fit anywhere) and decide which sentence best fits each gap.
- Mark your answers on your answer sheet.

Strategy

1 Read the title and subheading to get an idea about the topic of the text.

2 Read the main text carefully to make sure you understand what it is about.

3 Read the section before and after each gap and predict what information is missing from each gap.

4 Underline any nouns, pronouns, linkers etc. which will help you to find a link.

5 Read the eight sentences and look for clues that will connect them to the gaps. Look for topic words, synonyms and reference words.

6 If you are not sure about what goes in a gap, go on to the next question and return to it later.

7 When you have finished, read through the completed text to check that it makes sense. Make sure you have filled in all the gaps and not used any sentences more than once.

8 Try the extra sentence in each gap again to make sure that it doesn't fit anywhere.

9 Transfer your answers to the answer sheet.

Part 3 (Multiple matching)

What is being tested?

Part 3 focuses on your ability to search through a text (or texts) to find specific information, and on understanding writers' opinions and attitudes.

What do you have to do?

- Read four to six short texts around the same theme, or one longer text divided into four to six paragraphs. To answer the questions, you will have to read quickly to find specific information.
- Match fifteen questions or statements to the text or paragraph that it relates to. The text does not follow the same order as the questions.
- Write the correct letter for each answer clearly on your answer sheet.

Strategy

1 Read the title of each text and any subheadings.

2 Skim each text quickly to get an idea of what it is about.

3 Read the questions carefully and highlight key words.

4 Scan each section of the text to find the information in the questions. You do not need to read in detail. Look for words or phrases which are similar in meaning to the words or phrases in the questions.

5 Underline or highlight possible answers. Do not mark them on your answer sheet yet: you may find similar – but not exactly the same – information in other sections.

6 Read the information carefully to check which one is an exact answer to the question.

7 Leave any questions that you are not sure about; but always go back and answer them at the end as you will not lose marks for a wrong answer. Choose the most likely answer.

8 When you have finished, transfer your answers to the answer sheet.

How do I mark my answers?

Mark ONE letter for each question.

For example, if you think B is the right answer to the question, mark your answer sheet like this:

1	A B C D E F G H
2	A B C D E F G H
3	A B C D E F G H
4	A B C D E F G H
5	A B C D E F G H
6	A B C D E F G H
7	A B C D E F G H

Paper 2: Writing (1 hour 20 minutes)

Part 1 (Letter or email)

What is being tested?

Part 1 tests your ability to write an appropriate response to a letter or email with accompanying notes, and to carry out a number of specific functions such as advising, apologising, explaining, recommending or suggesting.

What do you have to do?

- Write a letter or email based on information and notes that you are given.
- Choose an appropriate writing style (formal or informal).
- Write 120–150 words.

Strategy

See Writing reference page 179

Part 2 (choice of task)

What is being tested?

There is a choice of tasks in Part 2, and the testing focus depends on the task. You will have to communicate clearly in a style appropriate to the task. You may also have to advise, compare, describe, explain, or recommend.

What do you have to do?

- Choose one task out of the four tasks you are given (question 4 has two options).
- Write an answer to the task using an appropriate format and style. The first three options could be from the following: a story, an article, an essay, a review, a report, a letter or email. For the fourth option there is a choice of two tasks based on the set book. The task could be a report, review, letter, email, article or essay.
- Write 120–180 words

Strategy

See Writing Reference page 179

Paper 3: Use of English (45 minutes)

Part 1 (Multiple-choice cloze)

What is being tested?

Part 1 tests your knowledge of vocabulary, including words with similar meanings. It also tests some grammatical features e.g. phrasal verbs and fixed phrases.

What do you have to do?

- Read a text with twelve missing words.
- Choose the correct word from each set of four options.
- Mark the correct letter A, B, C or D on your answer sheet.

Strategy

1 Read the title and the text quickly to get a general idea of what it is about, without trying to fill any of the gaps.
2 Read the text again. Stop at each gap and try to predict what the missing word might be.
3 Look at the options for each gap carefully. Try putting each of the options in the gap to see which one fits best.
4 Check the words on either side of the gap to see if the option you have chosen goes with these.
5 Read the whole text again to make sure the options you have chosen make sense. Do not leave a blank; if you are not sure, choose the one which seems most likely.
6 Transfer your answers to the answer sheet.

Part 2 (Open cloze)

What is being tested?

In Part 2, the focus is on grammar and the missing words will be grammatical words like auxiliary verbs, articles, prepositions, pronouns, phrasal verbs, etc. Again, there is also a lexical element.

What do you have to do?

- Read the text with twelve missing words.
- Put one word in each of the twelve gaps.
- Write the the correct word for each gap clearly on your answer sheet.

Strategy

1 Read the title and text quickly to get a general idea of what it is about, without trying to fill any of the gaps.
2 Think about what kind of word is missing e.g. preposition, article, pronoun, etc.
3 Write in the missing words in pencil. Only write one word in each gap.
4 When you have finished, read through the whole text again. Check it makes sense, and check the spelling.
5 Transfer your answers to the answer sheet.

Part 3 (Word formation)

What is being tested?

Part 3 focuses on both vocabulary and grammar and tests your knowledge of how words are formed using prefixes and suffixes, etc. You'll have to understand what kind of word is required in each gap (e.g. noun, adjective, adverb), and be able to form it.

What do you have to do?

- Read a paragraph with ten gaps.
- Use the word in capital letters at the end of each line with a gap to form a word which fits each gap.
- Write your answers on your answer sheet.

Strategy

1 Read the title and the text quickly to get a general idea of what it is about.
2 Read the text again. This time stop at each gap. Think about whether the missing word is positive or negative, plural or singular, a noun, verb, adjective or adverb. Use the words before and after each gap to help you decide.
3 Write the correct form of the word in the gap.
4 Read the text again to make sure your answers make sense and the words are spelt correctly.
5 Transfer your answers to the answer sheet.

Part 4 (Key word transformation)

What is being tested?

Part 4 tests a range of grammatical structures as well as vocabulary, and shows examiners that you can express yourself in different ways.

What do you have to do?

- Complete eight sentences using two to five words, including a key word which is provided. Your completed sentence must have a similar meaning to the lead-in sentence. You will usually have to change two things.
- Write your answers on your the answer sheet.

Strategy

1 Read the first sentence and the key word. Work out what is being tested, e.g. you may need a passive form in the future.
2 Identify what is missing from the second sentence.
3 Think about what kind of words need to be used with the key word.
4 Write down the missing words. Do not change the key words in any way.
5 Make sure you have not written more than five words (contractions, e.g. *don't*, count as two words) and that you have not changed the meaning at all.
6 Check your spelling and that the sentences make sense.
7 Transfer your answers to your answer sheet.

How do I mark my answers?

Part 1: Mark ONE letter for each question.

For example, if you think **B** is the right answer to the question, mark your answer sheet like this:

0	A	B	C	D

1	A	B	C	D

2	A	B	C	D

3	A	B	C	D

Parts 2, 3 and **4:** Write your answer clearly in CAPITAL LETTERS.

For Parts 2 and 3 write one letter in each box. For example:

0	E	X	A	M	P	L	E

13												

14												

15												

35	

36	

Paper 4: Listening (approx 40 minutes)

Part 1 (Multiple choice: short extracts)

What is being tested?

Part 1 tests a range of listening skills. You may be asked about the main idea, the attitude or opinion of the speakers, their relationship, etc.

What do you have to do?

- Listen to eight short extracts about different topics, twice. These may be monologues or dialogues.
- Answer one multiple-choice question about each of the eight extracts.
- Write the correct letter A, B or C on your answer sheet. (You are given five minutes at the end of the test to transfer your answers from the question paper to the answer sheet.)

Strategy

1 Read the questions and options and highlight the key words before you listen (you are given some time for this).

2 The first time you listen, mark the answer you think is best on your answer sheet.

3 Check your answers the second time you listen and make sure the options you have chosen answer the questions correctly.

4 If you aren't sure, choose the answer you think is most likely – you don't lose marks for wrong answers.

Part 2 (Sentence completion)

What is being tested?

In Part 2, the focus is on listening for detail, specific information and opinion in a longer text.

What do you have to do?

- Read the ten sentences with gaps about the recording.
- Listen twice to an interview or a report about a particular topic.
- Complete the ten sentences with a word or words from the recording.
- Write your answers on your answer sheet.

Strategy

1 Before you listen, read the sentences carefully. Highlight key words and think about the kind of information that's missing. You have some time for this.

2 As you listen, try to complete the sentences. The sentences are in the same order as the information on the recording. Write one to three words to complete each sentence. You should write the words you hear; you do not need to change these words.

3 If you can't complete a sentence the first time you listen, leave it blank.

4 The second time you listen, complete any remaining sentences and check your answers. Don't leave any of the gaps blank – you don't lose marks for a wrong answer.

5 Check that your spelling and grammar (e.g. singular/plural) is correct and that the sentences make sense.

6 Be careful not to make any mistakes when you copy your answers on to the answer sheet at the end of the test.

How do I mark my answers?

Part 2:
Write your answer clearly in CAPITAL LETTERS.

Write one letter or number in each box.
If the answer has more than one word, leave one box empty between words.

For example:

| 0 | N | U | M | B | E | R | | 1 | 2 | | | |

Part 2									
9									
10									
11									
12									

Part 3 (Multiple matching)

What is being tested?

In Part 3, the focus is on your ability to understand the main idea. You may also have to listen for specific details, understand a speaker's attitude or opinion, etc.

What do you have to do?

- Listen to five short monologues on a related topic, twice.
- Match one of six options to each monologue. There is one extra option which does not match any of the monologues.
- Write the correct letter A–F for each answer on your answer sheet.

Strategy

1 Read the rubric carefully. This tells you what topic the speakers will talk about.

2 Read each option. Highlight key words/phrases and think of synonyms/paraphrases for these words.

3 The first time you listen, try to identify the main idea of what the speaker is talking about, and mark the option which you think matches most closely.

4 During the second listening, check that the options match exactly what the speaker says. Don't choose an option just because it contains a word from the monologue.

Part 4 (Multiple choice: longer text)

What is being tested?

Part 4 focuses on your ability to follow a longer text and listen for the main idea, for a speaker's attitude or opinion, or for specific information.

What do you have to do?

- Listen to a monologue or dialogue about a topic twice.
- Answer seven multiple-choice questions.
- Write the correct letter A, B or C for each answer on your answer sheet.

Strategy

1 Before you listen, read the introduction to the task to get information about who the speakers are and what they will talk about.

2 Read the questions and options and highlight key words/phrases. Think about the kind of information you need to listen for.

3 Listen for paraphrases of the words and phrases on the recording and choose one of the options A, B or C. If you are not sure of an answer, continue answering the other questions and come back to it in the second listening.

4 During the second listening, check the options you have chosen. If you aren't sure, choose the one that seems most likely.

How do I mark my answers?

Parts 1, 3 and 4:
Mark ONE letter for each question.

For example, if you think **B** is the right answer to the question, mark your answer sheet like this:

Part 3					
19	A	B	C	D	E	F
20	A	B	C	D	E	F
21	A	B	C	D	E	F
22	A	B	C	D	E	F
23	A	B	C	D	E	F

Paper 5: Speaking (around 14 minutes)

Part 1 (Interview)

What is being tested?

Part 1 focuses on your general interaction and on social language skills.

What do you have to do?

- The examiner will ask you and the other candidate for some personal information.
- You will be asked different questions about things such as where you live, your family, what you do in your spare time, your work/studies, future plans.
- This will take around three minutes.

Strategy

1 Speak clearly. Try to relax and speak confidently.

2 Try to sound interested and interesting. Try not to speak in a monotone.

3 If you don't know a word, say it in another way. Don't leave long pauses.

4 Listen carefully both to the examiner and to your partner.

5 If you don't understand the question, ask for it to be repeated.

6 Give relevant, personal answers. Avoid giving one-word answers, but don't speak for too long.

Part 2 (Individual long turn)

What is being tested?

In Part 2, the focus is on your ability to organise your ideas and express yourself clearly. You will have to compare, describe and express your opinions.

What do you have to do?

- The examiner gives you two photographs on the same topic.
- Listen to the examiner explaining the task, which is also printed on the page with the photographs.
- The task has two parts; first you compare the photos, then you answer a question about them.
- You have one minute to do both parts of the task.
- You then listen to the other candidate speaking, and look at their photos.
- When they have finished, you will be asked to give a short answer to a question related to the topic.

Strategy

1 Listen carefully to the instructions. It's important that you understand exactly what you need to talk about. Ask the examiner to repeat the instructions if necessary but remember that the question is also written above the photographs.

2 Summarise the main similarity and any differences between the two photos. Talk about the general ideas and don't be tempted just to describe the photos or go 'off topic'.

3 You may need to speculate about the photos if you are not sure what they show.

4 Make sure you save enough time to do the second part of the task, in which you give your opinion on something.

5 Keep talking for the whole minute. Use paraphrases and 'fillers' if necessary. The examiner will say 'thank you' when the minute is finished.

6 Listen carefully while the other candidate is speaking. Look at their photos, but don't interrupt. When the examiner asks you a question related to the photos, give a short answer (about twenty seconds).

Part 3 (Collaborative task)

What is being tested?

In Part 3, you'll be tested on your range of language and your ability to interact with another person. You'll be expected to exchange and discuss ideas and opinions, and invite and respond to your partner's contributions.

What do you have to do?

- In this part of the test, you work with a partner to discuss something together.
- The examiner gives you both a task and some pictures to look at. The task is also written on the page with the pictures.
- The task has two parts. The first part will usually involve talking about each of the photos in turn. The second part may involve solving a problem, making a decision, choosing the two most important factors, etc.
- Discuss the task with a partner for about three minutes and reach a decision, although you do not have to agree.

Strategy

1 Read and listen carefully to the instructions. Ask for clarification if you do not understand.

2 You have three minutes for this part of the test. You should spend around two of these discussing each of the pictures in some detail (but don't spend too long on any one picture).

3 One of you should start the discussion. Then take turns to give your opinions, agree, disagree, etc. You are tested on the language you use to work together.

4 Turn-taking skills are important. Avoid dominating the discussion or interrupting rudely. It is important to involve and encourage your partner and follow up on what they say.

5 Explain things in a different way if you can't think of a word or phrase and don't leave long pauses. Use words such as *right* or *OK* to 'fill the gaps'

6 Try to use a range of functional language, such as asking for and reacting to opinions, agreeing and disagreeing, suggesting, speculating, opening and summarising the discussion.

7 Make sure you talk about all the options before reaching a conclusion. You don't have to agree.

Part 4 (Discussion)

What is being tested?

Part 4 focuses on your ability to discuss issues in more depth by giving and justifying opinions, agreeing and disagreeing, etc.

What do you have to do?

- In this part, the examiner asks you both questions which develop the topic in Part 3 and may lead to a more general discussion.
- You may add to what your partner has said or agree/disagree with their ideas.
- The discussion will last for around four minutes.

Strategy

1 If you don't understand the question, ask the examiner to repeat it.

2 Give opinions and express your feelings about issues. Give reasons or examples.

3 Listen to what your partner says and ask them questions or give follow-up comments.

4 Use a wide range of language, but don't dominate the discussion.

Pearson Education Limited
Edinburgh Gate
Harlow
Essex CM20 2JE
England
and Associated Companies throughout the world.

www.pearsonELT.com/examsplace

© Pearson Education Limited 2012

First published 2012

ISBN: 978-1-4082-9789-6

Set in Myriad Pro
Printed in Slovakia by Neografia

Acknowledgements
The publishers and author(s) would like to thank the following people and institutions for their feedback and comments during the development of the material: Nora Brussolo, Adriana Lado (Argentina); Henrick Oprea, Atlantic Idiomas (Brazil); Anna Kraśko, Katarzyna Machala (Poland); Eleonora Olaru (Romania); Idiomas O'Clock team, Kamal K Sirra (Spain); Tina Casura-Risch, Riana Paola (Switzerland); Pauline Bokhari, Fiona Johnston, Jacky Newbrook, Judith Wilson (UK)

Author Acknowledgements
The authors would both like to thank Jacky Newbrook and Judith Wilson for their helpful suggestions, our families for their support and all the team at Pearson for their hard work.

Text
Extract in unit 1 adapted from "From mod to emo: why pop tribes are still making a scene", *The Guardian*, 26/02/2010 (Rogers, J.), copyright © Guardian News & Media Ltd 2010; Extracts in units 2 and 3 adapted from "Relative Values: Colin Firth and his sister Kate", *The Sunday Times*, 21/08/1994 (Fox, S.); "Relative Values: Jonathan Self and his brother Will", *The Times*, 18/10/2007 (Neustatter, A.); "Relative Values: Zoë Heller and her sister Emily", *The Sunday Times*, 27/09/2009; "Relative Values: Will Young and his twin brother, Rupert", *The Sunday Times*, 28/09/2009; "Relative Values", *Sunday Times Magazine*, 15/03/1998 (Williamson, N.); and "All you need is love (and a scarf)", *The Times*, 25/05/2005 (Rudd, A.), copyright © The Times, 1994, 1998, 2005, 2007, 2009, www.nisyndication.com; Extract in unit 4 adapted from *Esquire presents: What it feels like* (Jacobs, A.J. (Eds) copyright © 2003 by A.J. Jacobs and Esquire Magazine. Reprinted by permission of Three Rivers Press, a division of Random House, Inc. and International Creative Management, Inc.; Extract in unit 5 adapted from "12-Year-Old's a Food Critic, and the Chef Loves It", *New York Times*, 16/11/2008 (Dominus, S.), copyright © 2008, The New York Times. All rights reserved. Used by permission and protected by the Copyright Laws of the United States. The printing, copying, redistribution, or retransmission of this Content without express written permission is prohibited; Extract in unit 5 adapted from Hard Rock Cafe London, http://golondon.about.com, copyright © 2011, Laura Porter. Used with permission of About Inc., which can be found online at www.about.com. All rights reserved; Extract in unit 6 adapted from "The future of entertainment Middle-class struggle", *The Economist*, 26/11/2009, copyright © The Economist Newspaper Limited, London 2009; Extract in unit 7 from *Brooklyn*, Viking (Colm Tóibín 2009) pp.27-31, copyright © Colm Tóibín, 2009. Emblem edition first published 2010. Published by McClelland & Stewart Ltd. Used with permission of the publisher, Penguin Group (UK) Ltd and The Free Press, a Division of Simon & Schuster, Inc., All rights reserved; Extract in unit 9 adapted from "How a suburban street in Reading became a wellspring of champions", *The Week*, 08/05/2010, copyright © Dennis Publishing Ltd and Extract in unit 9 adapted from "Mental Imagery" by Brian Mackenzie, 2002, www.brianmac.co.uk/mental.htm, copyright © Sports Coach, reproduced by permission; Extracts in unit 10 adapted from "Would you rent a friend?", *The Guardian*, 21/07/2010 (Dowling, T.); and "Virtual people, real friends", *The Guardian*, 02/01/2009 (Pickard, A.), copyright © Guardian News & Media Ltd 2009,2010; Extract in unit 10 adapted from *Long Way Round*, Time Warner Books (Charley Boorman and Ewan McGregor, 2004). Reproduced with permission by Little, Brown Book Group Limited; Extracts in units 11 and 13 adapted from "The kid who climbed Everest (It was his dad's idea)", *The Times Magazine*, 16/10/2010 (Watters, E.); "They all look the same to me", *The Sunday Times*, 17/12/2006 (Maltby, A.); and "Who are you again?", *The Times*, 11/08/2006 (Sieghart, M.A.), copyright © The Times, 2006, 2010, www.nisyndication.com; Extract in unit 12 from *One Good Turn: A Jolly Murder Mystery* (Kate Atkinson, 2010) pp.22-23,38. **Published by Doubleday.** Reprinted with permission from The Random House Group Limited; Extract in unit 13 adapted from "The art of digital forgetting", 20/10/2010 (Peter Haber, translated by Ulrike Anderson), first published in German at http://weblog.hist.net/archives/4610, English translation published on http://weblog.hist.net/archives/4681. Republished under the Open Licence CC BY-NC-SA and by permission of Dr Peter Haber; Extract in unit 14 adapted from "Watch your (body) language", *The Guardian*, 07/03/2009 (Wilson, S.), copyright © Guardian News & Media Ltd 2009; Extracts in Progress Test 1 adapted from "Yakutsk: Journey to the coldest city on earth", *The Independent*, 21/01/2008 (Walker, S.); and "Dining on insects: Anyone for crickets...?", *The Independent*, 21/10/2010 (Taylor, J.), copyright © The Independent

www.independent.co.uk.

The Financial Times
Extracts in unit 3 and Progress Test 2 adapted from "The seven secrets of a happy life", *The Financial Times*, 28/08/2010 (Powdthavee, N., and Wilkinson, C.); and "France: Claudie Haigneré", *The Financial Times Weekend*, 02/04/2011, p.35 (Kuper, S.), copyright © The Financial Times Limited 2010. All rights reserved.

In some instances we have been unable to trace the owners of copyright material, and we would appreciate any information that would enable us to do so.

The publisher would like to thank the following for their kind permission to reproduce their photographs:

(Key: b-bottom; c-centre; l-left; r-right; t-top)

Alamy Images: Pablo Scapinachis Armstrong 38, Asiaselects 33l, Dan Atkin 80bc, Hans Blossey / imagebroker 71r, Alexander Caminada 23b, Marvin Dembinsky Photo Associate 155tr, JanuszGniadek 80tr, Gavin Hellier / Jon Arnold Images Ltd 153br, D. Hurst 12, IS2008-10 / Image Source 130bl, tl, tcr, tr (superimposed), IS797 / Image Source 130tl, tcl, tr(superimposed), JAUBERT IMAGES 133t, Tiffany Jones 143r, Corinne Malet / PhotoAlto 154, Maskot 105tr, moodboard 105bc, Oberhaeuser / Caro 153bl, davidpearson 15, VadimPonomarenko 23 (mother and daughter), John Powell Photographer 80tc, Radius Images 23 (twins), 143l, john rensten / Cultura Creative 101, Maurice Savage 54, SergiySerdyuk 128, DmitriyShironosov 132, David Stares 80tl, Stockbroker / MBI 105tc, studiomode 32, Jochen Tack 133b; **Bridgeman Art Library Ltd:** *Fire, Full Moon*, 1933 (oil on canvas) byPaul Klee (1879-1940) / Museum Folkwang, Essen, Germany 59/2, *Confidences* (oil on board) by Edward Henry Potthast(1857-1927) / Private Collection / Photo © Christie's Images 98; **Corbis:** Alloy 114b, StephaneCardinale / People Avenue 58t, Still Life with Kettle and Fruit by Paul Cezanne (1839–1906) / Barney Burstein 59/3, Sean De Burca / Ivy 105br, Kevin Dodge / Comet 64, Nicolas Ferrando / Fancy 155bl, Frank Hurley / Bettmann 36t, Image Source 24, 35, Andreas Kindler / Johnér Images / Alloy 28, Howard Kingsnorth / cultura 23 (young couple), Bob Krist / Terra 127, FransLanting / Terra 147, David Leahy / cultura 80bl, moodboard 62t, Ocean 30bc, 53r, Jose Luis Pelaez, Inc. / Flirt 23t, PoodlesRock / Corbis Art 36b, Radius Images 43, *Self-Portrait*, 1657 by Rembrandt van Rijn 59/1, Patrick Robert / Sygma 153tr, Paul A. Souders / Encyclopedia 117r, Shin Suzuki / Anyone / amanaimages 140; **Keith Ducatel:** 45; **Pam Fishman:** 50; **Getty Images:** Daryl Balfour / Gallo Images 118, Banana Pancake / Photographer's Choice 155tl, Banksymural / Marco Di Lauro 59/4, Neil Beckerman / Taxi 33r, Steve Bronstein / Blend Images 116, Cavan Images / The Image Bank 114c, Chabruken / Photodisc 18b, Martin Child / Digital Vision 16, Robert Churchill / the Agency Collection 82, Compassionate Eye Foundation / Rennie Solis / Digital Vision 18t, Daly and Newton / OJO Images 152bl, Jonathan Daniel 97, Peter Dazeley / The Image Bank 80br, 122, Peter Dazeley / The Image Bank 80br, 122, Digital Vision 13, George Doyle / Stockbyte 94, Alexey Dudoladov / the Agency Collection 79r, Mark Evans / the Agency Collection 30tr, Steve Fitchett / Taxi 114t, Floresco Productions / Cultura 19, Frank and Helena / Cultura 62b, Fuse 23 (father and son), Ron Galella / WireImage 22, Ron Gaunt / Getty Images for Long Way Down 104, Claire Greenway 6, JGI / Jamie Grill / Blend Images 105bl, Juan Gris / The Bridgeman Art Library 30br, Martin Harvey / Gallo Images 49, JakobHelbig / Photodisc 155br, Dan Higham / Flickr 61, Mike Hollingshead / Photographer's Choice 115, Roy Hsu / Huntstock 156br / Photographer's Choice 85, IIC / Axiom / Perspectives 120, Ikonica / Radius Images 30l, Image Source 48, Les and Dave Jacobs / Cultura 87, Nico Kai / Iconica 53l, Jonathan Kantor / Lifesize 30tc, Howard Kingsnorth / Photographer's Choice 137, Jonathan Kitchen / Photographer's Choice RF 11, John Knill / Stockbyte 126, Bob Langrish / Dorling Kindersley 154tr, Latitudestock / Gallo Images 84, Manchester Daily Express / SSPL 9b, Ryan McVay / Photodisc 42, Jason Merritt 90t, Anik Messier / Flickr Select 74, Ty Milford / Aurora 113, Heath Patterson / Photographer's Choice 123, PNC / Digital Vision 105tl, Justin Pumfrey / Taxi 153tl, Dan Rafla / Taxi 117l, Frank Schwere / The Image Bank 76, Design Pics / Dan Sherwood / Perspectives 136, Smith Collection / Iconica 31, HOWARD SOCHUREK / Time & Life Pictures 69 (photo on cover), Stockbyte 112, Patrick Strattner 135, Paul Sutherland 141, Tetra Images 152tr, *Wheatfield with Cypresses*, 1889 (oil on canvas) by Vincent van Gogh / The Bridgeman Art Library 59/5, Klaus Vedfelt / The Image Bank 154bl, Frank Whitney / The Image Bank 67, WIN-Initiative 9t, Michael S. Yamashita / National Geographic 72 (monastery), Mel Yates / Stone 138, How Heww Young-Pool 156bl; **iStockphoto:** ilbusca 58b, Matt Kunz 68; **Kobal Collection Ltd:** BBC FILMS / KUDOS / OPTIMUM / 8, The Social Network / COLUMBIA PICTURES 102, ITV Global 65, SEE-SAW FILMS 20; **Mirrorpix:** Mike Moore 95; **Pearson Education Ltd:** 81; **Penguin Books Ltd:** Cover to be used in its entirety of BROOKLYN by ColmToibin (Penguin 2009). Copyright Penguin Books 2009. 69; **Photolibrary.com:** Tom Murphy / Still Pictures 41, Purestock / Jupiter Images 152tl, Urs Schweitzer / Photolibrary 146, VisitBritain / PawelLibera 152br; **Photostage Ltd:** Donald Cooper 60; **Press Association Images:** Anthony Devlin / PA Wire 29, Jeff Gentner / AP 77, Tony Marshall / EMPICS Sport 92, Fredrik von Erichsen / DPA 121; **Rex Features:** 71l, Graham Chadwick / Daily Mail 90, Paul Cooper 91, David Hartley 154tl, GenovevaKriechbaum 70, Lehtikuva OY 88, Ken McKay / ITV 10, Offside 26, Tom Oldham 14, Sipa Press 78, 110; **Science Photo Library Ltd:** Peter Menzel 46, 47l, 47r, 79l; **Summersdale Publishers Ltd:** Cover of James Hilton's Lost Horizon: The Classic Tale of Shangri-La 72 (book cover); **The Random House Group Ltd.:** from One Good Turn: A Jolly Murder Mystery by Kate Atkinson, published by Black Swan. Reprinted by permission of The Random House Group Ltd 125;**www.CartoonStock.com:** Glenn & Gary McCoy 148, W.B. Park 144

All other images © Pearson Education

Illustrated by Oxford Designers and Illustrators